TABLE OF CONTENTS

Preface

PART ONE

PART TWO

PART THREE

PART FOUR

PREFACE

The very first post on The Reading Experience weblog was a "statement of purpose" that included the following justification of attempting to do literary criticism online:

> Literary criticism is greatly in need of revitalization, as mainstream publications confine their coverage mostly to gossip and the book business, their book reviews becoming more and more perfunctory when not being eliminated altogether, while the academy, once entrusted with the job of engaging with works of literature, has mostly abandoned it altogether in favor of "cultural studies" and other forms of political posturing. I would hope, in fact, that this blog could work as a kind of bridge between blogs and other general interest literary publications and what was once called "literary study"--which in my mind is simply the willingness to take works of literature seriously.

In a later post, I briefly chronicled my own disillusionment with academic literary study:

> My alienation from academe was in part a reaction against the prevailing modes of academic criticism, which in my view had essentially abandoned "literature itself" in favor of critical approaches that were mostly just a way of doing history or sociology by other means. I had pursued a Ph.D in literary study in order to study literature, not to validate my

political allegiances on the cheap, or to study something called "culture," an artifact of which literature might be considered but given no more emphasis than any other cultural "expression." I was looking to find a way to write literary criticism that continued to focus on the literary qualities of literature, and to that end had published several critical essays in publications that would still print such efforts when I happened upon the first literary weblogs. I soon enough concluded there was no reason the literary blog could not accommodate a form of literary criticism--longer than the typical kind of post I was seeing on the extant litblogs but shorter than the conventional scholarly article or long critical essay. Trying out these possibilities has been the ongoing project of this blog. . . .

If anything, the decline of book review sections I described in the first post has only continued apace, to the point that book reviews as part of newspaper "coverage" will likely disappear altogether within a few more years, while academic criticism remains as clueless about literature as it did when I abandoned it. Literary criticism that focuses "on the literary qualities of literature" still needs to be recovered, although the rise and development of literary weblogs since I created my own has indeed contributed to a process of such recovery. There are now more sources of serious discussion of new (and old) fiction on blogs and numerous other book review sites than were ever available when book reviewing was dominated by newspapers and a handful of magazines, and this discussion is at least as well-informed as the old print-based criticism and generally avoids academic pretension.

In my statement of purpose, I also indicated that I wanted to use the weblog form to try a "new kind of literary criticism, more compacted and concise, perhaps than conventional print lit crit, but serious criticism nonetheless." By "new" I did not mean criticism of some unprecedented or revolutionary insight but a less formulaic--in the case of book reviews--and a less discursively extended--in the case of scholarly criticism--approach that seemed appropriate for a medium that most readers expected to feature briefer and thus more "compacted" commentary. A weblog could "review" new fiction without reinscribing the conventions of the journalistic book review, and if the typical "post" on a weblog would not allow for an 8,000 word scholarly analysis, much of what is included in most scholarly essays is filler and rote rhetorical gesture, anyway. As became increasingly clear as I began to post the more "concise" critical essays I had in mind, the ease and immediacy of publication and the ability to link posts that characterize the weblog made it possible to revisit and serially expand on chosen issues, specific texts, or particular authors in a way that compensated for the need to abbreviate most individual posts.

After six years of posting criticism of this sort, I have concluded both that my original hope that what came to be called the litblog could enable a form of serious literary criticism had been warranted, and that my own blog was approaching an imposed limitation of sorts, imposed precisely by my practice of returning to those subjects that most engaged my interest as a critic. This practice was only reinforced by an assumption that many if not most readers were understandably not following all of my posts with the same degree of concentration I myself brought to them and thus a strategy of something like theme-and-variations would be necessary to keep the blog's most central concerns in steady circulation. While this strategy continued to provoke some lively discussions in comment threads and resulted in posts that still managed to advance my own thinking about the subjects considered, eventually I had to acknowledge they were nevertheless being overworked. Since The Reading Experience came into existence essentially as a vehicle for exploring these subjects, I also had to acknowledge that this weblog, at least in its originally conceived version, would have to be retired.

If the blog had reached the end of its usefulness, however, the writing I had posted to it retained its value, or so I believe, at least. In many ways, in fact, the writing, reduced to a core of representative selections, amounted to a coherent, extended articulation of those main concerns with which the blog had been occupied; in effect, the book I might have written had I not instead used The Reading Experience as medium could be fashioned from my TRE posts, a book that would both sum up what I had attempted to accomplish with the weblog form and perhaps stand on its own as a work of literary criticism. This is that book, borrowing the weblog's title--the significance of which as overarching theme should become clear enough as the reader progresses through the text--and otherwise distilling the blog's content to what I think of as its essence. I have arranged the selected posts in what seems to me a suitable order reflecting the coverage of issues readers of the blog encountered, in some cases have edited the posts substantially to integrate them more effectively into book form, and in other cases have added wholly new material to be found only in this book version.

Readers will have to judge for themselves whether this book affirms my original intuition that the literary weblog could support serious criticism and ultimately whether the book itself does hold up as an adaptation of the critical writing that began as posts on The Reading Experience weblog. I can say for myself, however, that the effort to produce criticism of substance on a regular basis, as well as the subsequent time spent reinforcing that effort by putting together the book version of The Reading Experience, have been even more rewarding than I might have imagined when first thinking about experimenting with a "new" kind of literary criticism.

PART ONE

Reviewing the Reviews

I New York Reviews of Books

This book is first of all about the state and practice of literary criticism, both in its more popular form of the book review and its more rarefied "academic" variety. In each of these versions, literary criticism is greatly in need of revitalization, as mainstream publications confine their coverage mostly to gossip and the book business (or gossip about the book business), their book reviews becoming increasingly perfunctory when not being eliminated altogether, while the academy, once entrusted with the job of honestly engaging with works of literature, has mostly abandoned it entirely in favor of "cultural studies" and other forms of political posturing.[1] It seems that both modes of criticism are more or less entrenched in their current practices, so that what is really needed is an alternative approach to criticism that might also act as kind of bridge between audiences looking to general interest literary discussion for illumination of books and writing and those more receptive to the intensified focus provided by what was once called "literary study, which to my mind is ultimately just the willingness to take works of literature seriously.

Of course, there would seem to be different ways of taking books "seriously." The perspective commonly expressed in what is known as "literary journalism" is perhaps best illustrated by remarks made by *New York Times* editors in 2004, who announced that the *Book Review* would be moving away from "literary fiction" (including especially "first novels") in favor of more coverage of popular fiction and "urgent and journalistic" nonfiction. Editor Bill Keller's stated preference for books that act as a "launching pad for discussion" indicates a belief that books are "serious" when they contribute to public discussion of "issues," and only books that so contribute can be serious. "Ideas" come from nonfiction, not fiction, and its "ideas" we want.

At best, what Keller has in mind, aside from more reviews of airport books, is to convert the *Times Book Review* into something closer to *The New York Review of Books*, where indeed most of the review space is taken up with books of "urgency' or which deal with issues of "current interest." Unfortunately, the NYRB has become even less interested in fiction or poetry than the new Book Review Keller envisions. *The New York Review* has always ranged well beyond literature and literary issues, but I remember first becoming a regular reader back in the 1970s because it was a reliable source of discussion

---

[1] This situation has been altered by the rise of online criticism and literary weblogs, but I will reserve discussion of this development until later in the book.

about serious fiction and poetry, although it's possible my memory distorts. (However, a glance at the acknowledgements pages of William Gass's *Fiction and the Figures of Life* (1971), as well as *The World Within the World* (1976), reveals that many of the essays included were first published in *The New York Review of Books*, almost all of them reviews of Gass's fellow writers and other essays on decidedly literary matters.) To judge by the contents of a representative issue ("Spring Books," 2004), most readers must now come to NYRB because of an interest in history, cultural commentary, "learned" scholarship in non-literary disciplines, and politics (especially politics.).

Of all the works of fiction published during this spring season, can it really the case that the only one worth reviewing in the Spring Books issue was Jim Crace's *Genesis*? (And is it merely a misperception, or does NYRB not give more attention to British fiction than American fiction? A strong case of Anglophilia seems to be at work in the NYRB's judgment of what fiction needs to be reviewed.) In almost every issue of the NYRB, no more than two reviews of fiction are included, and frequently there's only one, as here. The proportion of fiction reviews in relation to nonfiction is consistently very low, probably less than ten percent, a ratio of which Bill Keller would no doubt heartily approve.

This issue does include reviews of other "literary" books. There's a review of two biographical studies of Mark Twain and an omnibus review of Shakespeare. In the Twain piece the reviewer, Larry McMurtry (a frequent contributor to NYRB, which is itself a whole other problem), writes that "Twain is one of those authors who is, invariably, more interesting to read than to read about." So why are we reading about him? The Shakespeare review, by James Fenton, is an interesting enough discussion of the viewing Shakespeare vs. reading him debate, but it trods well-worn ground. Why have these books been deemed worthy of review rather than works of fiction by living writers, particularly since they have a hard enough time getting read in the first place?

A literary scholar, Stephen Greenblatt, reviews Walter Laqueur's *Solitary Sex: A Cultural History of Masturbation* and, the prurience of the topic aside, his review points up another feature of *New York Review* reviews that make it a less than reliable "review" of books: many times these reviews are not reviews at all, merely excuses for the reviewer to substitute his own expertise and wisdom about the subject of the book for an actual critical evaluation of the book itself. The same thing is true of Garry Wills's "God in the Hands of Angry Sinners," which begins with some very interesting observations about *The Passion of the Christ* but then veers off into a lengthy discussion of the Legion of Christ, a radical Catholic group that is obviously of great interest to Will but the analysis of which can only appeal to those who share his fascination. Wills, like McMurtry, is an

NYRB perennial, and he is typical of the sorts of reviewers the editors rely on, establishment figures who are unlikely to add a fresh perspective or account for the unfamiliar.

Finally there's the obsession with ongoing politics, which crowds out less tendentious and more thorough discussion of other kinds of nonfiction, not to mention fiction and poetry. Part of the Spring Books issue is taken up with a continuing discussion of Michael Massing's dead-on accurate dissection of the news media's coverage of the Iraq invasion. The subjects of Massing's criticism have yet to adequately respond to it, but why was his essay even published in *The New York Review of **Books***? Why wasn't it published somewhere not only more appropriate for the subject, but where it might have gotten even more attention and had even greater impact? It's an important critique, but not at the expense of some worthy books that might have gotten the space instead.

Certainly some good essay-reviews are published in *The New York Review of Books*, and some worthy books get reviewed. But not nearly enough good writing--as opposed to just "books" in the perfunctory sense of pages with covers around them--is highlighted, and not nearly enough coverage of subjects that might help to foster a real literary culture is provided. It's become too much a "review" of the predictable and familiar by the smug and established. It's the very antithesis of "lively." Few and far between are the general interest publications that feature any extended analysis of contemporary literature, and those that do usually have an underlying ideological agenda to advance in the guise of literary criticism (*The New Republic, The Weekly Standard, The New Criterion.*) This is partly what makes the direction the *New York Times Book Review* has indeed taken so frustrating, since it had been one of the few publications to examine poetry and literary fiction without such obvious biases.

II Middling Intelligibility

It's always good when a reviewer voluntarily reveals his/her biases or preconceptions. Caroline Leavitt says this of Mark Dunn's *Ibid: A Life--A Novel in Footnotes*:

> The writing's playful and witty, and there's a good bit of inventive silliness to the tale. Young Jonathan misinterprets a wink as a sign that a young girl likes him, when actually it's a spasm. There's a wry running joke that all the loves of Jonathan's life are killed in freak Boston accidents, including the Great Molasses Flood. It's all sometimes dazzling fun, but the truth is, I wasn't lost in the book the way I wanted to be. I was always aware of the writer's sprightly mind at work here, when what I wanted was the feeling that his characters were real, that they might knock on my door any second and ask for a cup of tea. (*Boston Globe*, 4/4, 2004)

Ms. Leavitt is of course entitled to her preferences, but, really, what is a reader to do with this? The reviewer refers to what seem like exemplary qualities in the novel, but then in effect dismisses them. What if you are a reader who actually would enjoy a novel that's "witty," "inventive," has good jokes, is "dazzling fun," and reveals "the writer's sprightly mind at work"? Should you then disregard the reviewer's judgment that the novel lacks "real" characters and conclude this book is probably rather promising, despite the reviewer's ultimate "thumbs down"?

And what of this?:

What do we want from our books? Of course it depends on the reader, but personally, I think that new shouldn't just be novelty. Heart should override mind. And always, always, the characters -- be they investment lawyer or circus attraction -- should let us into their souls.

Disregarding the illogic of the claim that the new shouldn't be novel, isn't it just patently untrue that all good novels "always, always" feature characters whose "souls" we enter? Can't some good novels emphasize plot instead? Shouldn't some novelists be allowed to be "witty" and "inventive," qualities in some cases that might override the creation of character? Aren't novels that are primarily comic almost necessarily limited in their capacity to create "soulful" characters? (Such characters are by the requirements of comedy inherently two-dimensional.)

My problem is really not so much with Caroline Leavitt, who may like or dislike whatever she wants. But why does the *Boston Globe* print such a review? Of course reviews are matters of opinion (sometimes), and various opinions ought to be expressed. But the statements made in a review like this are enormously sweeping, to the point that they finally make the review almost impossible to use in any serious way to decide whether to read *Ibid* or not. If we don't share the reviewer's assumptions, are we likely to actually enjoy this novel? If we do share them, will we dislike it because it's too inventive and "fun"? The review fails in its presumably assigned task of informing readers about the book under review.

Or is this indeed the task of a book review? Is a book review primarily informative or evaluative? If the former, then the greatest hazard is that it will become a kind of book report, a record of the fact that you read and can summarize the assigned book. If a review should be primarily evaluative, then the danger is that, given the space usually allotted to book reviews, you'll wind up with something like Caroline Leavitt's review--all unsupported assertion with little effort to justify the underlying assumptions.

To indulge in my own very sweeping statement, my general impression of book reviewing in most print publications, both newspapers and magazines, is that it includes too little description of what the works reviewed actually do, what they are, and too much glib evaluation. Partly this is a result of the limited and shrinking space being given to the consideration of books and writing at all. Partly it is the consequence of too often assigning reviews to reviewers who seemingly have little acquaintance with or, frankly, much interest in literature in the first place. It's probably also a consequence of the general American propensity to have an opinion without feeling much need to support it.

That most book reviews are short on honest explication and long on unsupported evaluation applies exponentially to Emily Barton's review of Gary Lutz's *I Looked Alive* (Black Square Editions), printed in the Spring 2004 issue of *Bookforum*.

I must first say that I was mostly unfamiliar with Lutz's work until reading this book, but having done so my own judgment of the book couldn't be in starker contrast to Emily Barton's. I liked it a lot. While Barton claims the stories make for "rather anhedonic reading," I found them on the contrary to be even rather moving on the whole, in addition to being structurally and stylistically challenging (the latter description being meant as a compliment.) It's the kind of book that requires patience in the beginning but eventually becomes more compelling as you read it. "Experimental" fiction is often like that.

Even if I didn't like these stories so much, however, I would still have great problems with Emily Barton's review. It's reasonably short, so I will point out the lowlights in order, as they manifest themselves to the reader's notice. Although the review masquerades as a "description" of *I Looked Alive*, what passes for description is transparently a way of conveying to the reader that Lutz simply doesn't write fiction the way it ought to be written, at least according to the reviewer's assumptions.

Barton immediately informs us that Lutz's fiction "is difficult to read (to some the mark of experimentalism, to others shoddy craftsmanship). . ." The opposition between "experimentalism" and "craftsmanship" is patently obvious, of course, and we know before reading the rest of the review that we ought to avoid Lutz because he isn't a "craftsman." A craftsman doesn't write something that's "difficult to read." Never mind that this amounts to a wholesale rejection of the idea of experimental fiction in the first place, but it's a hopelessly reductive concept of what defines "craftsmanship" as well. If anything, experimental writers tend to be even more craftsmanlike in their approach, since what constitutes the "craft" of writing fiction is uppermost in their minds to begin with. Too many "well-made" stories or novels are not products of craft at all, but simple repetitions of formula.

Then there's "the fault of the narrative voice itself, which may make nominal switches from first to third person but sounds relentlessly the same from piece to piece." One of the blurbs printed on the book's back cover (from Sven Birkerts) suggests that "the overall effect of a Lutz piece is not unlike what we experience reading a John Ashbery poem." This actually seems right to me. The structure and execution of Lutz's stories have at least as much in common with poetry as with fiction. Do we criticize poets because the "voice" in their poems "sounds relentlessly the same from piece to piece"?

This problem, from Barton's perspective, is presumably related to the next: ""Lutz never provides the one, salient fact that would imbue a character with vigorous life, or even make him memorable." This is a very familiar lament of reviewers whose most basic assumption is that fiction will present us with "memorable" characters. In addition to being "craftsmen," fiction writers are also expected to be portrait painters in prose. Apparently this is the only thing that makes some readers interested in fiction in the first place, but of course the very notion of "experimental" fiction suggests that these ingrained expectations of what fiction is supposed to do are going to be challenged. If the writer isn't attempting to create memorable characters, it hardly seems a valid criticism to say that after all he doesn't do this.

If Lutz can't deliver up memorable characters, how about his ability to tell a story? "[It's] hard to know, moment by moment, what a Lutz story is even about," Barton observes. Putting aside the fact that this largely isn't true, that it's perfectly easy to see what a given story is "about" as long as you at least temporarily abandon the assumption that a story must proceed "moment by moment," this criticism really takes us to Barton's core complaint about *I Looked Alive*, which is further captured in this declaration: "Experimental fiction typically forgoes the comforts of storytelling in order to reveal the world in a new light. Sadly, Lutz reveals little." Thus Emily Barton would be willing to overlook the lack of storytelling, if the book would only conform in some other way to the conventions of realistic fiction, revealing the world through fiction's "light." But in fact experimental fiction doesn't first "reveal the world" in a new way. It attempts to reveal the possibilities of fiction in a new way. If it also gets us to look at the world differently, fine, but Barton puts her critical cart before the literary horse.

Perhaps the most damaging of Barton's criticisms, if it was true, is that Lutz "can't even write prose of middling intelligibility," fails to "maintain a crystalline clarity." Certainly Lutz could write prose of "middling intelligibility" if he wanted to, but he doesn't. He's deliberately confronting the standard of "crystalline clarity," asking why literary experiment can't include experiment with conventional uses of language. In the book's very first paragraph we are told by the narrator that "I had not come through in either of the kids. They took their mother's bunching of features, and were breeze-shaken things, and did not cut too far into life." This is not immediately "informative" in a "crystalline" way, but if you pause (and pause you must, throughout most of this book) and consider it, it makes perfect sense as a description of the way this man might see his children. It's just a "new" way of expressing features we are accustomed to seeing signaled in more familiar phrases.

One could decide that Lutz has failed in his experiments with language or character, that they don't accomplish what he seems to have set out to do, but it hardly seems useful to criticize him for even trying them out in the first place, which is what Emily Barton's review finally amounts to.

Laura Demanski's review of Elizabeth McKenzie's *Stop That Girl*, on the other hand, is an admirable example of what might be called the "fair negative" review. Demanski concludes that the book is "a disappointment despite all of its promising elements and McKenzie's obvious talent," but she also patiently describes what McKenzie seems to be attempting in the novel, arriving at her ultimately negative assessment only after showing that, in the reviewer's opinion, the execution of the author's purpose comes up short.

Early in the review, Demanski writes:

> . . .The nine stories that make up *Stop That Girl* cover Ann Ransom's life from age 7 until she's a 20-something mother. But we stop and look in on her only every couple of years, and a lot more happens offstage than on.
>
> It's an unconventional method that may leave completists unsatisfied. In the typical bildungsroman, we closely follow the major events of a young person's life and see how they form the adult she becomes. The success of that kind of novel depends in part on how convincingly the results follow from the causes. McKenzie's method shoots for different effects and delivers different pleasures. When the reader doesn't know everything--not even close to everything--mystery and surprise are added to the mix. (*Chicago Tribune*, 3/13, 2005)

From this description we understand that McKenzie is writing a variation of the "bildungsroman" (the coming-of-age novel), and that she is taking something of a risk in experimenting with the form. McKenzie's reader is going to be asked to read between the lines--or more precisely, between the stories--and make connections that in most such fictions are made more explicitly by the author him/herself. This provides what Demanski calls "breathing room," but obviously it would require some deftness on the writer's part to keep the reader interested after the more conventional strategy has been abandoned.

And it is precisely the writer's skill in maintaining the form she's adopted that is the basis of Demanski's subsequent judgment of this "novel in stories." She hasn't insisted that, in effect, the author should have written a different kind of book, merely that the results achieved do not really measure up to what seems to have been the writer's ambition.

Even so, Demanski's judgments are judiciously expressed:

What's left out between these stories isn't a problem; what's left out in them, however, sometimes is. McKenzie's deadpan, minimalist narration is well-suited to conveying Ann's chronic disenchantment with life; but over the course of the book it comes to feel stingy, shrunken and empty. To some degree this is a built-in problem with writing about disillusion and disenchantment: How does one represent them in one's characters without reproducing them in one's readers? McKenzie doesn't find a solution.

She also describes a selected number of stories from the book, giving the reader an opportunity, ultimately, to compare his/his own impression of them, and their relative degree of success, to the reviewer's. Or at least giving the reader some confidence that the reviewer has read the book carefully and has attempted to ground her evaluation in specific examples from the text.

Where one might question Demanski's evaluation is in a passage like this one:

> The standard novel about growing up tells a protracted tale of learning and gradual loss of innocence. Ann, however, experiences disillusionment so young--in the first story--that the usual tale is moot. Beyond a point that comes especially early for her, Ann is incapable of being truly thrown by life, or truly moved by it. What, then, remains to be narrated? Neither Ann nor McKenzie seem to know for sure; there's a fair amount of floundering on both sides.

It seems to me possible for the reader to accept this early disillusionment and to want to read the rest of the book anyway, not as the story of the protagonist's disillusionment per se but as the account of how she subsequently manages to deal with it or not--as the "narrative" of how innocence lost affects a human life that nevertheless continues on. Perhaps McKenzie does "flounder" in her effort to carry this out, but one wonders whether Demanski isn't finally missing something in the book, after all.

Still, I am actually more inclined to read *Stop That Girl* than I was before reading the review, the reviewer's qualified negative assessment notwithstanding. If nothing else, I would like to determine for myself whether Demanski's view of the possibilities of the modified bildungsroman is a sound one or not. Finally, Demanski has both convinced me that she has taken her responsibilities as a reviewer seriously, and that her conclusions are worth testing in a kind of reviewer-reader dialectic. In my opinion, this means the reviewer has not only decidedly earned her pay (meager as it probably was), but also my gratitude as her reader.

III Problems in the Story Line

In her book *Faint Praise: The Plight of Book Reviewing in America* (University of Missouri Press 2007), former *Boston Review* editor Gail Pool writes:

> Readers dismayed by the lack of criticism in reviews won't find more of it in other coverage, most of which is promotion, sometimes in disguise. Newspaper book features--profiles and interviews--are promotional. Readings are promotional. "Reviews" written by booksellers, even independent booksellers, are promotional. Book clubs are promotional. Even readers' guides are promotional: produced by the publishers to enhance the books' value for--and sales to--reading groups, they may be designed to encourage more thoughtful reading, but they don't encourage a critical approach. None of the guides seem to ask readers to question the quality of a book's prose, its cliched characterization, or the problems in its story line. They start from the premise that the books are good, and it's

their purpose to help readers "understand" why they're good, not discover they aren't.

Nor will readers frustrated by the quality of criticism in traditional reviewing find it improved by its nontraditional counterparts. On the contrary, in self-published reviews on the Web--the main nontraditional alternative--critical failings are and are bound to be exacerbated. It may be that editors too often fail to do their job in ensuring that reviews are unbiased, informed, well written, or critically astute, but I don't see how it can possibly be an improvement to eliminate the role of editor, the readers' only chance for quality control. Unscreened, anonymous, and unedited, self-published reviews can be--an often are--as biased, uninformed, ungrammatical, and critically illiterate as they like. (122)

Pool, as she does throughout her book, shares the delusion common among "professional" book reviewers that "criticism" and " book review" are synonymous terms--or at least that at their best newspaper and magazine reviews do embody what "criticism" is all about. Pool offers plenty of objections to the standards of book reviewing as currently practiced, but she never relinquishes the notion that reviewing, when done right, is an act of literary criticism, *sine qua non*.

For Pool, the defining feature of criticism is the more specific act of passing judgment. "Critical" in Pool's lexicon comes close to its overly literal and reductive meaning as "finding fault" (or looking for faults but happily not finding many). A novel has "problems in its story line" or fails to meet some predetermined measure of "quality" with which the critic is inspecting the text and pronouncing it fit or flawed. Discovering that a book might not be good becomes an urgent and noble endeavor that only the "critic," properly detached and unbiased, can venture to undertake.

Certainly critical judgment can never be avoided entirely; it always lies behind discussions of aesthetic merit. But in my opinion, judgment is only the precursor to criticism, its necessary spark but not at all its fulfillment, which is only to be found in the further elucidation of the way the work constitutes itself as a work of fiction or poetry, of the specific nature of the experience of reading the work attentively. The work may present itself in a way that is completely familiar or utterly alien, or somewhere in between. The critic at the least must give a plausible enough account of the text's perceptible qualities to make the critical judgment credible, but just as often judgment might be simply assumed, taken for granted, even neglected altogether. Criticism that is able to "encourage more thoughtful reading" is valuable criticism indeed, and if in many cases the critic discusses works he/she implicitly values highly in order to "help readers 'understand' why they're good," this is probably in the long run a much more worthwhile expenditure of critical energy than the effort to demonstrate that some works aren't. (This use of critical intelligence to illuminate the aesthetic accomplishments of literary works amounts to the "promotion" of literature in the very best sense the term can bear.)

Pool is especially determined to preserve the prerogatives of editors in providing "criticism" through book reviewing. To me, this is a *non sequitur*. Criticism is an unavoidably personal, very individualized activity. It's my encounter with the text, your encounter with the text, not this encounter as mediated by some third party presuming to act as gatekeeper. When Pool invokes "quality control" as the editor's job description, she's identifying this as a function within the hierarchy of a newspaper or magazine. Bias-, fact-, and grammar-checking are imperatives of journalism as practiced by a self-appointed group of so-called professionals in a self-limited sphere of work, not of literary criticism, which can be (in some cases should be) thoroughly biased, indifferent to "facts" except the facts of the text at hand, and resistant to hidebound rules of grammar when they interfere with the expression of difficult ideas or impede critical insight.

Even if we accept that newspaper or magazine book sections often benefit from inspired editing, Pool's own book often reveals that this sort of inspiration is sorely lacking in most book review pages. The "plight" of book reviewing is mostly a plight of editing, which fails to provide much in the way of "quality control" in the first place and has made book reviewing in America an activity without great relevance and characterized by a stale conformity of approach. At the top of Pool's list of needed reforms is "a better means of choosing books for review" (125). "Our current system," she writes, "inevitably leads to overlooking good books, overpraising bad ones, and undermining the book page." Well, who exactly is to blame for this "current system" in which the wrong books are reviewed, bad books are praised, and the book page trivialized if not the editors of the book pages? Don't they determine what gets reviewed and who does the reviewing? Aren't they responsible for publishing bland and vacuous reviews? Why in the world would we want to revive book reviewing by reinvesting in the very process that has caused the problem to begin with?

As far as I can tell, the concern among print reviewers and editors such as Gail Pool that book reviewing be saved, not least from the ragtag bloggers, comes from a fear that their identities as "book critics" are imperiled. It can't be from a fear that literature or literary criticism is imperiled, since *Faint Praise* itself demonstrates that book reviewing as now exemplified by working "literary journalists" has precious little to do with either. Since book reviewers are paid so little, and since, as again Pool herself attests, book reviewing is viewed by other journalists as occupying the bottom rung of the prestige ladder, the disdain for literary blogs and other "nontraditional" sources of literary discussion that drips from the pens of Gail Pool and Richard

Schickel and Michael Dirda must rise from a mounting fear that their sense of separation from mere "amateurs" is at risk: If you can't look down on bloggers, after all, who can you look down on?

Faint Praise at the same time both pinpoints the reasons why book reviewing in the usual print publications can't be taken seriously and argues that book reviewing can be saved only if the current "system" and the current mode of publication remain the same, with a little tweaking and a little "education' of reviewers who game the system to their own benefit and of readers who have otherwise come to see this system as the adjunct to "book business" hucksterism that it is. It demonstrates why book reviewing as a form of literary journalism is probably doomed: Its author can see the flaws in the "system" in which she works, but can't imagine a solution outside of that system, even when such a solution is probably the only kind available.

Bridging the Gap

I Theory About Practice

In his essay "Love and Hatred of 'French Theory' in America," Rolando Perez provides this very incisive account of the reception of Theory in the 1980s:

Those of us who were either in the U.S. academy as professors or as graduate students in the early 1980s were weaned on the milk of post-existentialist, French thought. For reasons that had little or nothing to with the individual thinkers behind the different theories, two camps formed all on their own. Or perhaps more accurately, according to the academic interests of the people involved. Those whose interests were primarily literary were attracted to, studied, and wrote on Barthes, Derrida, Jabes, de Man, etc. Much of what we think of as being "French theory" today is the result of the kind of literary criticism that was carried out in prestigious universities like Yale during the 1980s. Academicians and graduate students who were interested in Continental political philosophy found in Foucault, Deleuze, Guattari, Lyotard, and Baudrillard, the necessary keys they needed to critique contemporary, American capitalist society. Some of us attempted to bring these two strains of French thought together, either from the literary or from the political end. And there were good reasons for such attempts, even if at times the actual results were less than satisfactory.

He continues:

Certainly there were things to criticize in what came to be known as postmodern French theory. There were people who were churning out deconstructive readings of just about everything under the sun, and doing it quite badly: building careers, amassing publications for tenure, and saying nothing. And the same could be said of all the Deleuzean articles that made it to the pages of so many publications. Yet few would deny today the importance of contemporary French thought on American letters. Up until what some have called the "French invasion" of academia, American literary criticism was at a stand still, and Continental philosophy was merely what was left of the exhausted, no longer relevant post-war philosophy of phenomenology and existentialism. What *French Theory in America* and *Hatred of Capitalism* do is to show us in an eloquent manner what French thought has contributed, and continues to contribute, to academia and the art world. (*Borderlands E-Journal*, Vol. 4, No.1 2005)

Although I can certainly see how an endeavor like "Continental philosophy" might at a given time be "exhausted," in need of fresh insights and an altered focus, I find it harder to agree that "literary criticism was at a stand still." How could literary criticism--considered as a practice, not as a theory about practice--be at a "stand still"? Unless the term has come to mean only theory about practice, and the actual practice of explicating and evaluating texts is something else, something about which academe no longer concerns itself?

The latter kind of criticism doesn't need to be "advanced," its assumptions "updated." Explication is explication. The process of moving from consideration of textual features to an evaluation of the text's success in accomplishing its implicit purpose remains the same. Certainly insights garnered from a familiarity with theory or another critic's method might be brought to bear in a particular instance, but this will provide a new perspective on the individual work at hand, not on the practice of literary criticism per se. The new perspective has been produced by the application of an unchanging principle--read the text as intensively as one can, come to a conclusion based on an assessment of ends and means.

Developments over the past twenty-five years have produced a conception of "literary criticism" by which the object of criticism is no longer the literary work itself but the operations of criticism. The very notion of the "literary" is interrogated and competing notions of "value" are debated. These are perfectly acceptable things to do, but they have become the defining characteristics of literary criticism, not the appraisal of works of fiction and poetry per se, at least insofar as the very term "criticism" has become synonymous with "academic criticism"-- which I would argue has certainly happened. The debate over Theory is often framed as a conflict between the "higher eclecticism" John Holbo has written about and a more respectful appreciation of literature itself, but it would be more precise to say that one distinctive practice--literary criticism--has been replaced by another--theoretical speculation, with literature as its prompt.

I am not arguing that such speculation should not be carried out. Even if I did believe that, no amount of complaining by the advocates of "literature itself" is going to return us to the days when Literature was the disciplinary main attraction, the "literary" scholar its curator. For whatever reason, studying literature for its own sake has proven to be an unsuitable activity in the contemporary university. I do wonder, however, why the term "literary criticism" continues to be used in describing what academic scholars are now doing in most literature departments. Surely it isn't necessary to retain it for purposes of prestige or legitimacy. Why not just acknowledge that both Theory and cultural studies are what they are--which is to say, they are not literary criticism. They are both more and less than literary criticism: more in that they take all of culture as their domain, less in that by widening the scope of "criticism" so broadly they don't really notice individual writers and works much at all. If nothing else, relinquishing the title to "literary criticism" might revitalize criticism as a general-interest practice and in so doing might bring some needed attention back to the novelists and poets who could use it.

II Serious Criticism

Cynthia Ozick makes at least one very important point in her essay, "Literary Entrails," in the April, 2007 *Harper's Magazine*:

> . . .in searching for the key to the Problem of the Contemporary Novel (or Novelist), there are cupboards where it is useless to look. And there are reasons that do not apply: writers vying for the highest rung of literary prestige; potential readers distracted by the multiplicity of storytelling machines. Feuds and jealousies are hardly pertinent [e.g., Ben Marcus vs. Jonathan Franzen], and the notorious decline of reading, while incontrovertible, may have less to do with the admittedly shaky situation of literary fiction than many believe. The real trouble lies not in what is happening but in what is not happening.

> What is not happening is literary criticism.

Unfortunately, Ozick isn't very precise in explaining what she means by "literary criticism," beyond conjuring up a critic possessing "a powerfully persuasive, and pervasive, intuition for how [novels] are connected, what they portend in the aggregate, how they comprise and color an era." Even more unfortunately, she doesn't bother to bring poetry within the purview of criticism, which might have forced her to identify those elements of the critic's task that take criticism beyond taxonomy ("how novels are connected"), which is an important but by no means sufficient activity, and beyond noting what an era's fiction "portends," how it "colors" its time and place, which seems to me to be the job of sociologists and historians, not literary critics engaged in what I take to be their most indispensable work: reading individual novels (and poems) carefully and insightfully, giving other readers a sense of what a particularly dedicated reader experienced while attending closely to the text. The most effective critics also bring a familiarity with literary history to bear on the text at hand, but simply pointing out "connections" and keeping track of the "aggregate" won't really do.

Ozick invokes James Wood, apparently now almost everyone's default setting for the category "critic," as an exemplar of the kind of criticism she presumably has in mind, but she quotes some of his more pompous, oracular pronouncements-- "Belief is a mere appendix to magic, its unused organ. This is a moral problem" [referring to the work of Toni Morrison]--rather than any specific instance of critical analysis that might help us actually read the text more efficaciously, as opposed to admiring the critic's cute phrase-making or joining in on his moral sanctimony. Wood does frequently enough mix in plausible analysis with his moralizing, but it would seem that Ozick prefers his rhetorical posturing to his usable criticism.

Nevertheless, Ozick is right to distinguish between "literary criticism" and most book reviews and between literary criticism and academic criticism. While some book reviewers are also skillful critics (Sven Birkerts, Louis Menand, Daniel

Mendelsohn) able to use the book review form to more genuinely critical ends, Ozick is right to maintain that the judgments of book reviewers, even reviewers who are themselves writers, are too often "capricious," too often constrained by the formulaic structure of the book review. She is also accurate in her description of "advanced" academic criticism as limited by its "confining ideologies, heavily politicized and rendered in a kind of multi-syllabic pidgin," reducing literature to dogma. (One can only hope that she is correct in predicting such criticism is "destined to vanish like the fog [it evokes].") The success of academic criticism in appropriating "criticism" to itself, however much it has devolved into an insular discourse that long ago left any real interest in literature far behind, has created a situation in which the brief newspaper/magazine review has to suffice as "literary criticism." Ozick justifiably calls for the development of "a broad infrastructure, through a critical mass of critics," for the more amply developed kind of criticism she at least gestures toward in this essay.

This perceived need for a renewal of criticism is where I myself began when creating my literary weblog. To some extent, I have become only more aware of how the absence of such criticism, less deadline-driven and publishing-centered, has created a situation like the one Scott Esposito describes:

> Enough with the mad rush of literature where we barely have time to contemplate spring's hot titles before summer

assaults us with its books. Why not linger over those spring books (and the winter ones as well), think about them a little longer, say something about them that will last past the end of the year?. . . . (*Conversational Reading*, 4/20/2007)

Such a "mad rush" of superficial discussion can only result in a brand of reviewing that emphasizes the trendy and ephemeral, that elevates the "book business" and its trivialities over the long-term consideration of books that more people ought to read, of books that might even stand the test of time and still be read a generation from now, not just next year. One thing Ozick overlooks in her discussion of the current state of criticism is exactly where good literary criticism might appear. (One place to look would be Scott Esposito's own online critical journal, *The Quarterly Conversation*.) Certainly newspapers and magazines are not suddenly going to publish more of it. The current effort by the National Book Critics Circle to "save" the book section at the *Atlanta Journal-Constitution* is not likely to succeed, and if it did wouldn't make much of a difference--I can't remember the last time I read the AJC's book reviews with any seriousness. Literary quarterlies might usefully devote more of their space to criticism, but that really hasn't been happening very much, either.

In starting my blog (and joining up with other literary blogs in implicitly attempting to create a "broad infrastructure" of serious literary discussion), I was making a judgment that the blog post could come to approximate (in a perhaps more condensed form) if not replace the critical essay--the available forums for which have long been dwindling in number--as the vehicle for "literary criticism." Not only could an individual post attempt critical readings of various kinds and lengths, but that post could be linked to other posts (both of one's own, and of others considering the same subjects) in a kind of chain of critical discussion. I still believe that literary blogs can perform this function (especially since numerous other bloggers have since appeared taking what seems to be the same approach), although Cynthia Ozick either hasn't considered this option or shares the same blinkered attitude to online discourse expressed by Michael Dirda, Keith Gessen, and others. Her one mention of blogs is dismissive, as she refers to "blogging and emailing and text-messaging" as among the distractions the younger generations have succumbed to. I assume she's one of the print fetishists who can't imagine serious literary debate occuring online.

But I can't share either her snobbery or her conviction that, whether serious criticism survives or not, "novels *will* be written, whatever the conditions that roil around them." I think the existence of literary criticism is a necessary condition of the survival of both fiction and poetry. Without thoughtful discussion of what's being done by interesting writers, as well as continued discussion of what's been done in the past, "novels" as a form of "literature" will descend into further irrelevance. With no one to argue over what makes writing "literary" in the first place, or why such a concept even matters, novels will at best be only the first step in developing the script for the possible movie so many novels already want to be. Unless folks like Cynthia Ozick think rigorous print-based criticism is going to make a miraculous comeback in newspapers and magazines whose editors suddenly come to their senses and seek to safeguard the literary tradition, she ought to contemplate the possibility that "pixels" can form words and paragraphs and essays just as readily as ink.

Much of Steve Wasserman's essay, "Goodbye to All That" *(Columbia Journalism Review,* Sep/Oct 2007) is concerned with delineating newspapers' obligation to cover "books as news that stays news." He suggests that this means reviewing books "of enduring worth," which in turn suggests an emphasis on work of inherent literary value. I think most people would understand this to signify specifically works of literature--fiction and poetry, although some occasional works of nonfiction might also be included as achieving "enduring worth" as well. Indeed, in further indentifying "news that stays news," Wasserman asserts that "It is through the work of novelists and poets that we understand how we imagine ourselves and contend with the often elusive forces— of which language itself is a foremost factor—that shape us as individuals and families, citizens and communities. . . ."

But in his otherwise cogent enough defense of "serious criticism" in newspapers and other general-interest print publications, Wasserman doesn't really focus with much particularity on <u>literary</u> criticism. It is more or less conflated with discussion of "books" more generally, as if the latest academic tome on American foreign policy or most recent biography of William Randolph Hearst were equally the subject of "criticism" as a new novel by Richard Powers or new collection of poems by John Ashbery. As if the "news" conveyed by *The 9-11 Commission Report* were the same kind of news conveyed by *Falling Man*.

In fact, what Wasserman really has in mind is the kind of social analysis or cultural criticism described by Leon Wieseltier (as quoted by Wasserman): the "long, thoughtful, patient, deliberate analysis of questions that do not have obvious or easy answers." While most good novels do not offer "obvious or easy answers," I don't think it's the interpretation of fiction that Wieseltier has in mind here. Novels might sometimes provide grist for the cultural critic's rhetorical mill, but ultimately "criticism" as Wasserman and Wieseltier understand it is an "elite" discourse through which learned commentators discuss the cultural, political, and historical forces bearing down on "society" as it is reflected in all forms of expression. (I don't object to learned commentary per se, but I do like my learned commentary on literature to be <u>about</u> literature.) As Wasserman himself puts it, "the fundamental idea at stake in a novel—in the criticism of culture generally—is the self-image of society: how it reasons with itself, describes itself, imagines itself." It is the critic's role to sketch out this "self-image of society."

Suffice it to say I don't have much use for this conception of the critic's role, at least not if we're going to persist in calling such a critic a "literary" critic. It's telling that Wasserman singles out *The New York Review of Books* and *The New Republic* as exemplars of the kind of reviewing practice to which he aspired when the editor of the *Los Angeles Times Book Review* (and presumably still does). The NYROB (for a long time now) and TNR (increasingly) have more or less abandoned the task of reviewing fiction on any consistent basis. Only the most highly promoted, "big" novels, or novels by already established "big" authors get reviewed in these publications, and, especially in NYROB, the reviews are usually quite perfunctory, given length only by the tedious practice of dwelling on biographical details or surveying the author's career in an equally apathetic fashion. While both NYROB and TNR have sizable reputations for their supposedly weighty reviews and critical commentary, most of the weight comes precisely from discussions of books, mostly nonfiction, that illustrate how society "reasons with itself, describes itself," etc., not from "long, thoughtful, patient, deliberate" analyses of works of fiction or poetry.

Thus the whole ongoing debate about whether "serious criticism" can take place online or only in print is at best a red herring. Very little serious criticism of literature takes place in print to begin with, aside from the conventional, mechanical book-report review, which Wasserman concedes is, on the whole, "shockingly mediocre" as carried out by most American newspapers. "The pabulum that passes for most reviews is an insult to the intelligence of most readers," he writes. "One is tempted to say, perversely, that its disappearance from the pages of America's newspapers is arguably cause for celebration." The question is, at least for me, not whether print is superior to pixels or whether the online medium can sustain serious literary criticism, but whether there is or will be such criticism available at all to those who want more than the "pablum" spiced up as criticism to be found in newspapers or the "long, thoughtful" exercises in fake wisdom on display at the "premiere" mainstream print journals.

This is why I still hold out hope that blogs, or whatever subsequent online forms they might morph into, can serve as sites offering "serious criticism" of literature, both canonical and contemporary (but maybe especially the latter). Print may or may not be the more adequate medium for the kind of long and thoughtful meditation Wasserman and Wieseltier obviously prefer, but since newspapers are only offering less and less space for such efforts, and since print magazines and journals seem to favor the meandering "think pieces" over focused literary analysis, those of us who would simply like to see both contemporary literature and literary criticism continue to flourish don't really have the luxury of waiting for print editors to see the light or for would-be literary critics to quit noodling around. If blogs are attracting people, both writers and readers, who are enthusiastically engaged in discussions of literature, then I can't see any reason why the literary weblog or the online literary journal (or both together) can't be credible forums for "serious criticism."

The recent spate of articles deploring online discourse have raised various objections to this notion. The most easily dismissed is the assertion that criticism requires "authority" on the part of the critic and that blogs are too numerous and too dispersed to acquire such authority. While I can agree with Wasserman or with Richard Schickel that not every critical opinion is worthy of respect unless backed up with accompanying support and analysis (in Schickel's case, a point articulated in an essay mostly lacking either), there's nothing that automatically confers authority on a book review or critical commentary simply because it appears in print or that detracts from that authority because it appears online. Wasserman claims to agree with this ("content rules"), but also apparently accepts the further claim that most litblogs don't attempt such criticism, anyway, and that they lend themselves primarily to a cacophony of strident voices. Rohan Matizen confesses that she, too, held such a view (actually she acknowledges she had no idea that blogs engaged in "serious criticism" even existed, a state of knowledge she also, as it turns out, shared with Schickel and Wasserman) but now, she writes: "I've been reading through the archives of some lively blog debates related to my own questions about the terms and tendencies of contemporary academic literary criticism. . .Following the long chains of arguments and rebuttals, examples and counter-examples, I'm struck with a familiar sense of futility: when so much has been said by so many so often, what can I hope to add? I'm also struck, though, by just how unaware I was that conversations of quite this kind were going on." (*Novel Readings*, "Even in Blogging, Everything New is Old," 9/2/2007)

Another objection, one that clearly underpins Steve Wasserman's essay, is that criticism must be "long" before it is "thoughtful" and since blogs by their very nature can't accommodate lengthy analysis they can't be thoughtful. It is still probably an open question whether the blog form will allow for the kind of analysis Wasserman has in mind (this will be settled at least as much by readers as by writers, depending on whether we overcome the "screen fatigue" that some readers profess to develop with longer forms of online prose), but it is certainly true there is no defensible case to be made that that sort of analysis is impossible on blogs. However, if blog detractors were to sample, say, the shorter posts sometimes offered by Steve Mitchelmore in his *This Space* or on a regular basis by Jonathan Mayhew in his self-titled blog, they would surely see that "deliberate analysis" can occur in shorter, more compacted blog posts as readily as in the conventionally drawn-out critical essays they champion. Mayhew's deliberately condensed bursts of insight are more discerning about poetry than almost anything else I read. Bloggers like these just may demonstrate in the long run that "thoughtful" literary criticism doesn't always have to be "long" and that the "patience" requested by certain windy critics might not really be worth the time.

A final objection lodged against literary blogs is that the kind of reading they encourage is too frenetic, that the hyperlinks they provide make them hyperactive. Such skipping hither and yon interrupts the cogitative process, turns critical analysis into a game of tag, a cross-blog competition for links. To me, however, the interactive and recursive features of blogs are their most valuable and distinctive, the features most likely to result in the internet/blogosphere making a real contribution to literary criticism. Of course they can be used as excuses for gossip, shortcuts to thinking, or for cheap self-aggrandizement, but ultimately their additional, more purposeful potential for exploring implications and extending lines of thought will surely be exploited more fully as well. Links, whether external to other sites considering in-common subjects and themes or internal to archived posts representing previously-expressed thoughts on a given issue, provide an opportunity to extend debate and reintroduce relevant ideas in new contexts. They can lead to substantive discussions of both the immediate subject at hand and other, related subjects to create a reading experience almost impossible to duplicate through traditional print sources. This sort of experience, by which one is led to parallel analyses and direct response, often without having expected to encounter such a vigorous exchange of views, is one I have myself increasingly come to appreciate in my own reading of literary blogs, and I would like to think that blog skeptics, if they bothered to investigate what good literary blogs actually have to offer, would eventually themselves find this form of critical discourse as substantial and satisfying as I do.

In one of the installments of the apparently eternal series of "panel discussions" on book reviewing sponsored by the National Book Critics Circle, Dwight Garner proclaimed that he and his colleagues at the *New York Times Book Review* turn to blogs not for criticism but "for news of the publishing world and gossip." Other panelists seemed to agree that this is what blogs are good for (Richard Grayson, My Space, 9/15/2007). On the one hand, this is just more evidence of the incuriosity of Garner and his ilk, the self-appointed "gatekeepers" of mainstream book criticism. If they were truly interested in the "serious criticism" of literature, they would actively be looking in more than the usual places for anyone, in print or on blogs, who might be offering it. But they aren't, and they don't. On the other hand, that they can and do find blogs that supply them with their gossip is evidence enough that the literary blog as it has evolved over the 4-5 years of its existence indeed encompasses a large category of blogs that do little more than gabble on about the "book business" and its hangers-on practicing what is called "literary journalism." If anything, many of these blogs are even more sycophantic than the literary journalists themselves.

This has been a fairly predictable development of the approach taken by many of the founding literary bloggers, but it is neither a necessary nor a sufficient one. Most of the early bloggers did not simply link to "literary news" as an excuse for mindless chatter. They offered smart, often trenchant and contrarian takes on this news. If they hadn't, literary blogs would never have captured readers' attention the way they obviously enough did. (They certainly would never have attracted my attention as they did.) The collective existence of these weblogs, each contributing distinctive observations on books and book discussion, gave readers who happened upon them a perspective on the current literary scene that print criticism clearly was not providing. The literary blogosphere has now expanded to include more comprehensive and sustained commentary (including by many of the original bloggers themselves), but most of its critics seem fixated on what they perceive as the "chatty" qualities of the link-and-comment style of blogging. It allows them to continue in their condescension toward blogs, but I think I can even now hear the sound of their perches of "authority" crumbling.

Critical Assumptions

I Aesthetic Analysis

Although I agree with Barrett Hathcock's conclusion that the kind of "cultural criticism" represented by Greil Marcus's *The Shape of Things to Come* "too energetically [mines its] material for the cultural rather than the aesthetic," I can't agree with the critical typology that underlies his analysis:

> . . .The first level is the most base, the easiest, and perhaps the most valuable--the thumb. A thumbs up or thumbs down? This is the criticism of a friendly recommendation; this is the criticism of year-end lists, whether they're constructed by some blog or by *The New York Times.*

> The second, slightly higher level of criticism is that of specific, aesthetic analysis. How does this particular piece of art work? How does it function as a radically constructed whole? (Or how does it not, and why?) This is, I'll admit, rather undergraduate-heavy--art

seen through a lit seminar, where students pop open the hood of a sonnet to see how it works.

The third and highest level of criticism, in my radically simplified piñata here, is criticism as cultural interpretation, where a piece of art is situated in a larger cultural context, both compared to other pieces of the culture, and prism-like, made to shine in the various rays of that culture. I think this third type of criticism is the most complex of the three, the one that rewards the most re-reading, the one that soars above mere book reviewing (this was about that, and it was good), and speaks to what it means to be alive right now in this crazy, kooky world we live in, etc.. . . . (*The Quarterly Conversation* 7, Spring 2007)

"Specific, aesthetic analysis" is only "slightly higher" in its effect than list-making and crude value judgments? I understand that the "recommendation" function of book reviewing is important to many readers, who want to know whether a particular book is worth reading in the first place, but the kind of judgment that can be expressed through the thumb hardly qualifies as literary criticism. Indeed, I'm not likely to take anyone's recommendation seriously at all unless it's accompanied by some "specific, aesthetic analysis" that reveals to me just why how and why the reviewer reached his/her conclusion about a book's thumbworthiness in the first place.

Thus, I also take issue with the notion that "aesthetic analysis" is an act of pulling apart a work of art "to see how it works." To my mind, "aesthetic analysis" and "literary criticism" are synonymous terms. A literary critic doesn't so much "pop open the hood"--although something like this is probably inevitable when the critic tries to illustrate his/her responses to the text: this is what worked on me the way it did--as report on the aesthetic experience the work has provided. This may require some re-reading of the text to clarify what prompted the particular experience it provoked, but ideally "aesthetic analysis" is not an end in itself, something that settles once and for all how a particular work "functions as a radically constructed whole," but the means to another critical end: to provide other readers with an informed account of what the work is like, perhaps to encourage the reader to approach it with a sharper critical eye and heighten his/her own experience of it.

My biggest problem with Hathcock's schema, however, is the privileged place it gives to "criticism as cultural interpretation." In my view, this kind of "criticism," at least as it is applied to literature, isn't either literary or criticism. As soon as a work of literature "is situated in a larger cultural context," what follows isn't likely to be about the work at all--about what causes us to call it literary--but about the "context." It will be sociology, not literary criticism, intended to illuminate the "culture" that produced the art, not the art itself. This may or may not be more "complex" than actual criticism (I myself don't think it is; "situating" art in its cultural context may give such a piece of sociological analysis a patina of learnedness or the appearance of sounding out Important Issues, but it's finally much easier to make broad generalizations about "culture" based on superficial comparisons than it is to truly engage in "specific, aesthetic analysis"), but it isn't finally about what makes art or literature worth our attention to begin with. It isn't the literary critic's job to tell us "what it means to be alive right now in this crazy, kooky world we live in," although perhaps it is part of the artist's job to do so. The critic focuses on how the artist goes about that job in a particular instance, how the artist's work encourages (or doesn't) a singular aesthetic experience.

Hathcock says he would "like Marcus to pay more attention to the second type of criticism in an effort to bolster the strength of his higher cultural criticism," but Marcus is obviously not much interested in doing so because he's not much interested in his objects of analysis as art. Whether Marcus himself thinks he's doing "higher cultural criticism" rather than mere aesthetic analysis is debatable, but I surely don't know what's "higher" about it. I wouldn't necessarily call it "lower" than aesthetic criticism, but unless you think it's more important to understand the cultural currents flowing through David Lynch's work than to appreciate the work itself, I can't see why we would place it on such a pedestal.

On the one hand, Rohan Maitzen's comments about the nature of "academic criticism" seem to me unimpeachably correct:

> . . .aesthetic judgment is not currently seen as a central (maybe even an appropriate) aim of academic criticism. We are too aware of the shifting nature of such judgments, for one thing, and of the many reasons besides aesthetic ones for finding a text worth studying. If asked whether a book is good, an academic is likely to reply 'good at what?' or 'good in relation to what?' or 'good for what?' It may be that this insistence on refining the question, or examining its implicit assumptions, is part of what makes academic criticism less appealing to the 'average intelligent reader,' if what they are after is actually a recommendation. . . . (*Novel Readings*, "Novel Readings in the *Guardian*," 12/20/2007)

On the other, that "aesthetic judgment is not currently seen as a central (maybe even an appropriate) aim of academic criticism" is probably the ultimate reason why "academic criticism" as specifically an act of literary criticism is not likely to survive much longer.

The only period in the history of academic criticism (which runs roughly from the 1920s to the present) in which "aesthetic judgment" was seen as the "central" goal of criticism was really the period dominated by New Criticism, which was in turn the critical method that solidified academic criticism's place in academe's disciplinary structure. Before the rise of New Criticism, those who opposed converting English departments from philology (the study of the etymology of words) to literary study proper (the study of texts as texts) did so precisely because something as nebulous as "aesthetic judgment"--or "appreciation"--was not considered an appropriate focus of academic inquiry. New Criticism provided a plausible method of quasi-rigorous scrutiny of texts that finally satisfied most criteria of what constitutes a properly "academic" field of study.

Yet even New Criticism did not really rest on "aesthetic judgment" as its foundation. New Criticism's strategy of "close reading" was not primarily used to make judgments about the objects of its scrutiny, to declare some texts "good" and others not. The New Critics generally assumed the value of the works they examined (in fact mostly poems), although in some cases their readings did seek to demonstrate to perhaps skeptical readers that the work at hand possessed the requisite degree of "complexity" that New Criticism most fundamentally valued. (And in some instances, such as Cleanth Brooks's reading of Wordsworth's Intimations Ode, they also attempted to show that even works less generally esteemed according to New Critical standards could still be worthy of serious attention.) But the New

Critics would never have conceded to the notion of "the shifting nature" of value judgments. The point of New Criticism was to establish that it was the critical method applying authentic "literary" criteria to the reading of literary texts. Some readers might find value in such texts for extrinsic reasons--political, historical, cultural--but for the New Critics, readers assessing them through the rigors of close reading would hardly come to the kind of relativistic conclusions Maitzen's comment entails.

Still, as the New Critics implicitly recognized, it's difficult to justify the study of literature as part of an academic curriculum if the primary purpose is to arrive at "value judgments." Something more tangible than "appreciation" has to be the fruit of literary study or it does indeed become such a "soft" discipline that few serious-minded students will want to pursue it and even fewer scholars from other disciplines will consider it a respectable practice. However, the very fact that New Criticism was able to establish itself as a suitable "approach" to the study of literature ultimately became the seed of its own undoing. If appreciation is not the only possible goal of literary study, then neither is form-oriented close reading. "Refining the question," or even changing it altogether, is not only possible but, given the academic imperative to create "new" knowledge, almost inevitable. More than anything else, I would say, this changing of the critical guard, the cycling through of formalism, structuralism, post-structuralism, historicism, cultural studies, is what makes academic criticism "less appealing" to non-academic readers. It is a disciplinary debate between academics the ramifications of which are of importance only to academics.

However, I also think it's a little unfair to say that the "average intelligent reader" is interested merely in a "recommendation." This only reinforces the divide between "criticism," which is perforce practiced primarily in the academy, and reviewing, the goal of which is presumably to provide a recommendation. It is the existence of this divide, whereby the academy is considered to be the place where genuine literary criticism is practiced, while general interest book discussion involves. . . something else, that has helped to make academic criticism seem so insular, so reluctant to make itself intelligible to "ordinary" readers (no relevant recognition from other "experts" will ensue) and that has made what passes for general interest criticism so pallid and formulaic. (Although certainly academic criticism follows it own kind of formulas as well.) What both contemporary literature and literary criticism need is not for academic critics to become more "accessible" but for literary magazines and journals to publish more non-academic criticism that goes beyond book chat and conventional journalistic reviews but that also avoids the navel-gazing "refinements" of academic criticism.

And even though there are "many reasons besides aesthetic ones for finding a text worth studying," I further believe that most readers of poetry and fiction are drawn to them for the aesthetic reasons first of all. Some may later on take an interest in all those other things a text is "good for," but in my opinion most habitual readers of literary works want most immediately to have a fulfilling reading experience and, to the extent that criticism is pertinent to this goal, to use literary criticism as a way of enlarging and enhancing this experience. Thus, if "many non-academic readers would in fact like to think in more careful ways about their reading," as Rohan Maitzen acknowledges, and if that's "where academic expertise presented in an accessible manner comes in," then the kind of "expertise" such readers might find helpful would be an ability to describe the aesthetic strategies and effects at work in a text, based ultimately on the ability to pay careful and focused attention to the text, in effect to let it reveal its own aesthetic nature. A knowledge of literary history and of the ways in which all poetry and fiction is finally implicated in that history could also be valuable, as long as that knowledge is put in the service of illuminating the work at hand, not of demonstrating the critic's own superior powers of discernment.

Suffice it to say that academic criticism has long abandoned this modest though still worthwhile mission. It has almost abandoned literature itself, except where it can still be used to illustrate the critic's particular theoretical construct or cultural diagnosis. Pretty clearly, "literary criticism" as practiced in the academy has shifted its emphasis to an analytical perspective more like philosophy for some, more like sociology for others. Since most "non-academic" readers read works of literature for their literary qualities (which, although they can't be defined precisely, at least not to everyone's satisfaction, are still readily enough apparent to those who are looking for them) and not as opportunities to do philosophy or study social patterns, academic criticism isn't going to become more accessible to these readers, only less so. The real question becomes whether a new kind of literary criticism will arise, one less concerned with being "rewarded professionally" by the academy and more concerned with the elucidation of literature, less concerned with providing consumer guidance (buy this, don't buy that) and more concerned with assisting the consumers of fiction or poetry to guide themselves.

II The Biographical Fallacy

In a review of Jay Parini's biography of William Faulkner, J. Peder Zane writes:

> We hope that biographies such as Jay Parini's *One Matchless Time: A Life of William Faulkner* will illuminate such episodes. Where did Faulkner get the fortitude to continue chasing what the world and experience saw as only windmills? How to explain the grand artistic leap that produced *The Sound and the Fury*?

Perhaps if we know how he did it, we might be able to accomplish the same! (Raleigh *News and Observer*, 12/19/2004)

Surely this can't be the reason why otherwise intelligent people would want to read a biography of a writer, particularly one about a writer so distinctive in his accomplishments as Faulkner. Perhaps the idea is that the reader might learn not how to write like Faulkner, but how he summoned up the "fortitude" to continue writing in the face of all evidence that it wasn't getting him anywhere. One could imagine some readers who might be curious about such a thing, but if they have to see the reality of a writer dedicated enough to his talent and his vision to keep at it despite what the world seems to think of him corroborated in a biography, those readers aren't likely to be the type to "accomplish the same" to begin with.

Why should we want to read biographies, perhaps multiple biographies, of writers whose primary claim on our attention is that they were writers, presumably producing work good enough that we continue to read it? I can't think of any viable reasons why we should. The facts of writing itself, the wheres and hows and how oftens, aren't that interesting, and it is these facts that define the writer's "life" insofar as we ought to have any interest in most writers' lives at all. We should settle for the primary fact that a particular writer found the time and the appropriate circumstances in which to write. Everything else is gossip, at best a record of the sorts of things a writer did when he wasn't writing, which again ought not to be of much concern to us since what separates a writer from everyone else, aside from those facts of writing already mentioned, is the work left behind.

What do biographies usually tell us about that work? In my experience, very little. Perhaps there are some truly great biographical works--Ellman's on Joyce, Edel's on James--that provide insight into their subject's work, that provide us with a way of approaching the work we can't get elsewhere, but unfortunately such books are few and far between. I'm sure Parini's book is perfectly competent, will give its readers a satisfactory enough sense of what Faulkner's life was like. Since Parini is himself both a novelist and a critic, it's quite possible what he has to say about Faulkner's books is interesting as well. But if I want some additional commentary about the books, I'd rather turn to a critical book Parini might want to write about Faulkner's work rather than a biography, which almost inevitably gets caught up in discussions about where ideas came from, upon whom certain characters are based, what episodes in the writer's life were transformed into fiction. I'm more interested in the ideas themselves, in experiencing the characters in their artistically embodied forms. I'm more interested in the fiction.

Zane concludes his review by declaring:

Many questions surrounding Faulkner's life are even harder to answer. Parini does not adequately explain the source of Faulkner's signature achievement: Yoknapatawpha County. Parini focuses on that "matchless time" from the late 1920s to the early 1940s when Faulkner produced at least a half dozen masterpieces, but can't begin to explain why his writing fell off thereafter. And the biographer doesn't explore the suicidal tendencies that fueled his drinking and later his horsemanship (which almost killed him on several occasions).

But then, you can't get blood from a stone. Parini's biography is about as good as it will get, which suggests the need for a different approach. Faulkner requires the kind of attention that has been lavished on another enigmatic William, Shakespeare-- a speculative biography modeled after Stephen Greenblatt's brilliant *Will in the World* or a novel such as Richard Nye's masterful *The Late Mr. Shakespeare*. Only by discarding convention can we hope to one day know this unconventional man.

I suppose readers interested in such voyeuristic subjects as Faulkner's drinking or his "horsemanship" might be disappointed in Parini's handling of them, but I can't imagine that anyone interested in Faulkner's fiction rather than his flaws as a human being would care even an iota about these things. And why Faulkner's "writing fell off" after the early 40s--although I would argue it merely became more uneven--is less important than the fact that it did. The "why" question can even be answered more immediately by looking at the writing itself: Faulkner wrote less well, the concrete explanations for which can be discerned by examining the work itself carefully.

What would it mean to "explain the source of Faulkner's signature achievement: Yoknapatawpha County." Explain what? Why it is his "signature achievement"? Read the books and find out. Where an analogy to such and such a location or dwelling or geographical feature depicted in the novels might be found in or around Oxford, Mississippi? Who cares? How Faulkner brooded on the history and social realities of Oxford and its environs and was able to transform it all into compelling fiction that also managed to capture something essential about the American south? This is indeed an interesting question, well worth a book, but unfortunately a biography is not the sort of book that is going to be able to answer it very effectively.

As to a "speculative biography" along the lines of Greenblatt's book on Shakespeare: Why on earth would we need such a thing? Greenblatt has written a "biography" meant to compensate for the lack of known facts about Shakespeare. We know the facts about Faulkner. No "unconventional" reshuffling of these facts is going to shed any more light on Faulkner's work. (If we knew the facts about Shakespeare, no such biography of him would accomplish much, either.) I don't know if it's true or not that "Only by discarding convention can we hope to one day know this unconventional man." I still can't figure out why anyone wants to know the "unconventional man" in this way in the first place.

PART TWO

John Dewey's *Art as Experience*

I Aesthetic Experience

The title of this book (and of the literary weblog in which it originates) reflects the influence of the American philosopher John Dewey and in particular his book *Art as Experience*. I first came to Dewey through the writing of Richard Rorty, whose effort to in effect rescue philosophy from the futility of useless assumptions and a residual metaphysics was in large part inspired by Dewey and seemed to me by analogy a potentially relevant model for extricating literary study from its overworked abstractions and misplace priorities. I found Dewey's philosophical pragmatism even more compelling, his aesthetic philosophy more fully developed and more useful in conceiving an alternative to the elision of the literary in current literary study.

Until then I had been more or less an exponent of what was left of New Criticism, the formalist mode of literary criticism that came to prominence in the 1940s but by the 1970s had already become "old school" in academic criticism. I can't say the academic program in which I was enrolled as a graduate student necessarily encouraged me to value New Criticism above all other approaches to literary study, although it did still focus largely on authors and texts rather than theory or cultural analysis. I was not so much "trained" to be a New Critic as I was simply introduced to New Criticism, discovering an interest in it I pursued through my own reading of the key New Critical texts. Not everything about New Criticism appealed to me: Its function for some New Critics of turning the study of literature into a quasi-substitute for religious contemplation could not have been more remote from my own purposes in reading, and the notion of the literary text as "verbal icon," in addition to reinforcing the association with religion, seemed to me to make works of literature essentially objects to be passively admired.

Most New Critical practice did not really approach works of literature in this way, however. What I took from a book like Cleanth Brooks's *The Well-Wrought Urn* was that fully engaging with a poem, and by extension with fiction as well, is a dynamic process, the work itself both provoking the reader's effort to understand and resisting an easy assimilation into "meaning." All interpretations are partial, and unless it is undertaken with this is mind, interpretation can be a misguided assault on the integrity of the poem, which wants to be read, not translated into ordinary discourse. Although New Criticism had by the time I encountered it been designated for assignment to the dustbin of history by the even newer cutting-edge academic criticism, I thought its attempt to show how literary texts escaped subordination to "intention" or to "statement" was entirely consistent with such new theoretical developments as Jacques Derrida's critique of the "metaphysics of presence" and that the variety of "close reading" employed in the practice of deconstruction had more than a family resemblance to that pioneered by the New Critics. For a while at least, I investigated the implications of poststructuralism for literary study, especially in the work of Derrida, who himself once pointed out the continuity between deconstruction and New Criticism in an interview in which he said "what is heralded. . .under the name of literature cannot be identified with any other discourse" (Attridge 2004).

It was only a short step from Derrida's exposure of the metaphysical assumptions behind Western discourse conventions to the anti-metaphysics of Rorty, and thus to Dewey. His account of the nature of art, including literary art, also seemed remarkably compatible with New Criticism's holistic method of explicating literary texts, but it avoided entirely the temptation to elevate works of literature into icons and precious objects. What Dewey ultimately clarified for me is that the aesthetic effects of art begin in the object, but they don't end there. "Art" is not identical with the object but includes the process by which the beholder apprehends the object in experience. Since the act of reading already involves an obviously mediated process--registering the words, connecting them into syntactical units, translating them into images, ideas, etc.--literature arguably provides an especially complex instance of art arising from the stimulus to aesthetic experience. For the same reason, it often enough is a source of resistance on the part of some readers and critics not just to the notion of art as experience but to the very idea that literature should be regarded primarily as art.

For Dewey, then, even the greatest art must, in a sense, pass the test of experience:

> By common consent, the Parthenon is a great work of art. Yet it has esthetic standing only as the work becomes an experience for a human being. (4)

All "classic" or canonical art must achieve its "esthetic standing" in the moment, as an experience. "Common consent" might keep certain works more consistently available for experience than others, but it cannot itself establish such works as "art" except in the most rudimentary, descriptive sense. It is certainly true that much great art and literature has survived precisely because it has continued to provide compelling aesthetic experience. However, often enough criticism and interpretation of art, especially traditional art, actually inhibits its ability to become "an experience for a human being." The works themselves become encrusted with tendentious commentary meant to advance one external ideology or another, protect one or another cultural bias, rather than allow viewers/readers/listeners to judge for themselves. A proper Deweyan critic would seek to help the audience for art have a more satisfying experience of it, not appropriate it for other purposes or simply declare it "great."

Thus art is not just the ultimate product, the finished sculpture, the musical score, the published book, although these are the immediate gateways by which we enter art's domain (and the achieved work to which we return.) Great art also invites reflection on the means by which the product has been realized, order wrested from "flux." Ultimately it must solicit what Dewey calls an act of "recreation":

> Without an act of recreation the object is not perceived as a work of art. The artist selected, simplified, clarified, abridged and condensed according to his interest. The beholder must go through these operations according to his point of view and interest. (54)

To say that aesthetic effects--what some might want to call "beauty"--cannot be fully realized without this phase of recreation is not to say that the work itself disappears as an object of embodied aesthetic form. Dewey makes this clear in discussing literary critic I. A. Richards's contention that "We are accustomed to say that the picture is beautiful instead of saying that it causes an experience in us which is valuable in certain ways." Dewey responds by making a distinction between a "picture" and a "painting":

> The painting as a picture is *itself a total effect* brought about by the interaction of external and organic

causes. The external factor is vibrations of light from pigments on canvas variously reflected and refracted. It is ultimately that which physical science discovers--atoms, electrons, protons. The *picture* is the integral outcome of their interaction with what the mind through the organism contributes. Its "beauty," which, I agree with Mr. Richards, is simply a short form for certain valued qualities, belongs to the picture just as much as do the rest of its properties. (250-51)

The picture is an intentional object, created to convey those "certain valued qualities" that are fully realized in the viewer's encounter with them in the perceived object. It is not simply the "vibrations of light" that in Richards's scheme would account for our experience of beauty. It is an "object in esthetic experience," not just the provocation to such experience.

Dewey continues: "The reference to 'in us' is as much an abstraction from the total experience, as on the other side it would be to resolve the picture into mere aggregations of molecules and atoms." The "total experience" includes both the viewer's subjective apprehension of the object and the "qualities" of the object itself. It is not merely a subjective response. Although even Richards doesn't suggest that aesthetic response is essentially subjective: "certain objects cause effects in us of one kind or another." This account actually strips the subject of its agency, casting its role in aesthetic experience as passive and mechanical. Indeed, aesthetic experience itself is described by Richards entirely in mechanical terms, as the incidental phenomenon produced by the laws of cause and effect. For Dewey it is an "integral outcome" of a mutually dynamic interaction, something subjectively felt but not simply a matter of "projecting the effect and making it part of the cause," in Richards's words.

It is thus possible through Dewey's conception of aesthetic experience to affirm that "appreciation" of a work of art arises in subjective experience but is also directed toward an object of which it can be said that such qualities as "form" and "style" and even "meaning" objectively exist, although no particular aesthetic experience is likely to fully encompass all of the relevant elements of each. Still, one could point to these qualities as a way of judging the soundness of a description or intepretation of the work. Beauty may be in the eye of the beholder, but our eyes must register the assertion of beauty in the first place.

II Means and Ends

The problem of "form" in art, especially in works of literature, disappears fairly quickly if we simply accept John Dewey's definition:

> . . .form is not found exclusively in objects labeled works
> of art. Wherever perception has not been blunted and

perverted, there is an inevitable tendency to arrange events and objects with reference to the demands of complete and unified experience. Form is a character of every experience that is *an* experience. Art in its specific sense enacts more deliberately and fully the conditions that effect this unity. Form may then be defined as the operation of forces that carry the experience of an event, object, scene, and situation to its own integral fulfillment. (*Art as Experience*, 137)

Thus it is quite impossible for "substance" to precede form. All experiences are given substance by their unfolding and consummation into form, as perception itself (when it hasn't been "perverted") naturally seeks form ("a complete and unified experience"). Art makes the human form-imposing impulse itself into a subject of contemplation. Thus in experiencing a work of art we are both witnessing an "event" brought "to its own integral fulfillment" and are invited to reflect on our own "inevitable tendency" to seek such fulfillment.

For me, this is one of the most important tasks undertaken by works of art and literature. I would even say that it is a process, fundamental to the way that art works, that also has "real world" implications, a carryover from literature to life. By encouraging us to occupy the second-order level of reflection on the manifestation of form, literary art reveals our predisposition to form, at the same it satisfies it in a particularly concentrated way. (In Dewey's formulation, it "clarifies" experience by allowing us to more fully realize what it's like for a "event, object, scene and situation" to be brought to "integral fulfillment.") Literature in particular also forces a recognition of the "formal" elements of language, the way language when arranged into complex written compositions becomes ever less transparent in its capacity to "mean," ever more mediated by the form of its arrangement.

By alerting us to the ubiquity and mutability of form, art also alerts us to our attempts to impose form on life, where it is often much less benign in its effect, much more likely to close off experience than to enhance it. (This is my own further amplification of the implications of Dewey's thought, not something he himself says in so many words.) At the same time, Dewey does not want us to understand artistic form as something conventional or predetermined. Indeed:

> A rigid predetermination of an end-product whether by artist or beholder leads to the turning out of a mechanical or academic product. . . A statement that an artist does not care how his work eventuates would not be literally true. But it is true that he cares about the end-result as a completion of what goes before and not because of its conformity or lack of conformity with a ready-made antecedent scheme. He is willing to leave the

outcome to the adequacy of the means from which it issues and which it sums up. (138)

Further:

> The consummatory phase of experience--which is intervening as well as final--always presents something new. Admiration always includes an element of wonder. As a Renascence writer said: "There is no excellent beauty that hath not some strangeness in the proportion". . . . (139)

In my opinion, the resistance to form in some quarters of American fiction comes from a failure to consider this aspect of aesthetic form. Form does not refer to the mindless recapitulation of strategies deemed appropriate (by whatever shadowy cabal responsible for enforcing the rules) for composing what we agree to call a "novel," a "short story," or a "poem," but to what emerges from the "adequacy of means" adopted by the artist, the "consummatory phase" that always--at least in the most admirable works of literary art--results in "something new," a something new many reviewers and critics will find "strange." Form ought not be dismissed because it is upheld by the literary world's elitist powers-that-be but should be embraced because it so often confounds them.

Closely related to Dewey's analysis of form is his focus on "medium." In Chapter IX of *Art as Experience*, "The Common

Substance of the Arts," Dewey discusses the artist's special awareness of his/her medium, a preoccupation with "means" utterly unlike our ordinary utilitarian notion of "means" as "preparatory or preliminary," simply a way to get from here to there we would gladly skip if we could "get the result without having to employ the means." According to Dewey, "sensitivity to a medium as medium is the very heart of all artistic creation and esthetic perception." For the artist, a medium--paint-and-canvas, sound, words--is an employment of "means that are incorporated in the outcome." They don't disappear into the results. They are the results.

Dewey illustrates his point by noting the methods of "inferior" artists:

> Something which Delacroix said of painters of his day applies to inferior artists generally. He said they used coloration rather than color. The statement signified that they applied color *to* their represented objects instead of making them out of color. This procedure signifies that colors as means and objects and scenes depicted were kept apart. They did not use color as medium with complete devotion. Their minds and experiences were divided. Means and ends did not coalesce. The greatest esthetic revolution in the history of painting took place when color was used structurally; then pictures ceased to be colored drawings. The true artist sees and feels in

terms of his medium and the one who has learned to perceive esthetically emulates the operation. Others carry into their seeing of pictures and hearing of music preconceptions drawn from sources that obstruct and confuse perception. (200)

As with painting, so with fiction: The inferior writer fastens words onto his/her "represented objects" rather than making them out of words. In both cases, the artist fails not only to show "sensitivity to a medium as medium" but essentially denies the value of the medium as anything other than the laborious means one would readily avoid if the "represented object"--presumably locked up in the artist's head--could be accessed in a more immediate way. The medium and its "objects and scenes" are kept so far apart that the former collapses into its barest utility.

It is typical of Dewey that in this passage he stresses both the procedure of the artist and the aesthetic perception of the viewer. Throughout *Art as Experience*, he insists that an aesthetic act is not complete until the viewer/reader/listener is able to "emulate the operation" undertaken by the artist. When the painter and the poet succeed in incorporating "medium" in the outcome, that is, in creating a work of art, the work in turn provides the viewer and the reader with a potentially rich aesthetic experience that becomes all the richer when they are able to perceive the way the medium itself is being "used structurally" to create an aesthetic whole that precedes any "idea" the work putatively conveys.

Unfortunately, the "other" kind of audience that "carry into their seeing of pictures and hearing of music preconceptions drawn from sources that obstruct and confuse perception" is all too prominent, even including some critics. If anything, the preconceptions that obstruct and confuse are more seriously debilitating in literary criticism and discussion, which often introduce not just preconceptions about appropriate form but also about the non-literary ends to which artistic means are presumed to point. A preoccupation with ideas, with "themes" or social commentary or political efficacy or the author's biographical circumstances, deflects attention away from the work's primary reason for being, its exploitation of "medium," and reduces the experience of literary art to an ordinary form of communication.

Since "the movements of the individual body enter into all reshapings of material," all art, according to Dewey, could be described as performances, or at least as encompassing "the rhythm of vital natural expression, something as it were of dancing and pantomime" ("The Varied Substance of the Arts," *Art as Experience*). But the "shaping arts," which arise "when these movements carry over in dealing with physically external matters [in a medium]" transform and extend the possibilities of performance:

. . .print has acted--or reacted--to profoundly modify the substance of literature; modifying, by way of a single illustration, the very words that form the medium of literature. The change is indicated on the unfavorable side by the growing tendency to use "literary" as a term of disparagement. Spoken language was never "literary" till print and reading came into general use. But, on the other side, even if it be admitted that no single work of literature excels, say, the "Iliad". . .yet print has made for an enormous extension not merely in bulk but in qualitative variety and subtlety, aside from compelling an organization that did not previously exist. (228)

The "vital natural expression" we think we find more directly in performing arts--which is itself, of course, not exactly spontaneous--can still be attributed to poetry or painting or architecture--or at least to the semblance of "performance" embodied in the poem's lines, the painting's brushstrokes, or the building's contours. The reader or viewer "appreciates" the performance not as a passive spectator but by actively attending to the "shaping" that is the performance. Here lies, I think, the crucial difference between an aesthetic experience as conceived pragmatically by Dewey and an aesthetic "object" as implied by the practice of, say, the New Critics. The reader of a poem or novel in Dewey's formulation seeks to trace the "subtlety" of the work as manifest in the writer's aesthetic choices. The reader tries to re-create the writer's performance as much as possible. For the formalist, the object itself, the text, is the sufficient focus of interest, the "shape" rather than the shaping. The distinction here might seem itself rather subtle, but Dewey's insights help us avoid fetishizing the art "object" and push us harder to think through the implications of an aesthetic strategy in the context of strategies not pursued. They help us see "aesthetics" as an always renewable process rather than as the fixed qualities of a particular work.

One could say that reading involves becoming aware of that "organization that did not previously exist" when language was/is a specifically oral performance. As the most highly organized constructions of language, poetry and fiction especially solicit our attention to the way their "words" are organized. They allow words to become a medium. I tend to think that those who do "use 'literary' as a term of disparagement" ("merely literary") ultimately don't want to accept language as a "medium" in Dewey's account of the term. As a medium, the language of fiction and poetry precisely mediates between "natural expression" and the reader's response to what is expressed. The act of "saying something" becomes unavoidably dispersed in the entangling energies that literary "organization" brings forward. Many readers seem to find this frustrating.

But in reading fiction, we should not forget that neither people nor "things" are the subjects of perception. Words are. If, for example, we are reading a realist novel, we are not experiencing "the world" faithfully reproduced at all. We are not even, finally, experiencing a world of the author's creation, whether it's a world meant to be taken as a version of the real world or one the author has imaginatively brought into being. We are experiencing writing, which is "transformed" into a world of characters and their stories. In our haste to describe that realist novel as a convincing "picture" of reality or as something that "tackles" social problems, we should not forget that it's neither. As an object of aesthetic experience, it's just writing, skillfully arranged for your act of recreation.

III Old and New

By and large, John Dewey's pragmatic philosophy did not really have much room for a preoccupation with history. Dewey most emphasized the possibility of "growth," the forward-looking realization of potential, whether in education, politics, or art. History might hold some illustrative value, but only as it is relevant to the present or the future, only as history contributes to the enhancement of the present and future.

One might surmise, therefore, that Dewey would not particularly esteem "tradition" in the arts. And indeed he does in *Art as Experience* reject tradition as an end-in-itself, dwelling instead on the "adventurous" nature of the best art, art that takes account of the "emergence of new materials of experience demanding expression" by creating "new forms and techniques."

But Dewey understands that the "new" in art also relies on "a particular background of experience":

> Of this background, traditions form a large part. It is not enough to have direct contacts and observations, indispensable as these are. Even the work of an original temperment may be relatively thin, as well as tending to the bizarre, when it is not informed with a wide and varied experience of the traditions of the art in which the artist operates. (265)

The work of an artist insufficiently grounded in the "forms and techniques" of the past might nevertheless be original, but that originality risks being meaningless (simply "bizarre") because the existing audience fails to recognize it as participating in the broader practices of "the art in which the artist operates," although the artist who does so participate might indeed wish to alter or modify those practices. The alterations keep the tradition itself alive even as the tradition makes the "new" possible. Indeed, much of the critical commentary on modernism and postmodernism has consisted of efforts to show that works immediately received as so singular as to seem completely alien are actually comprehensible within the formal, stylistic, or national traditions from which these works arise.

About literary traditions in particular Dewey suggests that "'Schools' of art are more marked in sculpture, architecture, and painting than in the literary arts" but "there has been no great literary artist who did not feed upon the works of the masters of drama, poetry, and eloquent prose." Some writers merely imitate these masters, and for such a writer literary traditions "have not entered into his mind; into the structure of his own ways of seeing and making." Past practices "remain upon the surface as tricks of technique or as extraneous suggestions and conventions as to the proper thing to do" (265). One might object to Dewey's narrowing of the source of tradition to the "masters"; it isn't just the influence of the greatest writers that encourages the new contributions of current writers but, or so I would maintain, of literary history as a whole. "Tradition" does not rest in the indisputably "great" writers but in the continuity of fiction or poetry or drama even as manifested in lesser writers. As Dewey himself often insisted, it is best to think about human activities and institutions in terms of process rather than fixed result, so literary tradition is most usefully considered as an ongoing process of mutually reinforced conservation and change.

Artistic transformation occurs, then, when the artist with his/her "experience demanding expression" confronts tradition in an act of what Dewey calls "intuition," a

> meeting of the old and new in which the readjustment involved in every form of consciousness is effected suddenly by means of a quick and unexpected harmony which in its bright abruptness is like a flash of revelation;

although in fact it is prepared for by long and slow incubation. (266)

Like most accounts of artistic creation, Dewey's suffers from a perhaps unavoidable vagueness, although "intuition" may be as accurate a term for naming the act of discovery that culminates in the work of art as any other. What Dewey adds to nebulous descriptions like "a quick and unexpected harmony" or "flash of revelation" is that the "bright abruptness" of intuition comes only after "long and slow incubation." Artistic intuition occurs against a background of previous creation. It is prompted <u>by</u> that creation.

The reader or audience also has a responsibility to tradition: "The perceiver, as much as the creator, needs a rich and developed background which, whether it be painting in the field of poetry, or music, cannot be achieved except by consistent nurture of interest." Since Dewey's position is that the value of art resides in the <u>experience</u> of it, then that experience would be thin indeed without this "developed background" of tradition. The adventurous work of art could be equally meaningless if the "perceiver" <u>can't</u> recognize the broader practices made visible by tradition, even if the work does encompass them.

To say that both artist and audience need an acquaintance with tradition is not to claim that either must devote lifetimes to the study of literature and literary history (although to do so couldn't hurt). They need "a wide and varied experience of the traditions of the art," but this means that it is the experience of those traditions that count, regarding which quality counts for more than quantity. "Wide and varied" does not mean encyclopedic. At some point, in fact, a pursuit of tradition for its own sake is as likely to impede our ability to experience art deeply as enable it, as the customary practices come to seem "normal" and departures from them unwelcome. In this way, a fixation on "great art," or a certain kind of great art, makes it less likely the tradition it otherwise nourishes will continue to thrive.

T. S. Eliot seemed to recognize this danger when he maintained in his essay "Tradition and the Individual Talent" that

> The existing monuments form an ideal order among themselves, which is modified by the introduction of the new (the really new) work of art among them. The existing order is complete before the new work arrives; for order to persist after the supervention of novelty, the whole existing order must be, if ever so slightly, altered; and so the relations, proportions, values of each work of art toward the whole are readjusted; and this is conformity between the old and the new.

Both Dewey and Eliot suggest that without experiment in art and literature, the "supervention of novelty," the great works of the past merely ossify into a "tradition" that no longer inspires artists and writers to, in effect, outdo the "existing monuments," to bring those monuments into active communication with the present. (Harold Bloom's notion of the "anxiety of influence" probably fits in here as well, however much Bloom would prefer not to be associated with Eliot.) "Certain modifications of the old tradition" are needed to keep the "old tradition" from becoming merely old, as well as to invigorate "the new" through contact with the genuine achievements of the past. Thus both Dewey and Eliot view experiment as a way of maintaining the vitality of the tradition, but also see tradition as subject to the revision prompted by "the really new."

Eliot is usually taken as a conservative defender of tradition, of the notion of "an ideal order," but it seems to me unlikely that the younger Eliot, at any rate, would have much use for current notions of the "canon" Any canon of "great works" would have to be subject to the kind of modification both he and Dewey identify, which ultimately means the very idea of "greatness" in literature would have to be open to such modification. Certainly Eliot's own poetry would never have qualified as "great" if the criteria to be used in judging it remained those appropriate to Pope or Wordsworth or Tennyson. Modern literature as a whole, of which Eliot is the avatar and Dewey the advocate (at least in theory), would not have been possible if poets and writers (many of them now seen as "conservative" in their political and cultural views) had not seen literary tradition both as something to be honored and as something to be defeated.

This not to say that T.S. Eliot was a pragmatist, but that the only way to view both literary history and "the new aims" of present writers in a way that respects both the old and the new is a pragmatic way. The past remains vital to the extent it continues to resonate in the present. The present produces reputable work when such work can be seen as a creative extension of the past.

A more familiar, if not necessarily more precise, term for the faculty involved in the act of artistic creation Dewey identifies as "intuition" is "imagination," the latter of which Dewey discusses immediately after introducing the former in Chapter XI of *Art as Experience*:

> In what precedes, I have said nothing about imagination. "Imagination" shares with "beauty" the doubtful honor of being the chief theme in esthetic writings of enthusiastic ignorance. More perhaps than any other phase of the human contribution, it has been treated as a special and self-contained faculty, differing from others in possession of mysterious potencies. (267)

While Dewey himself is not above invoking "mysterious" processes such as "flash of revelation" in describing intuition, he does hesitate to attribute magical properties to imagination.

> It is the large and generous blending of interests at the point where the mind comes in contact with the world. When old and familiar things are made new in experience,

there is imagination. When the new is created, the far and strange become the most natural inevitable things in the world. There is always some measure of adventure in the meeting of mind and universe, and this adventure is, in its measure, imagination. (267)

The use of passive voice here--"old and familiar things are made new in experience," "the new is created"--is not simply clumsy writing (although Dewey's prose does sometimes have a clumsily hurried quality, as if he is choosing the words that most immediately come to mind), but expresses Dewey's restraint in considering the nature of imagination. He resists the idea that it is a "power" that acts on experience but instead sees it as a function of experience: "[A]n imaginative experience is what happens when varied materials of sense quality, emotion, and meaning come together in a union that marks a new birth in the world."

Unless regarded as this kind of "union," imagination becomes merely the "imaginary," which "gives familiar experience a strange guise by clothing it in unusual garb, as of a supernatural apparition." With the imaginary, "mind and material do not squarely meet and interpenetrate." The artist "toys with material rather than boldly grasping it." A truly imaginative artist does not distort or supersede experience for the sake of fancy. (Dewey cites Coleridge's distinction between imagination and fancy.) However much the "real" may be transformed by imagination (Dewey is not making a case for realism), it is not reduced to mere fantasy. Imagination makes the intangible tangible because "possibilities are embodied in works of art that are not elsewhere actualized." Art makes the real visible.

Dewey more specifically identifies the difference between the imaginative and the imaginary by making a further distinction between what he calls "inner" and "outer" vision.

> There is a stage in which the inner vision seems much richer and finer than any outer manifestation. It has a vast and enticing aura of implications that are lacking in the object of external vision. It seems to grasp much more than the latter conveys. Then there comes a reaction; the matter of the inner vision seems wraith-like compared with the solidity and energy of the presented scene. The object is felt to say something succinctly and forcibly that the inner vision reports vaguely, in diffuse feeling rather than organically. The artist is driven to submit himself in humility to the discipline of the objective vision. But the inner vision is not cast out. It remains as the organ by which outer vision is controlled, and it takes on structure as the latter is absorbed within it. (268)

The artist who insists on his "inner vision," who remains satisfied with that inner vision, is likely to only indulge in the imaginary. The artist who is willing to "submit himself in humility to the discipline of the objective vision" (who must accept the demands of the outer vision or there is no art) will, potentially at least, discover the fuller possibilities of the imagination. The imagination isn't confined to the reveries of the fantasist. It requires the "solidity and energy" of the "objective vision," of the art object itself, the making of which is the ultimate exercise of imagination.

The artist who devotes his/her attention to the "objective vision" finds "the object is felt to say something." Dewey is probably using the construction "say something" very loosely, to indicate that the work as shaped turns out to express the sharpest and most far-reaching vision, but it might mislead us into thinking that the vagueness of the inner vision becomes the more clearly enunciated "theme" through outer vision. Something closer to the opposite is true. The disciplined artist allows the work itself to find what it will say; its meaning will develop "organically," not as the figural rendering of the artist's "intention." The artist <u>feels</u> that the object has spoken. If inner vision "takes on structure as the [outer vision] is absorbed within it," the artist ends up "saying" what the work has said.

IV The Role of Criticism

Dewey perhaps articulates his notion of "art as experience" most straightforwardly near the beginning of the chapter devoted to art's "challenge to philosophy" (ch. XII):

> . . .esthetic experience is experience in its integrity. Had
> not the term "pure" been so often abused in philosophic

literature, had it not been so often employed to suggest that there is something alloyed, impure, in the very nature of experience and to denote something beyond experience, we might say that esthetic experience is pure experience. For it is experience freed from the forces that impede and confuse its development as experience; freed, that is, from factors that subordinate an experience as it is directly had to something beyond itself. To esthetic experience, then, the philosopher must go to understand what experience is. (274)

It should be said that art is "pure experience" if and when the reader/viewer/listener allows the experience its "integrity." This does not always happen, of course. Many predispositions can work to "impede and confuse" aesthetic perception, especially the aesthetic perception of works of literature, as readers subordinate the experience itself to various concerns that are finally extraneous to a concern for the work's aesthetic integrity, from the expectation that a novel should have an "exciting plot" or "characters I can care about" to the assumption that a literary work should be scrutinized for what it "has to say" or what it "reveals about our society." Since it is art's aesthetic integrity--its ability to unify disparate elements into a seamless whole--that for Dewey makes art valuable in the first place, these obstacles subvert the very purpose of literature as an artistic form.

Most literary criticism, especially academic criticism in its current iterations but also much general-interest book reviewing as well, can be characterized as anti-literary in this way. Critics and reviewers seldom assess a work of fiction (the situation of poetry is not so dire in this regard) for its creation of (or lack of) aesthetic unity. The reviewer settles for plot summary and a cursory evaluation, usually based on unstated or unexamined standards, while the academic critic interrogates the text for its value as a cultural symptom. Later in this chapter, Dewey writes that "Since a work of art is the subject-matter of experiences heightened and intensified, the purpose that determines what is esthetically essential is precisely the formation of an experience *as* an experience." Unless critics attend to the way in which a literary work stimulates "the formation of an experience *as* an experience," and subsequently evaluate the quality of the experience so induced, they are missing what is "esthetically essential"--and for Dewey to miss what is aesthetically essential is to miss what is essential about all art.

(There are legitimate forms of literary criticism that appropriately do not focus on aesthetic analysis. Certain kinds of historical or cultural criticism attempt to locate the work contextually, which is a perfectly good thing to do, but I would call this kind of criticism a supplement to aesthetic criticism, not a substitute for it.)

Dewey makes his view of the role of criticism explicit in a chapter devoted to the subject:

> The function of criticism is the reeducation of perception of works of art; it is an auxiliary in the process, a difficult process, of learning to see and hear. The conception that its business is to appraise, to judge in the legal and moral sense, arrests the perception of those who are influenced by the criticism that assumes this task. The moral office of criticism is performed indirectly. The individual who has an enlarged and quickened experience is one who should make for himself his own appraisal. . .The moral function of art itself is to remove prejudice, do away with the scales that keep the eye from seeing, tear away the veils due to wont and custom, perfect the power to perceive. The critic's office is to further this work, performed by the object of art. (*Art as Experience*, Ch. 13 325)

One might prefer to think of the critic's task as simply the education of perception, although Dewey no doubt uses "reeducation" deliberately. So much of modern life inhibits the process of "learning to see and hear," making it all the more difficult than it is already given the influence of "wont and custom." Too often critics themselves work as impediments to clear perception, in particular those who intercede a "judicial" (Dewey's word for the approach to criticism that replaces explanation and analysis with a simplistic rendering of critical decision) and moralistic discourse between the work of art and those who need most to see and hear so they may finally judge for themselves. Both critic and audience need to be reeducated away from these habits.

For Dewey, a more useful form of "judgment" consists in distinguishing "particulars and parts with respect to their weight and function in formation of an integral experience." The critic must develop "a unifying point of view" with which to consider the work of art. However,

> That the critic must discover some unifying strand or pattern running through all details does not signify that he must himself produce an integral whole. Sometimes critics of the better type substitute a work of art of their own for that they are professedly dealing with. The result may be art but it is not criticism. The unity the critic traces must be in the work of art as its characteristic. This statement does not signify that there is just one unifying idea or form in a work of art. There are many, in proportion to the richness of the object in question. What is meant is that the critic shall seize upon some strain or strand that is actually there, and bring it forth with such clearness that the reader has a new clue and guide in his own experience. (314)

While a critic of the "better type"--the type that is lauded for his or her own critical writing to the extent that it comes to take precedence over the writing under review--might be tempted to "judge" a work by comparing it to the work the critics thinks should have been produced but wasn't, the critic who sticks to the "object" (in literature, the text) actually in front of him/her is the one who is finally engaged in the act of criticism. The literary critic is obliged to honestly examine the characteristics the text exhibits, although he/she is not obliged to account for every characteristic that might be felt. The "unity" the critic posits is not a global unity that exhausts the work's formal or thematic possibilities but could be simply a "strain or strand" that does give the text coherence when shown to connect its particulars in a satisfying way. As Dewey says, there are many such strands, "in proportion to the richness of the object in question," and one critic's analysis of "unity" can be supplemented by additional kinds of unity demonstrated by other critics.

In addition, the truly valuable critic avoids what Dewey thinks are the two "fallacies" of criticism. "Reductive" criticism occurs "when some constituent of the work of art is isolated and then the whole is reduced to terms of this single isolated element," or when the work is reduced to its historical, political, or economic circumstances. Dewey finds psychoanalytic and sociological criticism especially reductive. With the former, "If the factors spoken of are real and not speculative, they are relevant to biography, but they are wholly impertinent as to the character of the work itself." As to the latter:

> Historical and cultural information may throw light on the causes of [the work's] production. But when all is said and done, each one is just what it is artistically, and its esthetic merits and demerits are within the work. Knowledge of social conditions of production is, when it is really knowledge, of genuine value. But it is no substitute for understanding of the object in its own qualities and relations. (316)

Thus academic criticism of the historicist and cultural studies varieties may result in something that could be called knowledge (although not always), but it is not knowledge of literature.

The second fallacy, "confusion of categories," can be related to the first when the critic fails to acknowledge this autonomy of the aesthetic. It happens when "critics as well as theorists are given to the attempt to translate the distinctively esthetic over into terms of some other kind of experience." The most common manifestation of this fallacy is the assumption

> that the artist begins with material that has already a recognized status, moral, philosophic, historical, or whatever, and then renders it more palatable by emotional seasoning and imaginative dressing. The work of art is treated as if it were a reediting of values already current in other fields of experience. (318)

Thus the religious poet is declared to be the spokesman for a set of religious values, the philosophical poet for a particular philosophy, etc. But

> medium and effect are the important matters. . .I imagine the majestic art of *Paradise Lost* will be more, not less admitted, and the poem be more widely read, when rejection of its themes of Protestant theology has passed into indifference and forgetfulness. . .The *mise-en-scene* of Milton's portrayal of the dramatic action of great forces need not be esthetically troublesome, any more than is that of the *Iliad* to the modern reader. There is a profound distinction between the vehicle of a work of art, the intellectual carrier through which an artist receives his subject-matter and transmits it to his immediate audience, and both the form and matter of his work. (318)

Protestant theology is Milton's "intellectual carrier." *Paradise Lost* is what it is, aesthetically. The literary critic who confuses these things, who allows the "carrier" to supersede "the intrinsic significance of the medium" (319) is not a <u>literary</u> critic.

V Deep Reading

Sven Birkerts has been developing a critique of "electronic media" for quite a long time, publishing *The Gutenberg Elegies* in 1994, well before the rise of blogs, stand-alone news sites, and critical webzines, so his cyber skepticism is not to be dismissed as simply more defensive posturing by an endangered gatekeeper. I have myself taken issue with some of Birkerts's more uninformed outbursts, but his concern for "unhurried" reading is usually expressed in an equally unhurried analysis of the act of reading (specifically reading fiction), not as the high dudgeon of a book critic protesting his imminent loss of status.

This is especially true of a recent essay by Birkerts in *The American Scholar*, "Reading in a Digital Age" (Spring 2010). The essay is framed as yet another inquiry into the way the digital information "environment" is making serious reading harder to accomplish, but ultimately it is really a candid inquiry into his own reading habits and an attempt to generalize from his conclusions to a theory of sorts both about reading and about the nature of fiction. Much of this theory seems to me perceptive, and generally correct, but parts of it as well seem an overly roundabout way of describing our experience of fiction that would benefit from a consideration of John Dewey's own "experiential-phenomenological" analysis in *Art as Experience*. There is overlap between the accounts offered by Dewey and Birkerts, but finally Dewey's comes closer to doing full justice to the role of "imagination" in reading, both writer's and reader's.

Birkerts associates imagination with the mental state of "contemplation," which he in turn contrasts with "analytic thought." Contemplation is "intransitive and experiential in its nature, is for itself"; analytic thought "is transitive, is goal directed. . .a means, its increments mainly building blocks toward some synthesis or explanation." Contemplation is, or should be, the preferred mode of reading fiction, by which "enhancement" and "deepening," end-states in themselves, are achieved. But Birkerts finds this "deepening" moving in just one direction: the purpose of fiction "is less to communicate themes or major recognitions and more to engage the mind, the sensibility, in a process that in its full realization bears upon our living as an ignition to inwardness, which has no larger end, which is the end itself."

Birkerts's insistence that the reading of fiction leads to experience and not "explanation" is wholly appropriate and does seem to coincide with Dewey's contention that art is an "enhancement" of experience. However, while Dewey might accept "sensibility" as the name for the human receptivity to art, he would not characterize our response to art and literature as primarily an opportunity "to engage the mind," especially if this means a retreat into an "inwardness" that is <u>itself</u> the ultimately desired state, cut off from the projected space occupied by the work instigating the experience in the first place. A Deweyan representation of the reading experience (the experience of art in general) would balance the inwardness Birkerts evokes with an outwardness that also seeks satisfaction in the perception of form and style. If "contemplation" involves the heightened awareness both of the palpable qualities of the created work and of our own awareness of those qualities, then the term might accurately capture the nature of aesthetic experience, but I think Birkerts privileges the activity of "mind."

When Birkerts writes that fiction provides "an arena of liberation. . .where mind and imagination can freely combine," he is not describing an interaction between the reader's "sensibility" and the work as an act of imagination but is positing "mind" and "imagination" as faculties exercised by the reader. When a little later he allows that "I tend to view the author as on a continuum with his characters, their extension," it seems to me he is explicitly discounting the artistic shaping that is finally the role of "author." In merging the author and his characters, Birkerts is putting most value on fiction's ability to induce "empathy," which in his case means the opportunity to connect with another "mind": "It is the proximity to and belief in the other consciousness that matters, more than its source and location." It is presumably this proximity to the "other" as evoked in fiction that constitutes "imagination" for Bikerts, not the unencumbered immersion in aesthetic experience as a whole.

On the other hand, I do identify with Birkerts's account of the "residue" his reading experiences leave:

> . . .the details of plot fall away first, and so rapidly that in a few months' time I will only have the most general précis left. I will find myself getting nervous in party conversations if the book is mentioned, my sensible worry being that if I can't remember what happened in a

novel, how it ended, can I say in good conscience that I have read it? Indeed, if I invoke plot memory as my stricture, then I have to confess that I've read almost nothing at all, never mind these decades of turning pages.

What does remain is "A distinct tonal memory, a conviction of having been inside an author's own language world, and along with that some hard-to-pinpoint understanding of his or her psyche." "Tonal memory" seems to me a good way of characterizing the lingering impression a strong work of fiction leaves, although it is a memory the work has indeed impressed upon the memory rather than the sort of mechanical effort of "recall" the recounting of plot entails. For myself, not only do I usually have trouble retrieving specific episodes from novels I have read more than a few months in the past, I often enough lose all but a general sense of the voice or behavior of the characters, in the case of minor characters sometimes forgetting their existence altogether. Yet I continue to feel a tangible connection to the "language world" I have encountered, which to me is the surest sign my experience of the text was worthwhile.

The storage model of reading thus threatens to reduce the reading experience to the acquisition of "information," which Birkerts rightly resists. But I would take Birkerts's invocation of the "language world" as the ultimate source of value in fiction even farther. Reading a work of literature should always imply the possibility, even the desirability, of re-reading. Suspension in the language-world rather than the collection of facts about the work is much more likely to encourage later re-reading, both because one wants to abide there again and because the work in its particulars hasn't already been thoroughly assimilated and duly packed away. I can read it again and still have a worthwhile literary experience. (Presumably Birkerts might think that re-reading would give him further insight into the author's "psyche" as well; I cannot accept this particular element of his theory of reading, as I cannot see how the created language-world that is the text could possibly reveal anything about the actual author's mental states, except through free-floating speculation irrelevant to the text itself, nor why I should care even if it could.)

Birkerts concludes by encapsulating his claim about "deep reading":

> Serious literary work has levels. The engaged reader takes in not only the narrative premise and the craft of its realization, but also the resonance—that which the author creates, deliberately, through her use of language. It is the secondary power of good writing, often the ulterior motive of the writing. The two levels operate on a lag, with the resonance accumulating behind the sense, building a linguistic density that is the verbal equivalent of an aftertaste, or the "finish." The reader who reads without directed concentration, who skims, or even

just steps hurriedly across the surface, is missing much of the real point of the work; he is gobbling his foie gras.

While there are still assumptions here that seem to me unwarranted--why must the core element of fiction be its "narrative premise," which would only re-introduce "plot" as a barrier between the reader and the "language world"--ultimately this is a credible description of what is involved in serious reading. Unfortunately, Birkerts seems motivated to offer this description mostly in order to bolster his conviction that this kind of reading is endangered by the transition to screen-reading. I am unconvinced, to say the least. If Birkerts were suggesting that deep reading is succumbing to the general human inclination to give in to distraction, to settle for what's easiest, he would perhaps be on firmer ground, although this weakness has always plagued us and can hardly have been induced by the presence of computers. But he clearly enough wants to insist there is something inherent in cyberspace and e-books that make them inimical to "serious literary work" and the reading it requires.

A generation or two from now, serious readers--and they will still be around--will look back at Birkerts's claims and find them deeply puzzling. They will find the notion that literary texts published on pieces of glued-together paper are somehow metaphysically superior to those published electronically difficult to comprehend. I find it hard to comprehend the idea now. I can understand continuing to find the printed book more convenient, or more comforting, but to maintain that serious, sustained reading can take place only when enabled by print-on-paper just isn't plausible. Birkerts is a trustworthy literary critic and a reliable authority on the pleasures of reading, but as a seer into the future of literature he will surely prove inadequate.

PART THREE

Experimental Fiction

Prologue

The aesthetic philosophy expressed in John Dewey's *Art as Experience* is, on the whole, quite sympathetic to experiment and innovation in the arts, in fact in large part is absolutely dependent on it. Without experiment (without what is sometimes called "progress" in the arts), art would ossify into dead monuments we are to extol for their putative greatness but that would not provoke the kind of experiential engagement Dewey thinks is art's ultimate validation.

Furthermore, experimentation is itself responsible for the succession of artistic accomplishments we think of as "art history" (or literary history) in the first place:

> . . .The dependence of significant technique upon the need for expressing certain distinctive modes of experience is testified to by the three stages that usually attend the appearance of a new technique. At first there is experimentation on the side of artists, with considerable exaggeration of the factor to which the new technique is adapted. This was true of the use of line to define recognition of the value of the round, as with Mantegna; it

is true of the typical impressionists in respect to light-effects. On the side of the public there is general condemnation of the intent and subject-matter of these adventures in art. In the next stage, the fruits of the new procedure are absorbed; they are naturalized and effect certain modifications of the old tradition. This period establishes the new aims and hence the new technique as having "classic" validity, and is accompanied with a prestige that holds over into subsequent periods. Thirdly, there is a period when special features of the technique of the masters of the balanced period are adopted for imitation and made ends in themselves. . .In this third stage (which dogs creative work after the latter has general recognition), technique is borrowed without relation to the urgent experience that at first evoked it. The academic and eclectic result.   (142)

Dewey also recognizes that artists who merely attempt to imitate the great accomplishments of the past, who don't go beyond the techniques previous artists discovered, are bound to fail:

> . . .Greek sculpture will never be equaled in its own terms. . .That which Venetian painters achieved will stand unrivaled. The modern reproduction of the architecture of the Gothic cathedral always lacks the quality of the original. What happens in the movement of art is emergence of new materials of experience demanding

expression, and therefore involving in their expression new forms and techniques. . . (143)

Recognizing the rather clinical connotations of the term "experimental" when applied to the arts, Dewey suggests an alternative:

> If, instead of saying "experimental," one were to say "adventurous," one would probably win general assent--so great is the power of words. Because the artist is a lover of unalloyed experience, he shuns objects that are already saturated, and he is therefore always on the growing edge of things. By the nature of the case, he is as unsatisfied with what is established as is a geographic explorer or a scientific inquirer. The "classic" when it was produced bore the marks of adventure. This fact is ignored by classicists in their protest against romantics who undertake the development of new values, often without possessing means for their creation. That which is now classic is so because of completion of adventure, not because of its absence. (144)

In discussing "experimental fiction," I am essentially using "experimental" in Dewey's sense as "adventurous." I am always looking for adventurousness in the new fiction I choose to read (although I'm pretty sure my critical lens is sometimes too cloudy to see it when I'm making decisions about what to read, and I thus simply don't read some fiction I'd probably like), so I tend to ignore much of the most highly-acclaimed, most widely-reviewed fiction, which usually strikes me as more of the same, new iterations of work that "will never be equaled in its own terms" and therefore of little interest to me. Perhaps I could be accused of systematizing Dewey's emphasis on "new forms and techniques" too literally. If every work of fiction were "new" in these terms, there would be no "mainstream" and thus no doubt many fewer readers of fiction. I'm not sure I would find such a state of affairs all that lamentable, but there are surely many readers of "literary fiction" who would, and who would find my preference for the adventurous to be needlessly strict.

And it is certainly the case that some "experimental" fiction fails, manifests a desire to create "new values" but "without possessing means for their creation." In fact, most experimental fiction probably fails in this way, or at least doesn't demonstrate <u>enough</u> of the skill required to produce something so transformatively new as to initiate the cycle Dewey describes in the first passage quoted above. Still, I would rather have these failed "adventures in art," fiction that attempts to reach that "growing edge of things," than give in to a complacent reshuffling of the tried and the true, which, as Dewey points out, will never really be "true."

I Context

In a post on his weblog (July 12, 2008), Ron Silliman observes that "the history of poetry is the history of change in poetry." He further contends that the critics of innovation in literary practice are themselves writers and critics likely to be swept away by the historical currents that favor innovation and are thus mostly engaging in "tantrums" over their own unavoidable fate.

Literature certainly is more the history of its own evolving forms than it is an assemblage of "great works," although I would substitute for "change" John Dewey's notion of "growth" as the inevitable outcome of artistic traditions that manage to extend themselves over time--"growth" not as simplistic "progress" by which one generation of art makes the preceding generation obsolete but as the expansion of available approaches to the form, an increase of insight into the variety of its possibilities. Indeed, even if we were to consider literary history as the accumulation of great works, in most cases these works are great precisely because they represent some new direction taken by the form employed. Surely English drama was not the same after Shakespeare finished stretching its boundaries, nor was English narrative poetry (narrative poetry in general) after *Paradise Lost*. Although we now think of the realistic novel as the epitome of convention in fiction, there was of course a time when it was on the cutting edge of change and writers like Flaubert, Tolstoy, and Henry James were writing what was for the time experimental fiction.

Thus I am less willing than Silliman to dismiss the "well-wrought urn" as a metaphor for aesthetic accomplishment in works of literature. A poem or novel may indeed be "well-wrought" without conforming to pre-established models. Perhaps the passage of time does allow us to see more clearly the craftedness of some works of art that at first seemed simply model-breaking, but ultimately I see no conflict between innovation in poetry or fiction and the skillful construction of individual poems, plays, short stories, or novels.

On the other hand, Silliman is certainly correct in characterizing most of the critical resistance to change in literary forms as a kind of lashing-out against writing implicitly recognized as destined to be remembered precisely because it exposes most of the otherwise critically favored writers of the moment as aesthetically tame and unadventurous, tied to the critical nostrums of the day (which, especially with fiction, are typically not only aesthetically conservative, but often not really focused on aesthetic achievement at all but on what the writer allegedly has to "say" about prominent "issues"). American experimental fiction of the post-World War II era has been especially subjected to these "tantrums"--if anything they have only increased in intensity--concerted efforts to marginalize this fiction by accusing it of lacking seriousness of purpose, of indulging in games and jokes rather than sticking to straightforward storytelling, of striving after effects that turn out to be "merely literary." In my opinion, however, it will be the work of writers like John Hawkes, Robert Coover, and Gilbert Sorrentino that will be recognized as the indispensable fiction of this period, not that of the more celebrated but less formally audacious writers such as Bellow or Styron or Vidal.

Eventually almost all postwar writers whose work departs significantly from convention have come to be labeled "postmodernist," a term that has definable meaning but that also has been used as an aid in this lashing-out, a way to further disparage such writers both by lumping them together indiscriminately and by identifying their work as just another participant in literary fashion. Silliman points out that a distinction can be made between fashion in the arts and the truly new:

> Each art form has its own dynamic around issues such as form and change. For example, one could argue that the visual arts world, at least in New York & London, has become self-trivializing by thrusting change into warp drive because of the market needs of the gallery system. There, capital demands newness at a pace that hardly ever lets a shift in the paradigm marinate awhile. I seriously wonder if any innovation in that world since the Pop artists let in the found imagery of the mid-century commercial landscape has ever had a chance to settle in. That settling process seems to be an important part of the run-up in helping to generate the power of reaction, to

motivate whatever comes next. The problem with the visual arts scene today is that innovation is constant, but always unmotivated.

Poetry has the advantage of not being corrupted by too much cash in the system. That ensures that change can occur at a pace that has more to do with the inner needs of writers as they confront their lives. . . .

The New York art world has become so dependent on "the latest thing" that aesthetic change becomes "unmotivated" except by the need for individual artists to enter the system that confers purpose on their work. While fiction is probably more tied to the cash nexus than poetry, most serious literary fiction is much less so, and the degree of change and resistance to change among writers and critics, although perhaps somewhat less pure than in discussions of poetry, is largely determined by honest beliefs about the direction fiction ought to take.

In this context, to regard experimental fiction as "fashion" is essentially to believe there can be no "shift[s] in the paradigm" in the development of fiction, that the experimental must always represent an irritating deviation from the accepted unitary model of how fiction should be written. It forecloses the possibility that the established paradigm might "shift" if something genuinely new were to appear and transform our assumptions about the nature of the novel and/or the short story. Even if it is allowed that the occasional genius comes along to produce work that stands out from the mainstream, such work is considered a singular achievement, a momentary departure from the otherwise settled paradigm granted only to the genius. The exceptional, extraordinary talent thus helps to preserve the status quo since no one else can be expected to rise to his/her level.

In reality, the "postmodern" period in American fiction came close to establishing a new paradigm insofar as it seemed to validate the experimental impulse behind modernism, its own even more radical experiments extending the reach of literary experiment beyond modernism and implicitly suggesting it can always be extended farther still. But ultimately experimental fiction can provide a paradigm only if it is one that rejects the creation of paradigms except in the loosest possible sense of the term--the model fiction writers should follow is the absence of a model. However desirable such a model might be in the cause of aesthetic freedom, it isn't likely to offer much stability to literary culture, and thus it was almost inevitable that some sort of reaction against the postmodern would set in to restore good critical order. The past thirty years or so has not seen a shift in paradigm but a reinforcement of conventional practices, a widespread return to narrative business as usual.

Such an embrace of convention--of the assumption that the art of fiction = storytelling, that the writer's job is to create characters who can be regarded as if they were persons, persons with "minds," etc.--can't really be said to be a part of the kind of dialectical process Ron Silliman describes. Postmodernism in fiction didn't "settle in" and then become the impetus for a new and refreshed practice but was considered a temporary aberration until writers could be brought back to producing "normal" fiction. Experimental writers have not disappeared altogether, but those sometimes still called "experimental"--Lethem, Saunders, Wallace--are surely much less resolutely so, much more restrained, than Hawkes and Coover, et. al. Normal fiction is precisely what is taught to aspiring writers in most creative writing programs.

Literary change will continue to occur, of course, but in fiction it won't come in paradigm shifts but through the persistence of individual writers impatient with normal fiction. These fiction writers will be motivated by the need to preserve the integrity of their own work and by the desire to ensure that fiction has a purpose beyond providing the "book business" with a commercial product designed to be another entertainment option. Their work will continue to demonstrate that the aesthetics of fiction are manifested more in the continued reinvention of the form than in the successful reinscription of the existing form.

At a time when the idea of self-reflexive art has become less disruptive, it may be useful to reconsider the original appearance in contemporary literature of what came to be called "metafiction." Not only was this strain of American experimental fiction--taken up by several different writers, in slightly different ways--probably the first of all of the contemporary arts (including the popular arts) to explore the possibilities of self-reflexivity, but arguably it was this approach to fiction that initially provoked the coinage of the term "postmodern" to describe it. Since both "metafiction" and "postmodern" have by now clearly become terms of abuse as much as descriptive labels, perhaps reexamining what the writers associated with the use of metafiction believed themselves to be up to might clarify what is still valuable about their work, as well as what the literary strategy involved still has to offer current and future writers of fiction.

In my view, the foundational works of American metafiction are John Barth's story collection *Lost in the Funhouse* (1968) and Robert Coover's novel *The Universal Baseball Association* (1968), as well as Coover's collection *Pricksongs and Descants* (1969). These books of course themselves show the influence of various precursors in the work of, among others, Borges, Beckett, and Nabokov, but finally they are the books that brought together most explicitly those characteristics of all previous fiction that work against simply producing transparent realism, that point the reader away from the unfolding narrative and toward the artificial devices by which literary narratives are constructed and embellished. In so doing, Barth and Coover created a kind of "self-conscious" fiction that would decidedly--

and perhaps irretrievably--alter perceptions of the role of convention in fiction.

In Barth's fiction, these conventions were challenged directly, in stories that blatantly reveal themselves to be fabrications, that examine self-reflexively the process and the tools of storytelling, that delight in all the contrivances and tricks that are involved in storytelling even as they acknowledge that such contrivances are always involved. Coover's fiction indulges in these sorts of diversions as well, although his work is perhaps more likely to explore the ways in which fiction and fiction-making incorporate, perhaps inevitably, elements of ritual and myth, as in UBA or "The Magic Poker," and to explode the conventions of realism and traditional narrative from within, to produce a kind of kaleidoscopic surrealism, as in "The Babysitter," rather than the comic anatomies of storytelling to be found in *Lost in the Funhouse*. (Although Barth is certainly interested as well in the mythic/ritual origins of storytelling.) But even as both Barth and Coover were seemingly set on demolishing the established conventions of narrative fiction, both also clearly reveled in storytelling and in finding new ways for stories to be "relevant" in a period of upheaval and radical change, as the 1960s clearly was.

Thus, metafiction was simultaneously an attempt to clear the ground of the remaining inherited presuppositions about the "craft" of fiction and to make possible a more unrestricted viw of what actually constitutes literary craft, to open up the ground for new practices that might expand fiction's potential range, that might even lead to a renewal of storytelling in new forms and styles. Most importantly, Barth and Coover went about this without sacrificing fiction's "entertainment" quotient. (In my opinion, at least.) *The Universal Baseball Association* is an engrossing read (even if you don't like baseball), "The Babysitter" an intensely compelling story despite the fact that what's "really going on" is impossible to determine. A story like Barth's "Menelaiad" is great fun to read, as long as you're willing to go along with its almost literally infinite regress of story-within-story. Other readers might not find them as entertaining as I do, perhaps, but that the authors meant them to be entertaining in their own way seems to me indisputable.

A list of subsequent metafiction of equal value and accomplishment would have to include William Gass's *Willie Master's Lonesome Wife* (1971), Gilbert Sorrentino's *Imaginative Qualities of Actual Things* (1971) and *Mulligan Stew* (1979), as well as some of the work of Ronald Sukenick and Raymond Federman. These writers continued to ask questions not just about the conventions of fiction but about the very medium of writing, about the established usages of language itself. Gass and Sukenick play games with typography, Sorrentino adds to metafiction his outrageous humor and inveterate experimentation, Federman uses metafiction (or what he called "surfiction") to question the "reality" of reality. Taken together, they remain the literary touchstones of American metafiction. Their books may occasionally go out of print, but they will always be rediscovered because they still seem innovative despite the passage of time and the borrowing of their innovations by later writers.

By the 1980s a backlash of sorts had set in, both among other writers, who increasingly went for minimalist neorealism, and among critics, who increasingly called metafiction "self-indulgent" rather than "self-reflexive." Nevertheless, all of the metafictionists continued to write some very good books, and younger writers emerged who were clearly influenced by their earlier work. There are metafictional elements in the work of Richard Powers and David Foster Wallace, of Steve Stern and Steven Millhauser. A good deal even of Philip Roth's later work would clearly not have been the same without the prior efforts of the metafictionists. Other writers, from Michael Chabon to the early Ian McEwan to David Mitchell, would not necessarily be called metafictionists, but their books show a preoccupation with writing and with forms of storytelling that can be traced back to the related but different kind of preoccupation to be found in *Lost in the Funhouse* and *The Universal Baseball Association*.

However, the real promise of metafiction has not yet really been fulfilled. Its true legacy is to be found in the way it calls writers' (and readers') attention to the attributes of fiction <u>as art</u>, potentially making all of us more immediately aware of the limitless ways in which works of fiction can be shaped into artful verbal creations. Too often self-reflexive devices and strategies are still used simply as gimmicks, empty gestures, stratagems employed by those wishing to appear clever and knowing. Not enough effort has been made to redeem the still latent possibilities of fiction when approached as an aesthetically malleable form waiting to be adapted to various imaginative purposes. The unmitigated commercialism and careerism of the publishing "industry" as it now exists is not going to make this sort of effort more likely in the near future, nor will the disciplinary imperatives of academic creative writing, which mostly contributes to the homogenization of "product." But anyone who might like to strike out on a different path anyway, to understand how fiction might be freed of its encrusted layers of formula and routine, could do worse than to read (or re-read) the books of Barth and Coover, Gass and Sorrentino.

In an essay defending experimental fiction, Marc Lowe writes:

> . . .the majority of popular critics and readers the world over, ultimately, still seem to crave the same thing they always have when it comes right down to it: entertainment. Is it not true that most individuals are primarily, if not exclusively, interested in believable characters with memorable names and realistically portrayed attributes (e.g. Samuel Sellers, the rotund jeweler with a tic in his left eye who picks his flat nose

with the end of his pipe holder; Linda Lacy, the woman with the sequined stockings who sucks on peeled carrot sticks in order to satiate her oral fixation), plots that resolve themselves in a decisive, if blandly predictable, manner (too many loose ends make for angry readers, despite the public's ubiquitous cry—which still resounds in chain bookstores around the English-speaking world— for "realistic" and "believable" characters and situations), and, most of all, a clear and understandable (i.e. linear and tidy) storyline with a consistent style of narration (no abrupt shifts in tense/time, no blurring of who's who or what's what, etc.), so that there is little or no need to have to stop and think for even a single moment about what may lie hidden beneath the surface of the words written on the page?. . . . (Mindfire Review 5, 2006)

Although I am an advocate on behalf of experimental fiction, I think this analysis goes a little too far. More precisely, it doesn't accurately describe the situation as it exists among serious readers of fiction in the early 21st century.

The question isn't really whether "popular critics and readers" accept or reject experimental fiction. The mass audience rejects "literary fiction" of even the most conventional, most character-driven kind. The challenge for experimental writers and sympathetic critics is to convince readers who might be looking for more than "entertainment" to move beyond what now passes for "literary" fiction to consider alternatives that are just as literary, if not as immediately recognizable as variations on an established form. With these readers, the situation is not as dire as Lowe suggests.

Most such readers have surely assimilated the innovations of modernist/postmodernist fiction to the extent they do not expect characters like "Samuel Sellers" and "Linda Lacy." If anything, the norm is now what I call "psychological realism," a technique pioneered by writers such as James, Joyce, and Woolf that seeks to portray the world as it is experienced by the characters in a given novel or story, not necessarily to emphasize those characters' "realistically portrayed attributes" if those attributes are external to consciousness. And I really do believe readers are more tolerant of stories that do not "resolve themselves in a decisive. . .manner" than Lowe gives them credit for (unless the stories are themselves decisively situated in a generic framework that more or less demands resolution of plot details). Indeed, what has variously been called "minimalism" or "dirty realism" is more or less predicated on the assumption that in the end nothing much will happen--on the surface at least. Finally, it seems to me especially true that readers of literary fiction are open to narratives that are structured as something other than "a clear and understandable (i.e. linear and tidy) storyline with a consistent style of narration." Fragmentation, chronological displacement, shifts in point of view, and other forms of non-linear storytelling are quite common in contemporary literary fiction, so common that I would say the sort of naively realistic, unswervingly linear narrative Lowe describes is in a distinct minority among the books that appeal to today's literary reader.

I don't think it does much of a service to experimental fiction to offer as rhetorical straw men either the mass audience who would be just as impatient with John Updike as with Gilbert Sorrentino, or the "anachronistic 19th century model" Lowe complains of. (Aspiring experimental writers could in fact learn quite a lot, about character creation and narrative development, from writers like Dickens and Hardy.) Serious writers will never attract a "popular" audience (I don't see why they would want to), and contemporary fiction for the most part does not proceed according to the 19th-century model. (It is especially mistaken to conclude that 19th-century writers were both relentless storytellers and "realist" in their approach to representation; in many cases the one is in conflict with the other, and these writers can be illustrative of the ways the two impulses can or can't be reconciled.) Better to seek out those readers who may already be at least half-interested in what experimental fiction might accomplish and convince them to risk the other half as well.

II First Principles

In a post on his weblog *books, INQ.* (September 24, 2006), Frank Wilson suggests that "artistic experiment" is defined by the amount of "trial and error" involved. He takes the scientific "experiment" to be the model for the use of "experimental" as a classificatory term in the discussion of literature. Scott Esposito more or less accepts Wilson's definition, although he has no problem with "art experiments being praised as ends in themselves," something about which Wilson seems skeptical. Esposito also suggests that "unlike in science, we can continually come back to and learn new things from successful literary experiments, or simply admire their beauty" (*Conversational Reading*, September 26, 2006).

Actually, we can probably do the same with certain especially compelling scientific experiments, but I think both Esposito and Wilson are mistaken to view "experiment" in literature as essentially analogous to the way the term is understood in science. Scott is correct in asserting that "a lot of trial and error is involved in the writing of most novels," and for that very reason "trial and error" is not really very helpful in capturing what literary critics/scholars have meant by using "experimental fiction" in describing selected works of fiction, especially fiction written since 1945, "experimental." For the most part, critical commentary on postwar experimental fiction (more broadly "postmodern" fiction) has focused on "experiment" as, in Jerome Klinkowitz's words, the "disruption" of a "conservative stability of form" in literary fiction (*Literary*

Disruptions, 1980). Klinkowitz thought this stability had reigned since the 1920s, but it probably goes back farther than that, to the establishment of realism in the mid/late 19th century--experimentalists such as Joyce and Woolf could be said to have also "disrupted" this stability of form (often characterized as the "well-made story"), although their experiments did not disrupt the assumptions of realism itself, were in fact an extension of these assumptions into what is now called "psychological realism." From this perspective, "trial and error" is not so much the guiding principle of experiment (except insofar as it involves finding appropriate methods of disruption) as is the notion that "stability"--to which scientific experiments always return--is itself not a desirable state where the art of fiction is concerned.

It is true that the term "experimental fiction" is a catch-all term of convenience that doesn't necessarily signal anything very specific about what particular writers might be up to in their efforts to, if not "make it new," then "make it different." Thus Klinkowitz prefers "disruption," while other critics have written about "breaking the sequence" or "the art of excess" or "anti-story." In most cases, however, these critics are really interested in what Ellen Friedman and Miriam Fuchs in *Breaking the Sequence* simply accept as "innovations in form." Friedman and Fuchs also provide a handy description of the elements of "stability" against which most innovative writers are rebelling: "Plot linearity that implies a story's purposeful forward movement; a single, authoritative storyteller; well-motivated characters interacting in recognizable social patterns; the crucial conflict deterring the protagonist from the ultimate goal; the movement to closure. . . ." Perhaps the most succinct statement of the motivations underlying experimental fiction would be the remarks made by John Hawkes: "I began to write fiction on the assumption that the true enemies of the novel were plot, character, setting and theme, and having once abandoned these familiar ways of thinking about fiction, totality of vision or structure was really all that remained."

A critic who did use the term "experimental fiction" straightforwardly was Robert Scholes in his book *Fabulation and Metafiction*. In the chapter of that book called "The Nature of Experimental Fiction," he writes: "Forms atrophy and lose touch with the vital ideas of fiction. Originality in fiction, rightly understood, is the successful attempt to find new forms that are capable of tapping once again the sources of fictional vitality." Scholes's book popularized the term "metafiction" as a more specific term describing the tendencies in postwar American fiction that made readers think of them as "experimental": "Metafiction. . .attempts to assault or transcend the laws of fiction--an undertaking which can only be achieved from within fictional form." Writers like Gass, Barth, Coover, and Barthleme were "working in that rarefied air of metafiction, trying to climb beyond Beckett and Borges, toward things than no critic--not even a metacritic, if there were such a thing--can discern."

Eventually that air probably became too "rarefied." Many readers came to associate metafiction--and thus "experimental fiction"--as "game-playing," an obsession with "art" over "life." This perception probably informs Frank Wilson's disdain for experiments "as ends in themselves." (Also his disinclination to think of Joyce as an experimenter--Joyce "knew from the start what he was going to do and how he was going to do it" and would never have stooped to mere "experiment.") It may also explain why Christopher Sorrentino, in a comment on Scott Esposito's post, observes that "while I have met a great many novelists ranging in outlook and approach from Ben Marcus to Jonathan Franzen, not a single one of them to my knowledge has ever described his/her work as 'experimental.'" While the writers associated with the *Journal of Experimental Fiction* would probably be less skittish about the designation than Marcus or Franzen, it probably is now true that many "experimental" writers (putting aside whether Ben Marcus or Jonathan Franzen are actually very innovative in the first place), are uncomfortable with the word as applied to their work. I'd still accept the explanation given by Raymond Federman, who coined the term "surfiction" as an alternative to "metafiction" in identifying his own brand of experimental fiction:

> The kind of fiction I am interested in is that fiction
> which the leaders of the literary establishment (publishers,
> editors, agents, and reviewers alike) brush aside because it
> does not conform to *their* notions of what fiction should

be; that fiction which supposedly has no value (commercially understood) for the common reader. And the easiest way for these people to brush aside that kind of fiction is to label it, quickly and bluntly, as *experimental fiction*. Everything that does not fall into the category of *successful fiction* (commercially that is), or what Jean-Paul Sartre once called "nutritious literature," everything that is found "unreadable for our readers". . .is immediately relegated to the domain of experimentation--a safe and useless place. (*Surfiction*, 1975)

In his book on the work of Ronald Sukenick and Raymond Federman (*The Novel as Performance* (1986)), Jerzy Kutnik comments:

> . . .The rise of Action Painting, the Happening, The Living Theatre, John Cage's experimental music and Charles Olson's "projective verse," to name only a few examples of performance-oriented works of the 1950s and 1960s, forced many aestheticians to review the underlying assumptions of classic aesthetics. Performance was now seen as a category which could be made relevant to all art forms. Indeed, for the postmodern artist, performance was shown to be an essential element of all creative activity, a fundamental value in itself, an indispensable, even unavoidable, ingredient of the work of art.

But it should also be noted that performance is not something that, as a result of certain historical developments, was added as a new element in the creative process, for it had always been there, though ignored or suppressed. What was added, rather, was the awareness that all art is always performatory, that it not so much says something *about* reality, but, by its occurrence and presence, *does* something as a reality in its own right. . . (xxiv).

Federman is a writer who directly and self-consciously engages in a "performance" strategy--anyone who picks up *Double or Nothing* or *Take It or Leave It* will immediately encounter Federman's notational performance as his text spreads itself across and down the page in seemingly (but not actually) chaotic arrangements--but ultimately his work forces us (or should force us) to consider the extent to which the writing of fiction and poetry is always, as Kutznick points out, about doing rather than saying. While few fiction writers play around with "text" as explicitly as Federman (or Sukenick), poets have certainly always done so; thus, what Kutznick is really getting at is that the work of writers like Federman insists that fiction as well be a mode in which the writer "does something as a reality."

The great majority of literary fiction is overwhelmingly dedicated to the task of saying something. This is why the great majority of literary fiction is not worth reading. Not only do most writers of such fiction have very little to say in the first place--the "theme" of most literary novels can usually be reduced to platitudes--but whatever "performance" that is involved in the use of the elements of fiction is dull and familiar, at best focused on forwarding the theme most expeditiously. Much experimental fiction is also dull and familiar, reworkings of previous, and better, performances of other experimentalists. However, the departures from the norm to be found in even the most perfunctory experimental fiction does at least continue to remind us that it is possible to conceive of fiction as a practice in which form is contingent, the medium through which the writer may offer a fresh and distinctive performance.

Even from within the confines of conventional practices it is possible to write fiction that is more doing than saying. The enactment of point of view and narrative structure affords ample opportunities for "performance-oriented work," and the best fiction has always taken advantage of these opportunities. Style also can be an "ingredient" in the performance of literary art, as long as style is regarded as something other than, something beyond, "pretty writing" of the usual kind. Unfortunately, most attempts to manipulate these elements that I read (or start to read) are again usually carried out in the name of more colorfully reinforcing theme, not as a performance seeking out its own limits or capable of sustaining interest in and of itself.

As Larry McCaffery puts it in his foreword to Kutznick's book, writers like Sukenick and Federman (and, I might add, Gilbert Sorrentino and Stephen Dixon and David Foster Wallace, to name only three) show us that the most challenging fiction "seeks to be an experience for its own sake." This is precisely what John Dewey, the foremost proponent of "art as experience," had in mind when he extolled the achievement of "adventurous" art. Like all other such art, adventurous fiction enhances experience by encouraging us to attend more closely to performance, in the best cases a performance unlike any we've experienced before.

Richard Crary finds the term "novel" too confining, and wonders:

> Why should contemporary prose works necessarily be treated as novels? Why do we insist that of course a given work is a novel, just not the kind of novel some readers expect? Why, indeed, should adventurous or exploratory or so-called experimental prose writing be subject to the same expectations as a novel? Why called a novel at all? (As always, I am ignoring the needs of the publishing industry.) Are Thomas Bernhard's works novels? Or might it be better to call them, simply, "prose works"? What about Blanchot's récit? Is Josipovici's *Everything Passes* a novel? David Markson's *This Is Not*

A Novel was titled, so I understand, in response to a what one reviewer reportedly actually wrote in dismissing *Reader's Block*, his previous work. But what if we just saw the title as simply accurate and then worked from there? (*The Existence Machine*, December 16, 2008)

There's no doubt that life could be made easier, for both writers and critics, if the identifying tag "novel" were confined to that plot- and character-heavy sort of narrative into which the novel evolved between 1850 and 1950 and which a majority of readers still steadfastly associate with the term. Devotees of "exploratory" prose would not have to contend, or would have to contend less, with objections that a particular work of experimental fiction is not "really" a novel, because it would indeed not be such and could perhaps be more honestly assessed according to criteria appropriate to what it is rather than what it is not. Many of the currently contentious critical debates about the purpose and proper form of the novel would presumably disappear, and those who insist it continue to be what it's always been and appeal to the widest possible audience would have the field to themselves.

Such a dispensation would have the added benefit of eliminating obtrusive discussions of "art" where the novel is concerned, since whatever art it would still be granted would be confined to minor variations on pre-established methods, and everyone still reading novels would be able to concentrate their attention on the "ideas" they supposedly express, the political efficacy they're claimed to have, the sociological observations they're said to make, or just the nice stories they're counted on to tell, all of which, as far as I can tell, are of much greater interest to readers of conventional novels than aesthetic values or formal ingenuity. "Style" might remain a relevant consideration, as long as it's used to identify especially pretty prose. Otherwise "art" can be safely relegated to the "experimental prose writing" Crary invokes, along with the latter's contrarian habit of representing experience in ways that aren't appropriately "realistic."

I confess I find this potential reinforcement of boundaries, and subsequent realignment of the literary sphere, initially attractive and possibly liberating. The reduction of the novel to its simplist form--or at least its most readily accessible--would allow adventurous writers to follow their creative bliss in whatever directions they wished (to the extent that they, too, are finally willing to "ignore the needs of the publishing industry") and critics to extend their horizons beyond the already known. Yet I think I would ultimately resist abandoning the classification "novel" as an umbrella term naming a still-evolving literary form. For one thing, a hardening of the boundary defining the novel would surely give whatever lies outside it a bracing freedom to explore new territory, but eventually it seems likely that either new boundaries would be erected around certain kinds of "prose works," boundaries that could prove just as restrictive, or that something like literary anarchy would ensue. Perhaps this anarchy would still be tolerable, depending on the quality of what some writers manage to produce, but such a state of affairs would make it more difficult to maintain a critical perspective on new writing, which might in turn make it more difficult for "prose writers" to gather an audience.

In addition, although I am clearly enough a partisan of experimental fiction, my appreciation of the experimental in literature is still pretty firmly rooted in literary history itself, and I am hesitant to conclude that those impulses that motivated writers to begin writing what we now call novels, and that has guided the development of fiction in general, are entirely spent. Fiction, at least in the modern literary tradition, began as an experiment itself, an offshoot of "narrative poetry" that began to test out the possibilities of extended narratives written in prose. Indeed, many of the early works of prose fiction, *Gulliver's Travels*, *Robinson Crusoe*, *Jacques the Fatalist*, could be described as "prose works" seeking their own conventions rather than novels per se. The history of the novel, in my view, is the continued search for subjects, strategies, and techniques that would redeem the artistic potential both of the form and of prose itself as a literary medium. Many people seem to think that this search effectively ended in the late 19th/early 20th centuries, when novelists discovered realism, enhanced by modernist experiments in "psychological realism," and thus added these approaches to the earlier emphasis on storytelling, but I think that such an arbitrary circumscription of the novel's further development is effectively a renunciation of the form's own history as an "exploratory" practice.

Perhaps, given both the adamancy with which the gatekeepers of the "novel" in its ossified version insist on its right to the designation and the sheer abundance of alternatives to this version offered up over the last sixty years (including those written by the authors Richard Crary mentions), we ought just to accept this renunciation and get on with writing and reading whatever fresh "prose works" continue to appear. Maybe this is the price to be paid for the novel's brief period of popularity as a mass entertainment before the arrival of movies and television to usurp that role: the "book business" expropriated the label "novel" as a marketing device and has continued to force all subsequent efforts at expanding the form back into its slim container. (Although in light of what seems to be the imminent implosion of this "industry," it may no longer be able to devote many resources to any but the most gaudily commercial novels at all.) The novel has effectively been severed from its place in the unfolding of literary history and tied instead to the imperatives of capitalism.

But would we have to discard as well the more elastic term "fiction" while we're giving up on "novel" as hopelessly constraining? "Fiction" doesn't just mean "something made up"; it's a signal that, <u>as</u> a prose composition that shouldn't be judged by its conformity to the prescripts of "reality," the work at hand is free to distort, embellish, pare away, redirect, transmute, or transcribe the "real" in whatever way provides the work its integrity, at whatever length, and in whatever style or form. Or at least it could mean this if we didn't insist that "fiction" is synonymous with "story." Much of the "experimental prose writing" of the past few decades has, in fact, moved fiction closer to the practices of poetry (back, as it were, to the origin of prose fiction in poetry), away from narrative toward various other arrangements and rearrangements of language. If this tendency were to result in some hybrid form somewhere between poetry and prose narrative, and were to inspire a new name to solidify its status, I myself wouldn't complain, but I'm content to stick to "fiction" and to challenging unnecessarily narrow conceptions of its scope.

III Practice

In a review of Aimee Bender's *Willful Creatures*, CL Bledsoe concludes that "Bender is that most daring of writers, who will take any risk, regardless of the consequences" (The *Pedestal Magazine* 32). I couldn't disagree more. I've read *The Girl in the Flammable Skirt* and *Willful Creatures*, and I don't think she takes any risks at all. Her stories display only a kind of surrealistic whimsy that I, for one, find mostly cloying.

Take, for example, "Ironhead," a story from *Willful Creatures* that Bledsoe singles out for discussion, claiming it is a story in which Bender "portray[s] even the oddest characters not simply as running gags, but with emotional depth." It is hard for me to find the "emotional depth" in passages like this, which to the contrary exhibit only a cartoon-like sentimentality: "The ironhead turned out to be a very gentle boy. He played quietly on the his own in the daytime with clay and dirt, and contrary to expectations, he preferred wearing ragged messy clothes with wrinkles. His mother tried once to smooth down his outfits with her own, separated iron, but when the child saw what was his head, standing by itself, with steam exhaling from the flat silver base just like his breath, he shrieked a tinny scream and matching steam streamed from his chin as it did when he was particularly upset. The pumpkinhead mother quickly put the iron away; she understood; she imagined it was much the way she felt when one of her humanhead friends offered her a piece of seasonal pie on Thanksgiving." This is as much "emotional" portrayal of these characters as we get; the rest of the story continues to wring equally asinine changes on an already dopey idea. Once we've registered the unbeguiling notion that a boy has been born with an iron for a head, the story has little to offer. It continues to rely on faux-naive phrasing ("a very gentle boy," "played quietly") and an altogether formulaic plot--the iron-headed boy dies, of course, leaving everyone very sad. I suppose one could characterize the story as a "running gag," but then the gag would need to be funny in the first place.

Or take "The End of the Line," in which a "big man" goes to a pet store "to buy himself a little man to keep him company."

Nothing in this story (Bledsoe calls it a "surreal parable") is other than predictable and smarmy, once one allows for its tepidly surrealistic premise. "After about the third week. . .the big man took to torturing the little man." The little man contemplates his escape but is unable to accomplish it. The big man sets the little man free, but decides to follow the little man as he drives away in a "small blue bus"--he "just wanted to see where they lived." A (literally) little girl looks up at the "giant" who has found them and wonders at the "size of the pity that kept unbuckling in her heart."

For a "parable" like this to work, in my opinion, it either has to implicitly examine the structural and thematic assumptions of the parable itself (in the process reconfiguring the possibilities of the form) or it has to manifest some stylistic vigor to compensate for the formulaic nature of parables and fables. Kafka, Borges, Calvino, and Barthleme, for example, are writers able to carry out such tasks, but Bender's stories do neither. Plot exists to reveal the mawkishly cute characters and situations (cute even in their occasional freakishness), but is otherwise so conventional as to be simply perfunctory. And her style is even less interesting, usually just an excuse to "shock" the reader with a seemingly outlandish situation that is really just silly:

> The motherfucker arrived at the West Coast from
> the Midwest. He took a train, and met women of every
> size and shape in different cities--Tina with the straight-

ahead knees in Milwaukee, Annie with the caustic laugh in Chicago, Betsy's lopsided cleavage in Bismarck, crazy Heddie in Butte, that lion tamer in Vegas, the smart farm girl from Bakersfield. Finally, he dismounted for good at Union Station in Lost Angeles.

"I fuck mothers," he said to anyone who asked him. "And I do it well."

One could imagine a writer like, say, Stanley Elkin, taking this set-up and running with it, transforming it through his inimitable style and comic imagination into an extended fiction full of narrative ingenuity and aesthetic delight. But in Bender's rendering it becomes an utterly straight-faced account of a man with a quaintly unconventional sexual proclivity who is given to such statements as "Desire is a house. Desire needs closed space. Desire runs out of doors or windows, or slats or pinpricks, it can't fit under the sky, too large."

I do not mean to single out CL Bledsoe's review for criticism. It has become common for reviewers to identify Bender as a risk-taker, her fiction as an example of what passes for "innovative" writing among the graduates of the better MFA programs. (Bledsoe even comes close to accurately describing Bender's fiction when she calls it "like a rich dessert," except that, for me at least, it is more like sugar overload.) But calling such work innovative or experimental simply because it distorts ordinary reality in some fairy tale-ish sort of way doesn't really do the cause of experimental fiction much good. Experimental fiction challenges the formal constraints imposed by past practices; it does not seek out alternative methods in order, finally, to just tell the same old stories in only superficially different ways. Bender's fiction accepts those constraints and relates decidedly familiar stories dressed up in gaudy but cheap disguises.

In a recent *Los Angeles Times* article (April 22, 2007) about *Granta*'s "Best of Young American Novelists" issue, there is a great deal of talk about the "themes" that the included writers are said to be addressing. While immigration and its legacy seems to be the common theme of this particular "snapshot" anthology, we are also told that some of the issue's judges "were dismayed by the lack of attention to social class in the work of these young novelists across the ethnic and national spectrum." Laura Miller believes that neither of these subjects is really where it's at with current young fiction writers: "The real themes in American fiction these days, she said, are the seeking of 'authenticity' — which sometimes works itself out in stories about immigrant communities—and interpreting the highly mediated, pop-suffused culture."

Nowhere in this article about supposedly important new writing is there any discussion, not even the briefest mention, of the aesthetic features, formal and stylistic, that characterize the stories collected in "Best of Young American Novelists," features that presumably ought to count for something when determining what makes these particular selections the "best" that might be found. What formal innovations, if any, are these writers pursuing? What insights into the possibilities of language in representing human experience, immigrant or otherwise, might be found in the stylistic explorations of their work? Such questions are not addressed; from the comments made by those involved in putting the anthology together, one has to conclude they were not considered relevant to the larger question of what fiction writers of this next generation are trying to "say."

The view of fiction implicit in this article's discussion of the newest and the latest is that it is a forum for "expression." Writers "express" themselves, and through them their ethnic or class heritage gets expressed. Taken as whole, the writers included in the *Granta* anthology express the concerns and preoccupations of their generational cohort. Why exactly such writers would choose the indirect and rhetorically impure mode of fiction--which unavoidably is going to disperse and obscure your "themes" unless you run them diligently roughshod--in order to give "expression" to such things is never made clear. Nor is it ever quite clear why anyone would care about such expressions in the first place. If "saying something" is important to you as a writer, perhaps nonfiction is a better choice. Better yet, if sociology or cultural anthropology is what you're really interested in, become an actual sociologist and ponder the effects of immigration or class or interpret mass culture to your heart's content. Perhaps some people might even be interested in what you thus have to say. But don't reduce fiction to a more entertaining branch of social science.

In fairness, it's probably the editors and the critics who contribute most to this metamorphosis of literature into sociology and politics. It gives them something to write about at a time when most of them don't know how to write about the aesthetics of literature, anyway. It's an easy way to convert literary criticism into "literary journalism." And it's this focus on the "journalism" of literature and the avoidance of the "merely literary" that largely explains the impatience and incredulity with which so many editors and critics confront works of fiction that do manifestly ask the reader to consider their formal and stylistic qualities above whatever "theme" they may be assigned, especially if such works can be regarded as "experimental."

Joshua Cohen's *Cadenza for the Schneidermann Violin Concerto* (Fugue State Press) will surely strike most readers as experimental, and, although the novel does in fact raise issues related to immigration and ethnicity, few would ultimately conclude that the author's primary purpose is "expression" in the sense I've discussed. It is resolutely an attempt to reconfigure the formal elements of fiction (although not to dispense with them.) Like any good experimental novel, it first of all provokes us to ask: Is this a novel at all? And, as good experimental novels do as well, it ultimately leads us to answer our own question: Why not?

Distinguished virtuosi, acclaimed virtuosos and virtuosas of this greatest orchestra in the world, members and memberesses of this fine ensemble, tuxedos and dressed of the New York Philharmonic Orchestra, you behind me I've stooped to rehearse with for far too many seasons now and have yet to conquer, consider this your cue! to draw out the longbows: downbows for the 1st violins, upbows for the 2nds--the bowings are as necessary as they are Schniedermann's written into your parts, yes believe it or not, in his own hand, and such hands! (though I helped some, because among many other lacks in this country was a publisher) and, yes, let's have the final cadence, drawn out to the last and stiffest hair, to the frog and to the tip of the bow as they're called.

Okay! gasp, and we don't want anyone asphyxiating on us, now do we?

Will the orchestra please stop? desist?

Everyone finished?

Gasp, it's okay! If you all just remain seated, and listen, I promise that no one will get hurt. Trust me, everything's going to turn out fine.

So declares renowned violinist Laster as he is about to begin his solo (the cadenza) in his friend Schneidermann's concerto. As we will discover, the elderly Schneidermann is missing (he excused himself from a matinee showing of *Schindler's List* and Laster hasn't seen him since), possibly dead, and Laster has apparently decided that a proper tribute to the composer requires him to speak instead of play. Which he does, for 380 pages.

> You'll never find answers in music, only more questions, and so, yes, I have a speaking part, not quite notated, not quite mentioned in the program you've glanced through and idly referenced, riffled through the least piano of my pinanissimos and are manically flipping through to see if I have a history of mental instability, some schizoid personality disorder that would serve to explain this away.

> My decision to address you with my voice instead of with my violin.

Schneidermann, as it turns out, is a Holocaust survivor and, in Laster's view, an unjustly neglected composer, the "iconoclast even the iconoclasts worshipped," while he, Laster, has lived a relatively privileged life as a soloist:

> Good evening ladies and gentlemen, good evening kids of all ages, good evening my exwives and my wife and prospective wives, good evening some of my own children out there in the audience, good evening my

lawyer, my agent, my accountant, good evening my recordlabel execs, good evening my podiatrist (who just last Thursday she told me that my onychauxis it had developed into onychogryphosis, had a professional trim my nails). . . .

Through Laster's mammoth *spiel*, we learn about both Schneidermann's and his own past, about how despite Schneidermann's experience in the Shoah he considered himself one of the last Old World Europeans, about Jewish history, about music. It's a fragmented piece of storytelling, to be sure, but eventually we learn those sorts of things we need to know about the characters--and really Laster and Schniedermann dominate the story--and their circumstances that we would get from a more straightforwardly related narrative. Laster is an unusual first-person narrator, but that's what he is, and we ultimately must judge him and his roundabout tale in the same way we would judge a more conventional first-person account.

In other words, the conventional elements of fiction are in play in this novel (substituting for the real playing of the concerto, as it were), but they are rhetorically shuffled in Laster's discontinuous streams of speech. The reader is asked to show a little patience, do a little honest work for his/her pleasure. The novel implicitly asks that we take the reading of a novel to be a unique experience, not just another rote variation on an a pre-established theme, just as Laster's "cadenza" is unlike any previously heard.

And there certainly are pleasures to be found in this novel, however much the easy ones are deferred. Many of the anecdotes Laster relates are compelling, some hilarious; over the long run, Laster's voice, and thus Laster himself, is vividly rendered, leading us through what becomes an hours-long exhortation, even if what we finally remember is probably less Schniedermann (who remains, perhaps unavoidably so, somewhat distanced and enigmatic) than Laster's own desperate attempt to make us remember him. More than anything else, however, there is the language, the Yiddish-inflected, frequently over-the-top speaking style exemplified in the passages I have already quoted. Cohen is skillful indeed in deploying this language, and if readers are able to accustom themselves to Laster's strung-out, stop/start way of summoning up those events that have culminated in this night at Carnegie Hall, they will surely find themselves enjoying the jokes, the deliberate or not-so-deliberate malapropisms, the puns, the occasional passages of real eloquence.

Some readers might balk at a novel that at first seems so determined to avoid "entertainment." (Laster, after all, himself seemingly interrupts the entertainment in order to berate his audience with his words, to get them to pay attention to his verbal cadenza and not just passively admire his musical one. At the same time, one could regard Laster as a kind of Catskill *tummler*, a stand-up comic who in discarding his role as Serious Artist discovers another talent for *schtick*.) But I have to say that ultimately I found *Cadenza for the Schniedermann Violin Concerto* to be abundantly entertaining, both as a "story" that is satisfying if deliberately circuitous and as an experiment in storytelling. I enjoy witnessing a writer, any artist, imaginatively transform the medium in which he is working, and I believe Cohen does an impressive job at sustaining his experiment--to make this rambling kind of storytelling itself part of the "point" of the story--over 300+ pages. (The jokes and the fascinating tidbits of information help.) Cohen has succeeded in taking one man's headlong attempt at "expression" and, through relentless artifice, almost a parody of the will to express, created an aesthetically complex (and engaging, precisely because it is complex) work of fiction.

On the one hand, it is easy enough to see how Sara Greenslit's *The Blue of Her Body* (Starcherone Books) could be called a "poet's novel." It makes no effort to "tell a story" in the ponderous, pedestrian mode too often adopted by novelists who come to fiction through an interest in narrative (as exemplified either in other fiction they've read or in movies) rather than an engagement with language and the possibilities of language in creating verbal art and exploring fresh ways of representing experience. There's no facile psychologizing of characters portrayed as "real people," no faux-dramatic plot points, no perfunctorily inserted dialogue straining to be "believable." No exposition, rising and falling action, or contrived resolution of the artificially induced "conflict." Instead, *The Blue of Her Body* is an artfully arranged construction of words, a novel that asks the reader to infer the "story" between the lines of its brief prose passages.

On the other hand, one would not call this novel "poetic" because it indulges in conventional figurative phrasing, lunges after arresting tropes, offers up an ostentatious display of "fine writing." Greenslit's prose is more matter-of-fact, more objectively descriptive:

> Her rented house on the edge of town is small, chipped paint, all her own. She likes the windows, large and filled with trees. The morning light on the wood floor reminds her of her mother's caramel. The dog clatters through the house, pet hair collects in the corners. She no longer needs a vacuum. The broom is easier.
>
> She has chosen birds over the soft other.
>
> A week before her new job at the aviary starts, boxes are left stacked in the living room. She is afraid to put everything away. She fears the open space. She fears the silence she sought, the echoes. She had wanted these things, but now they loom and hover.
>
> She brought only what was hers. But everything reminds her of Kate.

One chapter consists entirely of mostly one-sentence "paragraphs":

Whenever it was summer, I fell into a trance watching leaves on windy days

The sky was cloudless and blue like the spaces inside loved ones

Peregrine hacking box, nestling feather fuss down, eyes and beaks

Mother's summer garden: Asiatic lilies, red as a South American carnival, coneflowers about to unfold

When I was in love, I couldn't imagine any hands but yours. I smelled you while I worked, I saw you in our bed.

When I left, you wouldn't look me in the eye.

I was fool, fool to my mood.

I ate my pills day after day, unable to see.

One could say that the novel unfolds in lines and stanzas, rather than sequential prose paragraphs that disappear in the narrative flow they are meant to serve, although this does not so much make it a kind of prose poem as provoke us into considering the sometimes fine line between prose and verse, fiction and poetry. Why can't a novel proceed via evocative, carefully crafted sentences rather than routine, narrative-bearing paragraphs? At what point does the novelist leave to the poet the care and tending of language at its most fundamental level, the habitation of the word, the phrase, the sentence?

Much of what *The Blue of Her Body* is "about" is expressed in the first-quoted passage above: "She has chosen birds over the soft other." The novel's unnamed narrator has broken up with her lover in the city and moved into the country to work at an aviary. In her isolation, she considers her own history of depression, broods on her relationship with her mother (also a depressive) and her failed relationship with Kate, and takes the opportunity to further cultivate her love of animals. The novel in effect chronicles the narrator's convalescence, concluding with a variation on Emily Dickinson: "Hope is a damaged bird. She heals and then stays. . . ."

The narrator's dilemma and her attempt to work through it, however, are presented almost entirely through inference and suggestion. The story is purely backstory. In addition to the brief expository passages and the declarative sentences (sometimes stated in the third-person, sometimes in first-person), there are fragmentary accounts of the activity in the aviary, haiku-like descriptions of animals and of nature in general, and cumulative bits of information about the various efforts to treat the narrator's depression. While Greenslit thus avoids converting the narrator's circumstances into narrative melodrama, ultimately her novel does present a coherent and convincing, if oblique, portrait of its protagonist's struggle to gather her life into some semblance of order and purpose.

I believe that the future of prose fiction will only lead it closer to a kind of *rapprochement* with poetry, where the novel began as a splintering-off of narrative from the storytelling mode of epic poetry (just as drama appropriated the "dramatic" in dramatic poetry). Now that film and television (as well as what is called "creative nonfiction") have in turn taken over the storytelling function, at least for the mass audience, fiction's continued relevance, aside from those novels seemingly written with the film adaptation in mind, will perhaps require that it return to its origins in the poet's attention to language per se. Experimental fiction almost always points us in this direction, as challenges to the hegemony of conventional storytelling usually entail a reinvigoration of the resources of language, highlighting the capacity of prose fiction to do <u>something else</u>. *The Blue of Her Body* is an admirable addition to this effort.

According to Jonathan Gottschall, a critical proponent of what has come to be called "literary Darwinism":

> Understanding a story is ultimately about understanding the human mind. The primary job of the literary critic is to pry open the craniums of characters, authors and narrators, climb inside their heads and spelunk through the bewildering complexity within   to

figure out what makes them tick. (*The Age*, April 21, 2007)

According to Sabrina Seelig, in an article on translated fiction:

> . . .the works in *The World Through the Eyes of Writers*, while dealing with the same painful things that are covered in the news all the time, take the same hashed-out facts and gave them sense, potency, life. Reading stories that do this lifts a curtain: not on some generalized world or broad state of a country, but on specific realities about the ways people live. There is a vast difference between reading about a killing in the news and listening to, getting inside the head of the mother of that victim. Not only getting inside her head, but picking through the rubble guided by a skilled author drawing out colors, textures, whispering names and prayers. (*The Brooklyn Rail*, May 2007)

I bring together these at first only marginally related quotes--both writers agree that reading fiction is about "getting inside the head," but Gottschall is ultimately taking literary critics to task for their insufficient understanding of human nature, while Seelig is (admirably) calling for more English translations of "foreign" fiction--because in their assumptions about the ultimate purposes of fiction they perhaps reveal why innovative or "experimental" fiction is so often dismissed by both readers and critics. And, as it happens, the inadequacy of both of these views of what fiction is for is brought into sharp relief by a very provocative (and translated) novel I've just read, *Vain Art of the Fugue* (Dalkey Archive), by the Romanian author Dumitru Tsepeneag.

Gottschall's notion that fiction presents the reader (the critic being a more skilled reader) with the opportunity to scrutinize characters as if they were real people whose "craniums" can be opened to discover "what makes them tick" is no doubt widely shared. "Psychological realism" in the modern novel provides us access to "the Mind," which apparently many critics think is a very profound thing to do and makes the novel distinctive from the other forms of narrative art that have arisen to challenge the novel's hegemony. The Literary Darwinists accept that something like psychological realism is the novel's raison d'etre, but they feel that most literary critics aren't sufficiently knowledgeable about the biological imperatives instilled in us by natural selection to be able to discuss "evolutionary psychology" intelligently. Only by understanding how these imperatives influence human behavior are we really able to understand fiction credibly.

Vain Art of the Fugue makes all of this utterly beside the point. There are characters in the novel, but they keep changing in their identities and behavior. In the first brief section, a man steps onto a bus, thinks someone has called out to him and so turns to look, sees nothing and moves on into the bus. The second section, at first still narrated by the man in the first, follows him

142

on his trip to the train station but is soon interrupted by a third-person account of what happened to the man prior to catching the bus. He was apparently visiting a woman named Maria (or is she his wife or his mistress?), who urges him to go before he misses the bus. He leaves the house, passes a dog "with the mouth of a fox," as well as a man killing a pig, being watched by "several women in pink dresses." Getting closer to the bus stop, he also encounters a a cyclist carrying fish in his saddle bag.

The first-person narration begins again, as the man urges the bus driver to hurry. Now it seems he is going to the station to meet a woman named Magda. He imagines the confusion he'll find on the train platform and projects seeing an old man "dragging along a kind of box with a handle." The narrator continues to nag at the bus driver, who finally tells him to stop. He looks outside the bus window and sees a woman smiling at him. "If I hadn't been in such a hurry, I think I'd have jumped off the bus and gone after her," he tells us. At this point the imagery begins to repeat itself in different iterations, as it will for the rest of the novel: The man is at the station where the woman is now looking at him "vacantly"; the dog appears again, blocking his path; he walks along the street, where "a cyclist is trying to pedal along," the fish in his saddle bag now joined by a loaf of bread on top of it. The narration continues to switch from first-person to third-person as the man is back to the beginning of the story, racing to catch the bus. As the section comes to an end, we are introduced to other characters who will make subsequent reappearances: the engineer, the conductor, the ticket-collector, an attractive woman with "tanned thighs."

These characters and their bare-bones actions are shuffled and reshuffled throughout the novel. This reshuffling is, in fact, the novel's fundamental structural principle. No plot beyond the effort to get to the station, no character development beyond what is added in each transmutation, which sometimes subverts and contradicts what we think we've learned before. We couldn't crack open craniums and "spelunk through the bewildering complexity" even if we wanted to (and the novel gives us no reason to want to) since the "bewildering complexity" is all external, in the mode of storytelling itself. The characters are the interchangeable bits, strips of narrative possibility, that make the storytelling possible.

The novel's title, of course, tells us that the specific formal inspiration for its unconventional approach is the fugue, the musical form in which an initial theme or "voice" is repeated numerous times through imitation and variation. As in a musical fugue, the effect of this strategy in *Vain Art of the Fugue* is to take our attention away from simple linear development (in fiction, "story") and to consider instead the way a theme or episode can be developed laterally, so to speak, through a kind of accumulation of slight changes. And the art of the literary fugue is "vain," that is, unapologetically aesthetic, without pretense to psychological enlightenment or social commentary (although the occasional image of a tank rolling through the streets of Bucharest does certainly evoke Communist-era realities). The primary interest in *Vain Art of the Fugue* is formal; it substitutes for the easy "entertainment" of story a delight in formal manipulation. The reader must give up an accustomed passivity for a more active alertness in the face of the novel's constant (and constantly inventive) metamorphoses, but is this really more onerous than relying on the critic-drudge who will "pry open the craniums of characters, authors and narrators" and reveal to us the secrets of human motivation? More boring?

Tsepeneag's novel also fails to provide the "news" that Sabrina Seelig thinks is the hallmark of translated fiction. Its focus is resolutely on the commonplace, the habitual, the universal elements of human experience. The "events" related in *Vain Art of the Fugue* literally could happen almost anywhere. There really are no "specific realities about the ways people live" except the realities about the way everyone lives. The novel does not act as a travelogue or newsmagazine, offers only a few ordinary names (that continually shift--sometimes Maria is Magda and Magda is Maria), whispers no prayers. The only thing that's "exotic" about this book--exoticism being what Seelig really seems to be after--is its aesthetic form, its challenge to casual assumptions about what fiction--translated or otherwise--is supposed to be like. You're not going to learn much about Romania as "other" from *Vain Art of the Fugue*. You'll just see yourself and your own immersion in the inescapable flux of existence.

Both Gottschall and Seelig are working with a conceptual model of fiction that sees it as a fixed form--in Gottschall's case a model that applies (partly) to the kind of fiction that was dominant prior to World War II but that has been shaken up and spun around in all the years since. It has recognizable characters whose psyches we can analyze (if we accept the Darwinist tools) and tells stories that "lift a curtain" on "the ways people live." *Vain Art of the Fugue* is one of those frame-breaking novels that demonstrate such a model only constrains the adventurous writer's imagination and encourages a dessicated understanding of fiction's still unexploited possibilities for aesthetic surprise. It's the sort of novel everyone who thinks he/she <u>knows</u> what novels should be like ought to read, and be utterly disabused of such certainty.

It's good that Delia Sherman and Theodora Goss print at the end of the book an interview with themselves about *Interfictions*, an "anthology of interstitial writing" they've edited and published through the Interstitial Arts Foundation. Otherwise I, for one, would have finished the book, including its nominal "Introduction," without having much of an idea what either "interfiction" or "interstitial" are supposed to mean.

Heinz Insu Fenkl's introduction tells us that a book of his was published as a novel, even though it was really a memoir. Later, a publisher wanted to "repackage" the book as a memoir. Presumably, then, the book is neither a novel nor a memoir, but something "in-between," even though Fenkl's account makes it perfectly clear that it is a memoir, its "tropes, its collaging of time and character" notwithstanding. Using what Fenkl thinks of as "novelistic" devices not make the book a novel. Not wishing to have it understood as a memoir does not make it other than a memoir.

After this thoroughly confusing initial illustration (confusing in terms of what an "interfiction" might be), Fenkl goes on to tell us in jargon-clogged prose such things as "The liminal state in a rite of passage precedes the final phase, which is reintegration, but an interstitial work does not require reintegration--it already has its own being in a willfully transgressive or noncategorical way"; "Interstitial works have a special relationship with the reader because they have a higher degree of indeterminancy (or one could say a greater range of potentialities) than a typical work"; "Once it manifests itself, regardless of the conditions of its creation, the interstitial work has the potential to create a retroactive historical trajectory"; "An interstitial work provides a wider range of possibilities for the reader's engagement and transformation. It is more faceted than a typical literary work, though it also operates under its own internal logic."

This is all well and good, but I finished Fenkl's essay still wondering what an "interfiction" is. How does it differ from other literary works that also manifest a high degree of "indeterminancy" but no one ever thought to call "interstitial."? (In my opinion, all great works of literature are indeterminate in this way. It's what makes them literature in the first place. And Fenkl's invocation of "a retroactive historical trajectory," by which literary works of the past are transformed by new works, seems to me just a restatement of T.S. Eliot's notion that "The existing monuments form an ideal order among themselves, which is modified by the introduction of the new (the really new) work of art among them," which applies to all new works, interstitial or otherwise.) Does it merely have to be "transgressive" of genre boundaries? Where do we mark those boundaries, anyway? And what exactly is a "typical literary work"? I always get the sense that when intense partisans of genre fiction, SF especially, get wound up about "literary fiction" and its discontents, they usually associate such fiction with "realism," against which all genre fiction transgresses in one way or another. But is *Finnegans Wake* realism? *The Unnameable*? *Catch-22*? *Infinite Jest*? If not, do they also qualify as interstitial or as interfictions? Are or they just not "typical" literary fiction? (In which case the whole notion of "transgression" becomes just a convenient buzz word. It only applies to the most rigidly conventional or the most really boring literary fiction.)

Sherman and Goss clear things up a little bit in their interview. "An interstitial story does not hew closely to any one set of recognizable genre conventions," says Sherman. This makes it sound like an "interfiction" blurs the lines between genres, although from my reading of the stories collected in the book it seems that most of them mostly revolve around a fantasy/science fiction/horror axis that, as an only occasional reader of these genres, I often have trouble seeing as radically opposed forms that need bridging or boundary-smashing. But then Sherman says of one of the stories ("Climbing Redemption Mountain," a kind of cross-breeding of John Bunyan and Erskine Caldwell) that "If I tried to read it as realism, I ran up against the fact that the writer had made up this world out of whole cloth. If I tried to read it as a fantasy, I ran up against the story's lack of recognizable genre markers." This suggests that the real "boundary" the book wants to question is again that between "realism" (literary fiction) and genre fiction with its identifiable "markers."

Reading the book as a collection of stories that are "willfully transgressive in a noncategorical way" did me no good at all. Notwithstanding that most of them were "transgressive," when at all, in rather tepid and formally uninteresting ways, I simply was unable to understand what they shared in common that made them "interfictions." The editors' narrowing of focus to the contest between "realism" and genre fiction did allow me to reexamine the stories in this more concentrated light. (Although not all of them. Apparently some of them are "interstitial" because they portray characters who feel "in-between" or because their authors themselves feel this way, as revealed in the authors' comments appended to each story.) But ultimately I am still puzzled by Sherman's explanation of how it is that interstitial fiction avoids "any one set of recognizable genre conventions." She continues:

> An interstitial story does interesting things with narrative and style. An interstitial story takes artistic chances. . .[E]very interstitial story defines itself as unlike any other. . .The best interstitial work. . .demands that you read it on its own terms, but it also gives you the tools to do so.

I am hard-pressed to understand how these characteristics of "interfiction" distinguish it from other, non-genre, "experimental" fiction that also "does interesting things with narrative and style" and "takes artistic chances." Experimental fiction (which ultimately I would have to say is a part of "literary fiction," representing its vanguard in exploring the edges of the literary) precisely "demands that you read it on its own terms" rather than according to pre-established conventions. If interfictions are just versions of experimental fiction, why coin this additional term to describe them? If there is some significant difference between interstitial and experimental fiction, something that has to do with genre, why not be more specific and delineate exactly what that is rather than fall back on the usual language about taking artistic chances, etc.? Or is the purported conflict between realism and genre really meant to blur the fact that plenty of writers, writers who are otherwise thought of as "literary," have already deconstructed this oppositon and created work demanding "you read it on its own terms"?

On the other hand, if the stories in this anthology were to be presented as simply "experimental," without the accompanying claims that they alone challenge the "typical literary work," it's not likely they could stand up to scrutiny. Adrienne Martini's review of the book in the Baltimore *City Paper* (May 30, 2007) asserts that the first story, Christopher Barzak's "What We Know About the Lost Families of --------House," "feels wholly unique, as if it is rewriting our expectations about what kind of story it is even as we're reading it," but it's really just a haunted-house variation on Faulkner's "A Rose for Emily." The second story, Leslie What's "Post Hoc," about a woman who tries to mail herself to her estranged boyfriend, strikes me as standard-issue surrealism, with perhaps a chick-lit chaser. (I guess this might itself be "interstitial," but it's not very interesting.) "Climbing Redemption Mountain" doesn't really go anywhere with its blending of allegory and rural Gothic except to a mountaintop rendezvous with banality.

Of the rest of the stories, Matthew Cheney's "A Map of the Everywhere" is pleasantly odd and Colin Greenland's

"Timothy" has an amusing premise (a woman's cat is transformed into a man) that unfortunately doesn't go anywhere. Most of the rest are forgettable exercises conducted on what seem (to me) familiar science fiction/fantasy terrain. Some of them, such as Anna Tambour's "The Shoe in SHOES' Window" and Catherynne M. Valente's "A Dirge for Prester John" are essentially unreadable, full of pretentious declamations substituting for narrative: "Truly, where chaos reigns, even at night, nonsense and evasion shine where people look for straightforwardness, but where they look for inspiration, something beyond the realm of daily existence, they are then shown only things, and who can feed his soul with that?" Too many of the stories, in fact, are like this, straining after Meaning where some "merely literary" formal and stylistic pleasures would go a long way toward deflating the pomposity.

Karen Jordan Allen's "Alternate Anxieties" is the best story in the book, but it also only highlights the book's overriding weakness. The story's protagonist is a writer attempting to write a book about "mortal anxiety," which also appears to be the defining condition of the writer's own life. The story is presented mostly as a series of notes and brief episodes to be incorporated into the book. In the course of accumulating these notes, the protagonist latches on to the "alternate universe theory," according to which "events may have more than one outcome, with each outcome spinning off its own universe, so that millions of universes are generated each day. . . ." This notion then leads the author-protagonist to further reflection on the events in her own life (are there other universes in which her actions led to different outcomes?) as well as on the capacity of fiction to embody such alternate universes. It's a compelling enough metafiction, but again I can't see what calling it an "interfiction" instead of a metafiction accomplishes. Nor is it that clear why it would even be categorized as science fiction, despite the toying with the theory of alternate universes. It's a pretty good story, and trying to espy its "interstitial" qualities adds nothing to its appeal.

In her review, Martini asserts that "The stories in *Interfictions* operate. . .by existing in the spaces between what we want our genres to be." Speaking for myself, I don't what my genres to be anything but sources of interesting fiction. When it comes down to it, I don't even want genres, just worthwhile stories and novels. Whether you want to call them "interstitial" or "metafictional" or "postmodern" doesn't really matter much, and I suppose by that principle calling a group of stories "interfictions" isn't finally that objectionable, although in this case it is a needlessly byzantine way of arriving at the conclusion that a good piece of fiction "does interesting things with narrative and style" and, unfortunately, turns out not to be the most efficacious way of finding good fiction.

In his review of Jonathan Lethem's *Chronic City*, Hari Kunzru maintains that what separates this novel from the postmodern novels Lethem clearly admires is that "it's too good-humored to attain real satiric bite and is often content to drop a name instead of wrestling with the slippery ideas that might make Lethem's heroes worthy of a true fan's regard" (*Bookforum*, September 2009). This is probably right, although to say that the novel lacks "satiric bite" doesn't mean it is not still essentially an attempt at satire, just as it's true that while *Chronic City* doesn't especially wrestle with "slippery ideas," the claim that so-called "systems novels"--a term coined by Thomas LeClair in his book on Don DeLillo, *In the Loop*--can be defined by their own grappling with such ideas is altogether questionable.

Lethem's work is often associated with the first generation postmodernists, particularly Pynchon, Barth, and DeLillo, as mediated by the science fiction of Philip K. Dick and superhero comic books. This amalgamation of high postmodernism and popular literature seems to be, in fact, what most readers and critics take to be his signature variation on postmodernism in fiction. However, while it may be the case that Lethem is inspired by the postmodernists to create his brand of literary fantasy fiction, there isn't much that's especially innovative about a book like *Chronic City*. It seems more like a tired pastiche of postmodernism than an attempt to extend the reach of postmodern experiment into a different era and changed circumstances.

Kunzru maintains that Lethem "knows he's writing belatedly and wants us to know he knows" and that this gesture perhaps makes the novel "a conscious tribute of some kind, a love letter to the writing that inspired Lethem to become a writer." If John Barth initiated postmodernism by positing a "literature of exhaustion" that exploited the "used-upness" of fictional form to generate new forms, Kunzru's suggestion might indicate that Lethem is in his own way converting postmodernism itself into an "exhausted" source of formal development, at least for his own work, except that, where Barth and company forced a new attention on form, style, and narrative strategy, Lethem settles for vaguely surreal machinations of plot (providing what some want to call an "alternative reality") and loudly "colorful" characters (most of them given obviously Pynchon-derived names). There is otherwise nothing that could be called formal innovation in a novel like *Chronic City*, nothing that really challenges readers to examine their assumptions about the form.

Lethem's status as an experimental writer, then, seems entirely based on his incorporation of genre fiction narrative conventions into novels that have generally been accepted as "serious" fiction. The plot devices of detective stories and science fiction allow Lethem to ostensibly bypass the requirements of ordinary realism, providing for an approach that blends caricature and pseudo-fantasy to produce what in my view can best be described as whimsy. But whimsy is not exactly a postmodern mode, and in *Chronic City* it betrays a certain aesthetic timidity. I think I agree with William Deresiewicz, who in his review of the novel comments that Lethem "wants realism, with the credibility it brings--wants us to take the world of the novel as a faithful copy of the world we know--but he also wants to stack the deck by deploying supernatural elements whenever he finds it convenient" (*The New Republic*, October 15, 2009). Thus the New York City portrayed in the narrative needs to be recognizable enough as New York City that we are able to associate the events and themes with the real place but not so much that the author can't introduce runaway tunnel robots, an illusory space mission doomed by the presence of Chinese space mines, or snow in August.

This sort of contained fantasia can't really be what the postmodernists had in mind as an alternative to conventional realism, nor is it credible as a revision or reorientation of postmodern challenges to inherited practice. It implies that postmodern experiment was simply a strategy designed to undermine the principle of verisimilitude, so that any work not strictly observing the rules of traditional realism could be called "experimental." And while Lethem's work is consistent with much postmodern fiction in that it is essentially comic, the comedy of a novel like *Chronic City* is indeed much too gentle, too shy of the more corrosive humor of much postmodern comedy. It isn't so much that the novel is short on "satiric bite" as that ultimately it is *merely* satire, a relatively mild critique of

156

post-9/11 New York under Bloomberg, which has become inhospitable to its misfits and nonconformists. The postmodern comedy in the work of Pynchon or Barth or Barthelme doesn't seek to "correct" behaviors and institutions that threaten individual autonomy or impede social progress; it portrays such threats and obstructions as inherent to human life and thus unfortunately not much subject to amelioration.

Darby Dixon expresses his disappointment with *Chronic City* as perhaps the consequence of his own inability as a reader to "patiently dissect its meaning and formulate its connections," to "place [its] ideas and themes on pedestals in whose shadows lurk plot and character" (*Identity Theory*, October 29, 2009). This assumes that what is really at work in this novel is an underlying deep structure of "meaning" and "ideas" the reader must uncover. It further implies that what must make it a suitably postmodern work is precisely this deep structure of "connection." But neither does Lethem's novel conceal any deep meaning not made apparent through choice of satirical targets, nor is this undertow of supposedly abstruse "matter" what animates postmodern fiction. The story of the relationship between narrator Chase Insteadman, former child actor, and Perkus Tooth, former bohemian intellectual now pothead, allows Lethem to canvass his "alternative" New York from top (Insteadman is something of a mascot for the city's high-society types) to bottom and to adjust his satirical focus accordingly. That the purport of the novel's "ideas and themes" doesn't go much beyond this surface satire is in its favor, as we aren't subjected to the kind of tedium the exploration of "ideas" in fiction usually entails. In this way Lethem is actually faithful to his postmodern predecessors: to the extent Barth or Pynchon or DeLillo incorporate ideas, they do so as inspiration for formal or narrative devices ("entropy" in Pynchon's story of that name, for example) rather than as abstractions with which to "wrestle."

However, *Chronic City* nevertheless suffers from its own kind of tedium, exactly of the sort Darby Dixon identifies when he admits he found it simply "boring." *Chronic City* never attains the structural or stylistic vitality that would be required for us to suspend our disbelief in its plot contrivances. Its narrative drags along and its narrator's language is leaden and unnecessarily prolix to the extent that I mostly had to force myself to finish the book. The narrator is himself an unengaging figure whose status as a blank slate on which his friend Perkus inscribes a more capacious understanding does not make him a character with whom one wants to spend over 450 pages. And Perkus himself is much less interesting than Lethem wants him to be. He's an essentially stock countercultural type--he likes to discourse on "Monte Hellman, Semina Culture, Greil Marcus's *Lipstick Traces*, the Mafia's blackmailing of J. Edgar Hoover over erotic secrets (resulting in the bogus amplification of Cold War fear and therefore the whole of our contemporary landscape), Vladimir Mayakovsky and the futurists, Chet Baker," etc., etc., etc.--and his recurrent cluster headaches and other mental problems make him seem merely pathetic, not heroic.

In his *Washington Post* review of *Chronic City* (October 24, 2009), Ron Charles acknowledges it is "a tedious reading experience in which redundancy substitutes for development and effect for profundity," but he nonetheless thinks Lethem "proves he's one of the most elegant stylists in the country," offering "perfectly choreographed sentences." I have in the past found Lethem a pleasing enough stylist, but the style exhibited through Chase Insteadman produces sentences that are anything but "perfectly choreographed." Here's Chase in one of his moments of reflection:

> I'm outstanding only in my essential politeness. Exhausting, this compulsion to oblige any detected social need. I don't mean only to myself; it's frequently obvious that my charm exhausts and bewilders others, even as they depend upon it to mortar crevices in the social facade--to fill vacant seats, give air to suffocating silences, fudge unease. (I'm like fudge. Or maybe I'm like chewing gum.) But if beneath charm lies exhaustion, beneath exhaustion lies a certain rage. I detect a wrongness everywhere. Within and Without, to quote a lyric. It would be misleading to say I'm screaming inside, for if I was, I'd soon enough find a way to scream aloud. Rather, the politeness infests a layer between me and

myself, the name of the wrongness going not only unexpressed but unknown. Intuited only. Forbidden perhaps. Perkus would have called me *inchoate*. He wouldn't have meant it kindly.

I could have settled for the first sentence. Or perhaps "Perkus would have called me inchoate." These descriptions tell me what I need to know about Insteadman (to the extent I need to have Insteadman telling me about himself in the first place). The rest is just prattle, and by the time I get to "I detect a wrongness" and the politeness infesting a layer "between me and myself" I just want him to shut up.

This sort of inexhaustible self-examination and droning exposition occurs throughout the narrative and more than anything else accounts for the lackluster reading experience *Chronic City* turned out to be. Perhaps it is a sign of the author trying too hard to create "meaning" and forge "connections," but I don't think so. I think it's just Lethem's failure to execute his "alternative reality" into something more than a labored fantasy.

IV Alain Robbe-Grillet

Regardless of whether his own novels will stand up as important instances of "a new departure," Alain Robbe-Grillet thoroughly understood what it would take for the novel to survive as a credible art form:

There is no question. . .of establishing a theory, a pre-existing mold into which to pour the books of the future. Each novelist, each novel must invent its own form. No recipe can replace this continual reflection. The book makes its own rules for itself, and for itself alone. Indeed the movement of its style must often lead to jeopardize them, breaking them, even exploding them. Far from respecting certain immutable forms, each new book tends to constitute the laws of its functioning at the same time that it produces their destruction. Once the work is completed, the writer's critical reflection will serve him further to gain a perspective in regard to it, immediately nourishing new explorations, a new departure. ("The Use of Theory," in *For a New Novel*, trans. Richard Howard)

So much for the notion, advanced by Lionel Shriver, that "the ultimate test of any writer may be taking on the most traditional of genres. . .and pouring new wine into old skins" (*Los Angeles Times*, August 19, 2007). This may be the "test" for a certain kind of commercially-minded writer, the "professional author," but as Robbe-Grillet explains, the writer who truly takes his/her form seriously is willing not only to reject the "old skins" but also to discard the "new wine" once it has been made. Continuing to use the same "recipe" only shuts down the process of "continual reflection" on the possibilities of fiction needed to keep it vital. What has already been done--by the writer, by previous writers--however much it might continue to please readers, for the writer serves ultimately as the motivation for "new explorations," without which the novel will devolve into mere product and survive only as an historical curiosity. "The writer must proudly consent to bear his own date," writes Robbe-Grillet elsewhere in this essay, "knowing that there are no masterpieces in eternity, but only works in history, and that they survive only to the degree that they have left the past behind them and heralded the future."

In his essay "On Several Obsolete Notions," Robbe-Grillet describes the novel in its "classic" phase:

> All the technical elements of the narrative-- systematic use of the past tense and the third person, unconditional adoption of chronological development, linear plots, regular trajectory of the passions, impulse of each episode toward a conclusion, etc.--everything tended to impose the image of a stable, coherent, continuous, unequivocal universe. Since the intelligibility of the world was not even questioned, to tell a story did not raise a problem. The style of the novel could be innocent.

He continues:

> But then, with Flaubert, everything begins to vacillate. A hundred years later the whole system is no more than a memory, and it is to that memory, to that dead memory, that some seek with all their might to keep the novel fettered. . . (*For a New Novel*)

It is tempting to say that Robbe-Grillet's account of the 19th century novel and the shadow it cast on subsequent novelists still seems relevant, fifty years later, and that many readers still think of the "innocent" narrative as the novel's natural form, from which any variation or experiment in form is merely a temporary departure. However, an honest consideration of Robbe-Grillet's bill of particulars would have to conclude that fiction over the course of the 20th century did in fact move beyond the model Robbe-Grillet associates with Balzac and other early novelists.

While much current fiction does continue to employ third-person narration--usually the "free indirect" variant through which a character's thoughts, recollections, and emotions provide a perceptual matrix but are not directly stated by the character--first-person narratives are probably more prevalent than ever before, as are experiments in shifting, alternate, and multiple points of view. Similarly, stories related in the present tense have become so common that what was once a notable divergence from the norm is probably no longer noticed by most readers. And while most novels still rely on "plot," their plots are by no means always "linear," such chronological development as they possess often enough supplied by the reader after piecing together the fragments of narrative presented without much immediate regard for chronological continuity. It could perhaps be argued that too many novels do still imply a "decipherable universe"--decipherable insofar as it can be adequately rendered through the protocols of realism--but most literary fiction is not so tied to a 19th century worldview as to portray human experience as "stable, coherent, continuous, unequivocal."

Indeed, to the extent that contemporary life seems to many of us discontinuous and indefinite, the modernist-derived strategies emphasizing subjectivity and fragmentation seem justified in the name of realism itself. And to this extent, Robbe-Grillet has been proven correct when in the same essay he predicts that this sort of modernist experimentation (with which he more or less associated his own fiction) will become "assimilated," viewed by critics still attuned only to the past as the most recent golden age of storytelling. Thus, esteemed critics such as James Wood point us back to Henry James or Virginia Woolf as writers who set a standard of inner-directed realism, a realism of the mind and its subjective perceptions rather than a realism of the material world presented as a collection of facts. Wood is certainly not alone in holding up the psychological novel as the apogee of the novel as a literary form. The notion that in fiction, and only in fiction, we can "get inside" a character, can "feel" what it's like to negotiate the world from a perspective other than our own, is very widespread. But, I would argue, this is because one part of the modernist project, the extension of realism into "psychological realism," has been successful, while that part setting a precedent for aesthetic innovation ("make it new") as a measure of artistic achievement has not been embraced as firmly by either writers or critics. The set of accepted conventions for the writing of fiction has been advanced from about 1825 to about 1925, but those voices that "seek with all their might to keep the novel fettered" to a "dead system" can still be heard, even if that "system" has incorporated some of the strategies for which Robbe-Grillet himself was an advocate.

Although "innocent" novels are still being written (particularly within some forms of genre fiction), very few serious writers have failed to notice fiction's loss of innocence. But the expansion of techniques available to the modern writer has developed into its own kind of "systematic" practice that can be just as stubborn an obstacle to the development of a "new novel" as the traditional story form Robbe-Grillet wanted to clear away. It is probably inevitable that strategies and approaches once regarded as mold-breaking will eventually become conventional, established techniques for the novelist to adopt when they suit his/her need. But this only makes it more important that writers like Robbe-Grillet or Donald Barthelme or Gilbert Sorrentino emerge to point out that such techniques have become hidebound and to offer fresh alternatives.

Robbe-Grillet is, of course, most famous as both theorist and practitioner of the "new novel." In his essay "New Novel, New Man," Robbe-Grillet defends his practice against some of the main criticisms directed at it (and at Robbe-Grillet's previous defenses of the practice). Among those criticisms was the charge that the New Novelists devalued the past, or, as Robbe-Grillet put it, that they "made a *tabula rasa* of the past." Robbe-Grillet replies that this charge can only itself proceed from an incomplete appreciation of the history of fiction:

> Not only has the development been considerable since the middle of the nineteenth century, but it began immediately, in Balzac's own period. Did not Balzac already note the "confusion" in the descriptions of *The Charterhouse of Parma*? It is obvious that the Battle of Waterloo, as described by Stendhal, no longer belongs to the Balzacian order.
>
> And, since then, the evolution has become increasingly evident: Flaubert, Dostoevski, Proust, Kafka, Joyce, Faulkner, Beckett. . .Far from making a *tabula rasa* of the past, we have most readily reached an agreement on the names of our predecessors; and our ambition is merely to continue them. Not to *do better*, which has no meaning, but to situate ourselves in their wake, in our own time. (*For a New Novel*)

Robbe-Grillet has himself, of course, now become one of those "names," one of the predecessors in whose wake writers inspired by his adventurousness might wish to "situate" themselves. But his account of the impulse behind experiment in fiction-the New Novel being a very prominent variety of experimental fiction in the post World War II era--is still compelling and goes some way toward clearing up a confusion about what motivates the best experimental writers.

Such writers do not consider themselves or their work either as cut off from the flow of literary history or as actively hostile to the accomplishments of the past. Indeed, as Robbe-Grillet points out, they are likely to see the history of fiction as itself a history of innovation and the greatest writers as the greatest innovators. Experimental writers such as John Barth or Donald Barthelme or Robert Coover saw themselves as continuing the adventurous spirit embodied in their esteemed predecessors (Borges for Barth, for example, the surrealists for Barthelme) and Barth, for one, reached back for inspiration all the way to the beginnings of the novel for his first foray into "experimental" fiction, *The Sot-Weed Factor.* I'm certain that most younger experimental writers similarly look to the past for innovative touchstones, including the work of Barth, Barthelme, and Coover.

Those who don't risk producing fictions that seem merely eccentric, idiosyncratic, unattached to the historical tradition that itself represents a "development" of a form without "strict and definitive rules" and that proceeds through challenges to "order." Experimental fiction that seeks to be perceived as irrevocably "other" implicitly does regard the history of fiction as without notable predecessors and its writer does suggest he/she can "do better" than Kafka, Joyce, Faulkner, et al. (or better than Balzac, for that matter). But absent this tradition, such doing better, as Robbe-Grillet reminds us, has "no meaning."

Robbe-Grillet begins his essay "From Realism to Reality" with what must be a truism:

> All writers believe they are realists. None ever calls himself abstract, illusionistic, chimerical, fantastic, falsitical. . .Realism is not a theory, defined without ambiguity, which would permit us to counter certain writers with certain others; it is, on the contrary, a flag under which the enormous majority--if not all--of today's novelists enlist. And no doubt we must believe them all, on this point. It is the real world which interests them; each one attempts as best as can to create "the real." (*For a New Novel*)

Robbe-Grillet believed himself to be a realist and his attempts at advancing a "new novel" an effort to preserve the possibility of realism in fiction against the insistence of some critics that the novel remain encased in its pre-modern form. "The discovery of reality will continue only if we abandon outworn forms," Robbe-Grillet writes. "Unless we suppose that the world is henceforth entirely discovered (and, in that case, the wisest thing would be to stop writing altogether), we can only attempt to go farther. .

.advancing in ways as yet unknown, in which a new kind of writing becomes necessary."

This "new kind of writing" is necessary for realism's sake. Even if it is true that each succeeding generation of writers "has different ideas of reality," that "the classicists believed that it is classical, the romantics that it is romantic, the surrealists that it is surreal," the task of coping with "the objective modifications of reality" that have continued to develop at an ever increasing pace since the 19th century requires that the novel remain open to the kind of formal innovation that might--for the moment, at least-- begin to "account for what is real today."

But Robbe-Grillet didn't think that the "realism" of novels consisted of merely <u>reflecting</u> the "real world" it encountered but that it actually worked to create reality:

> The style of the novel does not seek to inform, as does the chronicle, the testimony offered in evidence, or the scientific report, it *constitutes* reality. It never knows what it is seeking, it is ignorant of what it has to say; it is invention, invention of the world and of man, constant invention and perpetual interrogation. All those-- politicians and others--who ask of a book only stereotypes, and who fear above all the spirit of contestation, can only mistrust literature.

169

Robbe-Grillet comes a little closer to commenting on the kind of realism one finds in his own books when he reflects on a trip he once took to the Brittany coast:

> On the way I told myself: here is a good opportunity to observe things 'from life' and to 'refresh my memory.' But from the first gull I saw, I understood my error: on the one hand, the gulls I now saw had only very confused relations with those I was describing in my book, and on the other hand it couldn't have mattered less to me whether they did or not. The only gulls that mattered to me at that moment were those which were inside my head. Probably they came there, one way or another, from the external world, and perhaps from Brittany; but they had been transformed, becoming at the same time somehow more real *because* they were now imaginary.

Those gulls inside the head are the gulls that make it into Robbe-Grillet's novels, even if they are described with a kind of obsessive exactitude that makes us believe they're a copy from "real life." Or, for example, we get this, the opening paragraph of *Jealousy*, which describes the south side of the house that will be the immediate setting for all of the novel:

> Now the shadow of the column--the column which supports the southwest corner of the roof--divides the

corresponding corner of the veranda into two equal parts. This veranda is a wide, covered gallery surrounding the house on three sides. Since its width is the same for the central portion as for the sides, the line of shadow cast by the column extends precisely to the corner of the house; but it stops there, for only the veranda flagstones are reached by the sun, which is still too high in the sky. The wooden walls of the house--that is, its front and west gable-end--are still protected from the sun by the roof (common to the house proper and the terrace). So at this moment the shadow of the outer edge of the roof coincides exactly with the right angle formed by the terrace and the two vertical surfaces of the corner of the house. (Translated by Richard Howard)

Already we can see Robbe-Grillet beginning to "constitute" the reality of the novel's setting, which will extend to the banana plantation of which this house is the center, all described in the same painstaking, concentrated manner. And it is a particularly literal-minded kind of description: no fussy, unnecessary adjectives, no figurative flourishes to get in the way of a full-on apprehension of the house and its wooden walls, its veranda flagstones and "vertical surfaces." Robbe-Grillet's approach has at times been called "cinematic," but what could be less cinematic than this description of the banana trees:

In the second row, starting from the far left, there would be twenty-two trees (because of the alternate arrangement) in the case of a rectangular patch. There would also be twenty-two for a patch that was precisely trapezoidal, the reduction being scarcely noticeable at such a short distance from its base. And, in fact, there are twenty-two trees there.

But the third row too has only twenty-two trees, instead of twenty three which the alternately-arranged rectangle would have. No additional difference is introduced, at this level, by the bulge in the lower edge. The same is true for the fourth row, which includes twenty-one boles, that is, one less than an even row of the imaginary rectangle.

It is generally assumed that film provides a more immediate and more distinct rendering of perceptible objects (at least visually), but passages like this demonstrate that verbal depictions of such objects are, potentially at least, capable of a far greater range of effects, of bringing us much closer to the palpable qualities of things. In "From Realism to Reality," Robbe-Grillet writes of Kafka that "if there is one thing of which an unprejudiced reading convinces us it is the absolute reality of the things Kafka describes. . .Perhaps Kafka's staircases lead *elsewhere*, but they are *there*, and we look at them, step by step, following the detail of the banisters and the risers. Perhaps his gray walls hide something, but it is on them that the memory lingers, on their cracked whitewash, their crevices." The same is true of Robbe-Grillet's descriptions; they force our attention on what is <u>there</u>. We remember (or should) the arrangements and textures of the plantation house, the symmetries of the banana rows.

Some might say that Robbe-Grillet's descriptions don't qualify as "realism" at all, since they appear to reject the principle of selectivity of detail and renounce the effort to enhance the real through figurative language, both of which are believed by such guardians of literary realism to be among its most crucial enabling conventions. But this is to confuse the practice of a certain kind of commercialized storytelling with realism, the latter of which probably becomes more genuine the farther away it gets from storytelling. It is to pin the concept of realism down to a few customary gestures that assume a stability of reference to "the real" and denies that this is a state of affairs to be discovered rather than presupposed. In abandoning these gestures, Robbe-Grillet's "experimental" fiction is actually an experiment in the further possibilities of realism, a realism that accepts, as Robbe-Grillet puts it in his essay's conclusion, that "everything is constantly changing" and that "there is always something new."

The realism of *Jealousy* is about as far away from modern "psychological realism," and especially the mode of narration James Wood defends as the "free indirect" method, as it could be.

Our access to the characters and their environment remains entirely on the surface, our knowledge of what they are "thinking" confined entirely to what we can infer through their actions. This, is, of course, faithful to the way we do in fact experience reality, and the spurious notion that fiction is some magical way for writers to open up consciousness to our direct examination beyond what people say and do is duly dispensed with in Robbe-Grillet's novel. This is not to say that we don't ultimately gain access to a character's mental state, but this character is neither A. . . (not further named), the plantation wife, nor her possible lover, Franck (we're never entirely sure they are lovers), the ostensible protagonists of *Jealousy*. One could say that the true protagonist of the novel is the emotion named in the title, which we finally come to understand is expressed by the narrator, who is not the detached omniscient narrator we first assume him to be (or at least is also more than that) but the husband of A. . . and an observer of her suspicious behavior.

Thus do we almost literally inhabit the consciousness of this character, and we are determined in our experience of *Jealousy*'s fictional world by the skillful manipulation of point of view--in this case a third-person/first-person hybrid. But, since we can't rest comfortably in the author's probing of the character's mind in a "free indirect" way, the effect is if anything to provoke us into re-reading the novel in order to direct our attention more carefully on the details and the actions through which, and only through which, can our awareness of the narrator's jealousy be raised. *Jealousy* encourages the reader to be an active participant in assembling whatever "meaning" we're to get from it; it doesn't allow us to settle passively for the "insight" afforded us by Wood's preferred strategy of "inflected" narration.

What this hybrid point of view allows Robbe-Grillet to do most thoroughly, however, is to create an intimately "realistic" world that both mirrors the narrator's own fixated absorption in detail--his "perpetual interrogation"-- and uses that absorption to "invent" scenes and circumstances of dense realistic detail. So dedicated is Robbe-Grillet to the invention of these scenes that he repeats many of them, enlisting his narrator in a repetition and return to specific details and events--the remains of a centipede killed while walking across a wall, workers fixing a bridge, etc.-- as if making sure they have been surveyed for all of the attributes they can be made to reveal. The ultimate effect is of a scrupulously observed, enclosed world that is wholly imaginary, constituted through the writer's determination to invoke it in his words, and thus also wholly real.

Among the many unsupportable assertions made by Stephen Marche in his semi-infamous 2008 diatribe against Alain Robbe-Grillet was the following:

The "new novel". . . as Robbe-Grillet defined and explained it in his famous 1963 essay, was high art at its unpalatably highest. It applied rules and regulations, opposed subjectivity and tried to dissolve plot and character into description. (*Salon*, March 6, 2008)

I would challenge Marche to re-read Robbe-Grillet's fiction, especially those novels written before the publication of *For a New Novel*, and try to make a case that any of these points can be sustained. Most of them, in fact, are precisely the opposite of what one finds in novels such as *The Erasers*, *The Voyeur*, and *Jealousy*, but I will focus in particular on *The Voyeur* as a work against which accusations such as Marche's simply aren't credible.

Like its immediate predecessor *The Erasers*, *The Voyeur* is essentially a detective story, although the earlier novel (Robbe-Grillet's first) literally includes a detective in its cast of characters while *The Voyeur* asks the reader to do the detective work its story calls for. It includes a murder of a young girl and a possibly psychopathic killer, both of them elements that would seemingly be attractive to the "popular" readers Marche believes Robbe-Grillet spurned and as far from the assumptions of "high art" as one could get. What is missing from its mystery plot is a firm resolution of the mystery, and while this refusal to accede to the conventions of the genre might be frustrating to some readers, it also manifests a commitment to the depiction of life's complexities, which are not reducible to the neat resolutions of mystery stories. This commitment is not a characteristic of "high art." It is a characteristic of <u>art</u>.

What most readers who find themselves alienated by *The Voyeur* would cite as their source of disfavor surely would not be its application of "rules and regulations" but precisely the absence of such rules. A proper novel of this kind (a proper novel in general) should establish a stable relationship between reader and protagonist, should lay out its plot as a discernable series of events and should ultimately fill in whatever gaps might be left over, should use description to fill out the narrative not to substitute for it, should leave the reader with the impression its narrative has been appropriately developed and completed.

The Voyeur does none of these things. Its protagonist, a watch salesman named Mathias, initially provokes a mostly impassive response, although eventually we are led to exchange this neutrality for a more decisive attitude: either we are appalled and think Mathias is a monster on the loose or we have some sympathy for a character who is clearly insane and can't even remember whether he committed the act or not. Given that finally we don't know which person he really is, the original more affectless reaction seems the right one, but many readers might find this unregulated drift in our disposition toward the character unsettling.

The Voyeur begins as a relatively straightforward account of a day the watch salesman spends on an island off the French coast, which is initially presented as the place where the salesman himself grew up. However, this item of information is not the first we come to suspect might be questionable. Soon enough the narrative begins to circle around itself--reflecting perhaps the figure-eight pattern that Matthias uses to navigate the island on his quest to sell watches--and to shuffle between past and present. We become uncertain whether Mathias is simply following his route or whether he is engaging in dissociative reveries. We become concretely aware of the murder of the young girl about two-thirds of the way through the novel, but there may be hints that something untoward has happened through these reveries or in the spaces opened up by disruptions of narrative continuity. The murder is the narrative's central event, yet it is the one episode in the novel that remains undescribed.

Description is indeed a dominant strategy in *The Voyeur*, but only a passive and inattentive reader would conclude that it is used to "dissolve plot and character." Both plot and character are *revealed* through description, not annulled by it. Although the point of view in the novel is ostensibly third-person, we would be mistaken to take a passage like this, a description of the island's harbor as Mathias's boat approaches it, as originating in an "outside" narrator:

The pier, which seemed longer than in actually was as an effect of perspective, extended from both sides of this base line in a cluster of parallels describing, with a precision accentuated even more sharply by the morning light, a series of elongated planes alternately horizontal and vertical: the crest of the massive parapet that protected the tidal basin from the open sea, the inner wall of the parapet, the jetty along the top of the pier, and the vertical embankment that plunged straight into the water of the harbor. The two vertical structures were in shadow, the other two brilliantly lit by the sun--the whole breadth of the parapet and all of the jetty save for one dark narrow strip: the shadow cast by the parapet. Theoretically, the reversed image of the entire group could be seen reflected in the harbor water, and, on the surface, still within the same play of parallels, the shadow cast by the vertical embankment extending straight toward the quay.

This is what Mathias sees as he stares as the scene from the ship, but, more importantly, it is the _way_ Mathias sees it, complete with the attention to specific detail and obsession with geometric patterning. These qualities are not just those that are brought to passages of description like this--and the novel contains many, many more--but help to constitute Mathias's character, help constitute him _as_ a character. He is precisely the sort of man who keeps careful watch of himself and his surroundings and whose apprehension of the world takes special note of its geometric attributes--its existence as "a series of elongated planes alternately horizontal and vertical," etc. The "plot" in which he figures as the primary character, furthermore, is not "dissolved" into description of this sort but is enabled by it, the "mystery" at its center evoked by it. Does the omission of description of the act itself signal that Mathias didn't do it, or that he did but can't bring himself to confront it? If the "real" is what is able to impress itself on Mathias's awareness, then the fact that the murder has not done so means he had nothing to do with it, or that there's only some reality he can face?

These questions are not answered by one's reading of *The Voyeur*, and that is because, far from "oppos[ing] subjectivity," Robbe-Grillet builds this novel on it. The descriptions offered are not "objective" renderings of a reality presupposed to exist but indeed the subjective perceptions of an ultimately very flawed and uncertain character. The reality he constructs is a vividly rendered one, and it is the reality we as readers must also inhabit, but ultimately it is a rendered one. There is no reason why an approach emphasizing description must therefore necessarily be an approach seeking objectivity. A novel like *The Voyeur* leaves us with the conviction that subjectivity is all.

In her book *Inventing the Real World: The Art of Alain Robbe-Grillet* (1998), Marjorie H. Hellerstein explains that Robbe-Grillet "began by looking into the possibilities of expressing subjectivity while seeming to be objective in descriptions without emotion." That Mathias's perceptions are related "without emotion" is probably what bothers someone like Marche, a characteristic he translates into a rejection of subjectivity. Marche believes that Robbe-Grillet "convinced a generation of talented novelists that there was something vulgar about attracting a popular readership," and presumably the lack of "emotion" in Robbe-Grillet's work acts as an impediment to this "popular readership." It's too "puritanical," too hostile to the "pleasurable" in fiction.

I doubt that Robbe-Grillet would have objected had his books managed to reach a wider audience. This audience would, of course, have had to accept the books on their own terms, as harbingers of a "new" fiction that renounces the easy pleasures of traditional fiction as distortions and misrepresentations of the very reality it was purported to be portraying. But I don't see why these books can't be taken on those terms, why they can't be enjoyed for their own ingenuities and mischievous challenges to our expectations. There is pleasure to be had in allowing one's assumptions to be challenged and following a work's alternative logic where it will lead, especially if that alternative logic provides new insights into the still possible permutations into which fiction writers might shape their work, which I believe *The Voyeur* and Robbe-Grillet's work as a whole does. Finally it seems to me that Stephen Marche is being "elitist" when he assumes that "readers in the English-speaking world" are incapable of reading in this way.

PART FOUR

Realism

I Realisms

I was recently directed to a 1996 *Salon* interview with John Updike in which Updike remarks that

> "There are fads in critical fashion, but a writer at his peril strays too far from realism. Especially in this country, where realism is kind of our thing. Writing that gives you the real texture of how things look and how people acted. At least there's something there beyond yourself and your own wits to cling to, a certain selflessness amid the terrible egoism of a writer."

Updike doesn't necessarily speak contemptuously of postmodernists such as Donald Barthleme or John Barth, and if they were "out of fashion" in 1996, they are indeed even more so now. However, Updike's assertion that "realism is kind of our thing," especially if realistic fiction is considered to be merely "writing that gives you the real texture of how things look and how people acted," is simply wrong. It can't stand up to an analysis of American literary history in any way.

I'm not sure that Updike's own fiction validates a statement like this one, in fact. Certainly his work represents an effort to give "the real texture of how things look and how people acted," but a number of his books defy the label "realism" in any meaningful sense of the term: *The Centaur*, *The Coup*, *The Witches of Eastwick*, *Brazil*, *S*, most recently *Toward the End of Time*. Furthermore, Updike's sinuous prose style is probably not what most people have in mind when they think of "realistic" storytelling.

Much of the most important American fiction fits more comfortably into the category of "romance" than realism. (The term goes back to the medieval narrative form, and doesn't have any connection to the modern "romance novel.") Hawthorne famously set out the terms in which the romance is to be understood in his preface to *The House of the Seven Gables*: "When a writer calls his work a Romance. . .he wishes to claim a certain latitude, both as to its fashion and material"; this "latitude" allows him to present the "truth" of human experience "under circumstances, to a great extent, of the writer's own choosing or creation" and to "manage his atmospherical medium as to bring out or mellow the lights and deepen and enrich the shadows of the picture."

Going back to the beginnings of American fiction, "romance" would thus encompass the work of Charles Brockden Brown (often identified as the first important American novelist), Washington Irving, James Fenimore Cooper, Hawthorne, Melville, much of Twain, the later Henry James, Faulkner, Ellison, Flannery O'Connor, Malamud, much of the later Roth, and, in my opinion, almost all of the writers called "postmodern." Of the "great" American writers, only Crane, the earlier James, Edith Wharton, Dreiser, Steinbeck and Hemingway could plausibly be called "realists." (And there are those who think the latter would more aptly be called a "symbolist" rather than a realist.) Currently the followers of Raymond Carver or Richard Yates might fit the description.

(For a much fuller treatment of the romance tradition I've sketched out here, see Richard Chase's *The American Novel and Its Tradition*, which traces the Romance tradition is much more detail. That such books as this have fallen into obscurity is itself perhaps one of the reasons many people misunderstand what the history of American literature actually shows us--and thus what many contemporary writers are actually up to.)

Perhaps it's just that the term "realism" gets tossed around much too lightly, used to signal other assumptions about what fiction ought to do: tell dramatic stories, create sympathetic characters, depict current social conditions, reflect "life" as most readers would recognize it. If so, I can't believe Updike actually thinks that this kind of "realism" is either fiction's "proper" mode or that most readers actually do prefer fiction that really, truly, tells the "truth" about human existence or the common lot of most people in our beloved U.S. of A. In my somewhat jaded opinion, most readers still want "escapist" literature--to the extent they want literature at all--that nevertheless doesn't stray too far from ordinary experience. American "literary" writers have really never provided them with this, so the test of how many people are reading a given writer at a certain time is wholly irrelevant.

None of this is to say that realism is inherently inferior, an aesthetic mistake. Flaubert is a great writer, as is Chekhov, as is James, as is, in a much different way, Thomas Hardy. If the complaint is that current writers don't write like these folks, well, few writers could. If it's that writers like Bartheleme or Barth don't write conventional narratives with "real" people and identifiable "themes," then it's really a complaint that serious fiction doesn't remain clinging to the past.

While I would agree with Scott McLemee's contention in a *Chronicle of Higher Education* article (July 30, 2004) that, given the sociological and political approach exemplified by the realist writers McLemee discusses, it is surprising that academic critics do not give more attention to these writers, the reason that it is surprising is that the approach taken by most of these critics is itself emphatically sociological and political. On the other hand, it is not surprising that critics interested in the specifically literary and aesthetic accomplishments of fiction would shy away from such writers as Sinclair Lewis, Upton Sinclair, and James T. Farrell. Their work has little aesthetic appeal in the first place, although, to be fair to them, these writers really did not take up the writing of fiction for its aesthetic potential, anyway.

I'm not quite clear why McLemee chose to focus on these particular writers if the object is to bring some attention to "realism" as a literary mode. The realists in American fiction are writers like James, Twain, Crane, and Edith Wharton, or the "colorists" such as Sarah Orne Jewett and Willa Cather. Lewis, Sinclair, Farrell, and Theodore Dreiser are really "naturalists," a further development of realism to be sure, but one that is inherently programmatic, that is to say, it is an approach that deliberately uses fiction to illustrate larger ideas about, in this case, the biological determinants of human nature and the clash of the biological and the social. Most of the naturalists would be more accurately called commentators or polemicists rather than artists. Again, since the overwhelming trend in academic criticism is to view literature as, at best, an opportunity for polemics and social analysis, it is perhaps correct to say that these naturalist writers are unduly neglected, but if literary study was still mostly about literature these writers would quite rightly get little attention.

I think we should preserve a distinction between the kind of social realism discussed in Scott McLemee's article and "literary realism" more concretely understood. If analysis of social conditions is what you want from fiction, then probably social realism is where you should go. Realism as an aesthetic strategy, however, requires that both writers and readers first of all put aside the consideration of social conditions and political debates. Well-conceived and -crafted literary realism might finally lead the reader to reflect on the state of society or on political ideas, but this would be a secondary effect, a consequence of the fact that the writer has taken a particular aesthetic strategy--to create an illusion of "real life" sufficiently compelling that the reader is willing to put aside the knowledge that it's constructed, finally just words on a page--and allowed it to discover the integrity of its own internal logic, to go where it will. If social analysis is what the writer wants to provide instead, then that's what we'll get. But it won't be something that could plausibly be called literary art. And no argument is going to convince me, at any rate, that writers like Sinclair and Farrell (or for that matter Tom Wolfe and Norman Mailer) are anything but polemicists and would-be social philosophers.

As it happens, at least one of the writers to whom McLemee refers, Dreiser, managed to produce work that can be regarded as literary art, even though it's clear enough in reading his books that he had the ambition to be a social philosopher as well. But Dreiser is a good example of a writer whose instincts for fiction to some extent subverted his more schematic intentions. (Flannery O'Connor is another example.) Although Dreiser was surely not subtle, his narratives have a power that comes much less from any insights he may have had into the grinding away of the social machinery than from the impression his novels create that they have proceeded from their original arresting images--a young girl from the provinces on her way to start a new life in the city, a family of itinerant Christian proselytizers plying their trade on the streets--to dramatize the possibilities inherent in those images with great amplitude and discernment, the narrative unfolding in what finally seems the only way it could have developed. Both *Sister Carrie* and *An American Tragedy* seem "real" in that they are faithful to the particulars their subjects already--naturally--seem to possess, their worlds and their characters built up out of accumulated details that give them credibility as fictions, no matter how readily we are tempted to interpret them as vehicles for the author's social commentary.

Something like this has to be true of any realist fiction that makes a claim on us <u>as</u> fiction rather than an excuse for dubious political or cultural analysis--and the latter would have to be dubious because making up stories is first of all not a very efficient way of engaging in such analysis and because there's nothing inherent in the act of writing fiction that gives the writer any particular wisdom to convey about politics or social arrangements. Again, an artfully composed work of realist fiction might provoke in readers some reflection on these topics, but it would be the result of the work's success in literary terms, its capacity to stand up to subsequent readings because of its aesthetic interest. Otherwise it is inevitable that "realist" works such as *The Jungle* or *Babbitt* or *Studs Lonigan* are ultimately going to be of concern mostly to the kinds of historians who, as McLemee laments, "treat realist fiction strictly for its documentary value" and who, in the words of one scholar McLemee quotes, "[l]ike strip miners,. . .rampage through texts, interested in only the most obvious social references." Unless it can be shown that books like these work first of all as skillfully shaped and convincing examples of literary art (and I admit I don't think this can be shown), they will in the future attract few readers other than these kinds of historians.

A good illustration of the kind of distinction I am making would be a comparison of the stories of Chekhov with those of his contemporary Maxim Gorky. Chekhov's fiction reveals a great deal about the state of Russian society in the late 19th and early twentieth centuries, but we still read these stories because they're splendid examples of the artistic possibilities of a certain kind of realism. Gorky's stories will perhaps tell you something about a Russian radical's attempt to change this society through fiction, but only if you're able to actually read them as something other than propaganda--that is, if you're even able to read them at all.

In his conclusion, McLemee discusses a current scholar's attempt to show that "a careful reading of the American writers reveals a stronger influence that issued from an incongruous source: the deep current of literary romance, exemplified in American literature by the work of Edgar Allan Poe and Nathaniel Hawthorne." He claims further that "The genre of romance -- with its strong tendency toward symbolism and its eruptions of the fantastic and the supernatural -- seems like an improbable influence on, say, Frank Norris." But the very first book to propose the Romance as the dominant strand of American fiction, Richard Chase's *The American Novel and Its Tradition* (1957), included a chapter on "Norris and Naturalism." Writes Chase: ". . .the youthful father of naturalism was in dead earnest in describing his works as romances. . .And in the brief years of his growing maturity. . .he wrote books that departed from realism by becoming in a unified act of the imagination at once romances and naturalistic novels." And of Dreiser Chase writes "[He] performed the considerable service of adapting the colorful poetry of Norris to the more exacting tasks imposed upon the social novelist--very much as James assimilated Hawthorne's imagination of romance into novels."

Responding to Lee Siegel's assertion in the *New York Times* (May 8, 2005) that "Nowadays, often even the most accomplished novels offer characters that are little more than flat, ghostly reflections of characters. The author's voice, or self-consciousness about voice, substitutes mere eccentricity for an imaginative surrender to another life," Maud Newton in her weblog further describes the way in which she decided to focus her own attention on "books that delve into a character's thoughts and motivations and idiosyncratic take on the world" (May 7, 2005). Both Newton and Siegel are expressing a preference for "psychological realism" (a preference also shared by the literary critic James Wood, among others), an approach to the writing of fiction that perhaps gained its initial impetus in the late work of Henry James, but that probably became most identified with the work of such modernists as Joyce or Woolf.

(I think Siegel is wrong in claiming that 19th century writers "plumbed the depths of the human mind with something on the order of clairvoyance." Before James (or Flaubert, or Chekhov), the reigning narrative model was the picaresque, which surely emphasizes event over reflection, and which generally produces characters that are flat indeed--although not necessarily without color or vibrancy. One could say that writers such as George Eliot or Hawthorne or Melville plumbed the depths of the human soul, but they did not do so using the techniques of psychological realism as we have come to know them. It was as an addition to the strategies used by 19th century writers that stream of consciousness and what might be called psychological exposition--in which the writer describes what's going on inside a character's mind in the same way he/she might describe landscape or event--came to be identified as "modern" in the first place. And while Siegel blames Freud for the ultimate decline of "character" in fiction, he neglects to mention that the great modernist writers were partly inspired by Freud to try out the possibilities of "plumbing the depths" in the first place.)

I would argue that it is a misperception of most contemporary fiction to claim that it neglects either character or psychological "insight." Siegel identifies "postmodern and experimental novels" as the main culprits in fiction's deliberate turning-away from psychological depth, its refusal to "surrender to another life," but the vast majority of current fiction still focuses resolutely on character, and most of it uses the same strategies pioneered by Joyce and Woolf. Newton thinks that creative writing workshops put too much emphasis on "externalizing" through the "show, don't tell" rule, but most writers are neither minimalists nor postmodernists, and the chances are that if you were to pick out at random a work of literary fiction on your Borders shelf, you would find an entirely recognizable attempt both to establish character as the center of interest and to present the character's thought processes as the primary way of making him/her seem "realistic."

To this extent, Siegel's essay is just another backhanded slap at literary postmodernism (and some further by now superfluous stomping on the grave of Sigmund Freud), and in my opinion not to be taken seriously as a critique of contemporary fiction. However, Newton's concern for the "novel's psychological possibilities" is not misguided (and to her credit she correctly identifies the temptation to "endless, largely banal psychological reflection" as one of the pitfalls of psychological realism). That the novel has "psychological possibilities" is undeniably true. Indeed, the illusion of psychological depth is something fiction can provide more thoroughly than the other narrative arts, and if you think "imaginative surrender to another life" is finally what fiction is all about, then such illusion is one of the defining features of fiction as a form. But it is an illusion, and in my view if you're going to stories and novels to acquire your understanding of human psychology, you're going to the wrong place. First of all, what gives novelists themselves a superior understanding of the psychological make-up of human beings? Isn't this like expecting them to somehow possess a special wisdom about human life simply because they're novelists? Second, is merely recording in prose what one considers to be the typical operations of thought (which can finally only be done in a kind of shorthand, anyway) really probing human consciousness in anything but the most superficial way?

Better to think of psychological realism as just another strategy a writer might use to give a work of fiction a sense of unity or purpose--another way of getting the words on the page in a way that might compel the reader's attention. This might be done through other means, including the "self-annulling irony, deliberate cartoonishness, montage-like 'cutting'" Lee Siegel disdains. Privileging "psychological realism" over all the other effects a work of fiction might convey, all the other methods of creating an aesthetically convincing work of literary art, ultimately only diminishes fiction as literary art. It perpetuates the idea that fiction is a "window"--whether on external reality or the human psyche--rather than an aesthetic creation made of words. (Perhaps some still consider fiction to be an inferior or inappropriate form for achieving this kind of creation, at least as compared to poetry, but why should those who condescend to the form get to pronounce on its possibilities to begin with?) It reduces fiction to a case study in social science just as much as the insistence that it "reflect" social and political realities. There are plenty of great novels that reveal human motive and the operations of the human mind. But their authors didn't necessarily set out to make such revelations. They set out to write good novels.

In a review of Neil LaBute's collection of short stories, *Seconds of Pleasure* (New York Times Book Review, November 28, 2004), Jennifer Egan comments that "Writing Fiction would seem to offer LaBute a chance to plumb his characters' inner lives more fully, but the opposite proves to be true: being in the head of a LaBute protagonist is like flying in a plane with blackened windows--the rage so many of them feel toward the women who engross them obscures virtually everything else." Further: ". . .the protagonist's inner machinations [in one of the stories] are merely caricaturish. What's lacking here is the subtlety, the intimations of a larger world that gives the best short fiction. . .its insinuating power."

Egan thinks that the "inner lives of Labute's perennial manipulators. . .turn out to be less interesting in these transparent incarnations than when left opaque," as in LaBute's films. This is a convincing enough insight about the kinds of characters in which LaBute is interested, and perhaps if he were to turn his attention to a different sort of character he might produce more compelling works of fiction. But I think it is more likely that LaBute's conception of both character and story are inherently better suited to film, and that his forays into theater and, especially, fiction, only reinforce this perception and suggest he ought to stick to making movies. I do not necessarily mean to imply that writing good fiction is harder than writing screenplays, nor that screenwriting is finally inferior to fiction writing; I would say, however, that much mainstream fiction, even much "literary fiction," has been influenced in its formal and narrative assumptions at least as much by movies as by other fiction, and that this influence is not for the better where the future of fiction is concerned.

I would maintain that most fiction labeled "realistic" by critics and readers does not really belong to the tradition of "realism" as it was developed in nineteenth century fiction, but instead merely adopts the elements of conventional narrative as they are exemplified most recognizably in American movies. Such movies perhaps are themselves operating under the assumptions embodied in the traditional "well-crafted" story (at least where plot and character is concerned, both of which must follow certain patterns of "development" it is assumed an audience expects), but again our idea of what such a story is like is almost certainly more influenced now by the movies we see than the books we read. Moreover, realism of the classic variety, as illustrated by such writers as Flaubert, James, and Chekhov, doesn't really bear much resemblance to either mainstream Hollywood narratives or to what is called realism in much current fiction. I always encountered great resistance from students when I would teach any of these writers in introductory literature classes. Most often they would complain that in the assigned fiction "nothing happens," or there's "too much description." Clearly these students have become especially accustomed to a certain kind of story (where the focus is all on what does happen) arising from their movie-watching habits, but I think even more dedicated readers of current fiction might be surprised upon reading, say, Chekhov to find so little emphasis on plot, or even conventional character identification, of the kind films have prompted us to expect.

Two writers who seem to me to illustrate the phenomenon I am discussing would be Tom Wolfe and Richard Price.

However much Wolfe wants to imitate Dickens or Thackeray, his books are cinematic, focused on visual detail and dialogue in such a way that whoever attempts a screenplay adaptation of them must find they provide an enormous headstart. Price is a better writer than Wolfe, but he began his career writing novels that, if not exactly movie-like, were readily assimilable to film. This may be why his services as a screenwriter were solicited in the first place. The books he has published since his immersion in Hollywood script-writing certainly seem if anything more cinematic than his early books, as if they began as movie ideas that Price couldn't sell or thought would work better--would provide him with a larger canvas--as novels.

LaBute appears to aspire to a version of psychological realism. The problem is, judging from the passages Jennifer Egan quotes, he uses it very perfunctorily, with no apparent feel for the possibilities of writing at all. It is as if the thoughts attributed to the characters are merely lines of dialogue LaBute has instead decided to place "inside" the character's heads. What it again seems to betray is the notion that fiction is much like film, only a little bit different, affording the opportunity to make explicit what in LaBute's films is implicit. But what works pretty well in his movies--focusing on his characters' behavior without explaining it, giving it a creepily mysterious quality--can't survive the necessary exposition fiction usually requires, or that LaBute at any rate wants to provide. In this sense, he would definitely be well advised to go back to film, unless he wants to change directions completely and instead explore more fully what fiction might be capable of evoking in him as a writer, as a stylist, rather than as half-hearted exercise one takes up just for kicks.

II Flaubert's Children

In the first chapter of his 2005 book, *Realist Vision*, Peter Brooks writes:

> With the rise of the realist novel in the nineteenth century, we are into the age of Jules Michelet and Thomas Carlyle, of Karl Marx and John Ruskin, of Charles Darwin and Hippolyte Taine: that is, an age where history takes on new importance, and learns to be more scientific, and where theories of history come to explain how we got to be how we are, and in particular how we evolved from earlier forms to the present. It is the time of industrial, social and political revolution, and one of the defining characteristics of realist writing is I think a willingness to confront these issues. England develops a recognizable "industrial novel," one that takes on the problems of social misery and class conflict, and France has its "roman social," including popular socialist varieties.

To the extent that Brooks wants to link the rise of realist fiction to the rise of science and "theories of history," I can't really see how the former is influenced much by the latter, except specifically in the fiction of naturalist writers such as Emile Zola or, in the United States, Frank Norris and Theodore Dreiser. These writers did indeed try to depict human behavior as it was defined by science--especially Darwinism--and by the forces of history. But these were writers who were deliberately using realism to illustrate a view of human life as determined by such external forces, not exploring the purely literary possibilities of realism as a still relatively new aesthetic strategy. They may have in a sense been portraying "things as they are," but they were doing it from an abstract philosophical perspective, not as an attempt to first of all render life in all of its particularities.

I equally don't understand why a defining feature of realism would be the willingness to "confront" issues or to "take on" social problems. If works of fiction are truly "realistic," immersed in the details of life as lived, they will naturally, sooner or later and in one way or another, engage with the issues and the problems of the times. There is no need to take that extra step, to insist that "issues" be confronted, unless the writer's (and the critic's) real interest lies in "taking on" social problems, on using fiction as a tool of social amelioration rather than regarding it as a self-sufficient form of literary art. To me, a "defining characteristic" of any fiction that can make a claim to be literary art, that can still be taken seriously in the long run, after the "social problems" of the day have been replaced by the next set, is that it <u>not</u> "confront" any issues or problems other than the literary problems immediately at hand.

Brooks's own insistence here that realism must "take on" larger social and cultural questions is actually contradicted, it seems to me, by what he asserts just a few paragraphs later:

> You cannot, the realist claims, represent people without taking account of the things that people use and acquire in order to define themselves--their tools, their furniture, their accessories. These things are indeed part of the very definition of "character," of who one is and what one claims to be. The presence of things in these novels also signals their break from the neoclassical stylistic tradition, which tended to see the concrete, the particular, the utilitarian as vulgar, lower class, and to find beauty in the generalized and noble. The need to include and to represent things will consequently imply a visual inspection of the world of phenomena and a detailed report on it--a report often in the form of what we call description. The descriptive is typical--sometimes maddeningly so, of these novels. And the picture of the whole only emerges--if it does-from the accumulation of things.

This seems to me a pretty good account of what the best realist novels do: Draw the reader into a meticulously described world that the reader can accept as like the "real" world (keeping in mind that realistic description in fiction is just another device the writer can use, no more "authentic" than any other, given that what the reader is finally "confronted" with are just words on a page) and allow the reader to "see" the approximated world as fully as possible. If this sort of realism does bear philosophical implications, they are centered around the idea that the real is what is perceived. (Later, the "psychological" realists such as Woolf and Joyce would reject this; their fiction finds the real in <u>how</u> things are perceived, by focusing on the internal processes of consciousness.) But finally the art of realism lies in the way "things" are organized, in the manner and the skill with which the writer entices the reader to take note of the illuminating details.

Such an approach seems wholly at odds with the notion that realist fiction makes the reader aware of historical abstractions and social "issues." (The "generalized" rather than the "concrete.") "Things as they are" in the one seem on a wholly different scale than "things as they are" in the other. We <u>can</u> be made aware in fiction, subtly if implicitly, of historical change or social conflict, but only by acknowledging that the "defining characteristic" of realism is its particular approach to aesthetic representation, not its willingness to "take on" non-literary "problems."

Maintaining an analysis of realism that emphasizes "taking on" social problems as a defining characteristic requires a skeptical attitude toward the literary art of two of realism's ostensible founding figures, Charles Dickens and Gustave Flaubert, as Brooks demonstrates in chapter 3 of *Realist Vision*. Brooks writes of Dickens's *Hard Times*, perhaps his own most concentrated portrayal of the social conditions of Victorian England:

> By its play on the streets and surfaces of Coketown, the narratorial prose upholds that ideal evoked in the allusion to the *Arabian Nights*: the play of fancy, of metaphor, of magic and the conterfactual. The narratorial language is constantly saying to Coketown, as to Gradgrind and company, I am not prisoner of your system, I can transform it, soar above it, through the imaginative resources of my prose.

This is Brooks's ultimate judgment on Dickens as a writer who evokes the surfaces of realistic description, at times soars above them, but doesn't really grapple with the "issues" behind them: he writes too much. As Brooks puts it a little later, Dickens engages in "the procedure of turning all issues, facts, conditions, into questions of style." Rather than acknowledging that "Everything in the conditions of Coketown. . .cry out for organization of the workers," Dickens just plays his grandiose language games. He makes "the questions posed by industrialism too much into a trope."

For Brooks, *Hard Times* is not so much a "taking on" of the harsh realities of 19th century England as a retreat from them into. . .literature. Dickens doesn't attempt the politically-directed representation of these forces but instead the "nonrepresentation of Coketown in favor of something else, a representation of imaginative processes at work, a representation of transformative style at play on the world." It is difficult at times in reading this chapter to remember that Brooks intends such words as criticism. The "representation of imaginative processes at work" that Brooks describes here has always seemed to me one of the glories of Dickens's fiction.

Brooks gestures at granting Dickens his artistic preferences, but it's pretty clear from his discussion of *Hard Times* that he doesn't value these preferences in the same way he values fiction "that takes on the problems of social misery and class conflict," or at least that does so without turning them into tropes. Certainly Brooks doesn't want to admit Dickens's fiction, with its out-of-control "narratorial prose" and its stubborn insistence on imagination, into the club of respectable realism.

With Flaubert, Brooks is less impatient with his style per se but still essentially accuses Flaubert of writing too much, of being preoccupied with writing, in this case of being fixated on structure and on detail ("le most juste"). According to Brooks:

. . .it may be precisely in this disciplining of his imagination to something he loathes that the arduous perfection of *Madame Bovary* is forged. There is nothing natural about this novel. It is absolutely the most literary of novels, Henry James said--which he did not mean entirely as praise. There is indeed something labored about the novel, its characters, plot, milieux are all constructed with effort. Everything, as Flaubert understands it, depends on the detail. (Chapter 4)

Flaubert's insistence on detailed description makes Brooks think that *Madame Bovary* "is the one novel, among all novels, that deserves the label 'realist'," but this conclusion does not leave him sanguine. Flaubert's sort of realism is too insular, too much the excuse for building an elaborate aesthetic construction where "everything depends on the detail." Unfortunately, the detail doesn't add up to a "confrontation" with the world, doesn't even add up to a coherent whole at all:

Rhetorically, I suppose you would call all of those riding crops and cravats and shirt buttons in Balzac's world synecdoches: they are parts that stand for an intelligible whole. In Flaubert's world, however, they seem more like *apparent* synecdoches, in that often the whole is never given, never quite achieved. While Emma is frequently described, we never quite see her whole. She and her world never quite cohere.

Further: "It is as if the parts of the world really are what is most significant about it--the rest may simply be metaphysics." Flaubert's very approach to realism, then, precludes a fiction that takes on problems other than the problems of representation themselves, beginning with the representation of Emma Bovary: "Emma is surely one of the most memorable 'characters' of the novels we have read, we want to construct her fully as a person, we live with her aspirations, delusions, disappointments. Yet we repeatedly are given to understand that as a living, breathing, character-construction, Emma is a product of language--of her reading, and reveries on her reading, and of the sociolects that define her world." When Brooks claims there is "something labored" about *Madame Bovary*, he intends it as "le mot juste" in describing Flaubert's relationship with language: "Writing was such a slow and painful process for Flaubert because he had to make something new, strange, and beautiful out of a language in essence commonplace."

"New, strange, and beautiful," it would seem, are finally incommensurate with "realism" as Peter Brooks would have us define it. Despite their importance as writers moving fiction toward a greater realism of representation--the attempt to create the illusion of life as lived by ordinary people--neither Dickens nor Flaubert can finally be embraced as true-blue realists dedicated to confronting the issues of the age. Both of them seem too interested in writing to be reliable social critics, the role

Brooks appears to think supercedes all else in the realist's job description. Brooks almost seems to suggest that "art" and "realism" are mutually exclusive terms.

James Wood discusses Peter Brooks's *Realist Vision* in an essay, "The Blue River of Truth" (*The New Republic*, August 1, 2005). Wood introduces many of his own ideas into his discussion of "realism" as prompted by Brooks's book, and I would like to comment on a few of those.

1) Wood begins his essay by quoting two "anti-realist" statements (one by the novelist Rick Moody) and declares them to be "typical of their age." Realism, we are told, is now widely considered "stuffy, correct, unprogressive." It's a little hard to know whether Wood considers this attitude "typical" only of critics and other commentators on contemporary fiction or whether this is a "finely characteristic" belief about realism held by most writers and readers. If he means the latter, he couldn't be more wrong. Judging from the fiction that actually gets published and reviewed, the vast (vast) majority of literary fiction is still safely realistic, even to the extent of focusing on "Mind," the source for Wood of most of fiction's satisfactions. (I have referred to this kind of fiction as "psychological realism," but since Wood has expressed a dislike of the term, I won't use it here. Nevertheless, any honest assessment of the kind of novels

showing up on Borders' and Barnes and Noble's fiction shelves would have to conclude that psychological realism is still the order of the day. That Wood would disregard this fact is not that surprising, since most of these books are thoroughly mediocre and, if anything, illustrate quite persuasively that this mode of realism is indeed, as John Barth once put it, "exhausted.")

2) "The major struggle in American fiction today is over the question of realism," writes Wood. "Anywhere fiction is discussed with partisan heat, a fault line emerges, with 'realists' and traditionalists on one side, and postmodernists and experimentalists on the other." I think this is wrong as well. Postmodernism began to be superseded by various neotraditional practices in the mid-to-late 1970s, although some of the true postmodernists--Barth, Coover, Sorrentino--did continue to produce interesting work on into their literary dotage. And compared to the "experimental" work of these writers--*Lost in the Funhouse*, *Mulligan Stew*, etc.--the more adventurous writers who followed them are hardly radical innovators. I think Richard Powers is a fine writer, but he's hardly a programmatic metafictionist. T. Coraghessan Boyle has settled into a more or less conventional kind of satire. In my opinion, David Foster Wallace is closer to being a psychological realist--albeit of a somewhat twisted kind--than he is a postmodernist. There are other, less well-known writers who continue to explore the possibilities of self-referentiality or who have revived a form of

surrealism, but let's not pretend that they have a very high profile or constitute some kind of "movement" against realism comparable to the postmodernism of the 1960s and 1970s. If there is a "struggle" in current fiction, it is between those who write a conventional kind of character- or plot-driven fiction more or less auditioning to become movies and those who still seek to discover what the possibilities of fiction might be beyond its role as source of film adaptation, what fiction can do better than other narrative or dramatic arts. Realism itself doesn't necessarily have anything to do with this.

3) I agree with Wood that too many people think of realism as a "genre," confusing realism per se with "a certain kind of traditional plot, with predictable beginnings and endings." Moody is quoted as deploring realism's "epiphanies, its rising action, its predictable movement. . . ." But these things are more properly associated with orthodox narrative conventions (embodied in "Freytag's Triangle") than with realism strictly understood. Indeed, one could argue that truly realistic fictions would avoid neat divisions of plot and anything at all "predictable," since "real life" does not unfold like well-made stories. I also agree that the great 19th century realists were actually radicals in their time, overturning as they did the picaresque and romantic modes of storytelling they'd inherited from the first generation of novelists in favor of narratives that focused more on details of setting and on creating plausibly

"lifelike" characters. And I certainly agree that "There is no writing without convention," making it most important to "be alive to the moment when a literary convention becomes dead," not to assume that the ultimate goal is to free fiction from convention altogether.

4) Perhaps my biggest problem with James Wood's approach to fiction is embodied in this statement: "There is, one could argue, not just a 'grammar' of narrative convention, but also a grammar of life--those elements without which human activity no longer looks recognizable, and without which fiction no longer seems human." Much of the fiction Wood reviews unfavorably is, in one way or another, ultimately charged with this offense, that it doesn't "seem human." He so conflates a particular aesthetic strategy with the representation of the "human" that the writers of whom he disapproves are more or less declared "inhuman," their work morally grotesque. (This seems to me the upshot of Wood's recent dismissal of Cormac McCarthy, for example.) But this is a wholly unjustified substitution of "human" for "realistic." Since all writers are human beings writing about their own human experiences or those of other human beings, how can any work of fiction be something other than "human" at its core? It may not provide James Wood with a sampling of the human that meets his high moral standards, but to suggest that the dispute between realists

and anti-realists is over who gets to be more "human" seems to me supremely unjust, if not simply absurd.

Furthermore, it turns out that what a work of fiction needs to be "recognizable" as human is to conform to W. J. Harvey's "constitutive category":

> The four elements of this category are, he suggests, Time, Identity, Causality, and Freedom. I would add Mind, or Consciousness. Any fiction that lacked all five elements would probably have little power to move us. The defense of this broad idea of mimesis should not harden into a narrow aesthetic, for it ought to be large enough to connect Shakespeare's dramatic mimesis, say, with Dickens's novelistic mimesis, or Dostoevsky's melodramatic mimesis with Muriel Spark's satiric mimesis, or Pushkin's poetic mimesis with Platonov's lyrical mimesis.

As far as I can tell, what this means is that fiction needs to be "realistic" enough that it doesn't collapse into the "entirely random and chaotic." (Although in adding "Mind, or Consciousness," Wood again ups the ante. Now it must not only depict "plausible human activity," it must do so with psychological plausibility.) Does Wood really think there are many works of fiction that don't meet this minimal standard? Is experimental fiction merely a descent into chaos? In order to rescue the innovative fiction he apparently likes, Wood broadens his definition of "plausible" even further: "Kafka's "Metamorphosis" and Hamsun's *Hunger* and Beckett's *Endgame* are not representations of likely or typical human behavior; but they draw their power, in part, from their connection to the human." Well, of course they do. How could they do otherwise? The question is whether in so doing they have done it artfully, and whether the art involved had to be "realistic" in the less sweeping sense of the term. ("Melodramatic mimesis"?)

5) This is perhaps the most provocative thing Wood has to say in his essay: ". . .both sides in this argument are perforce Flaubert's children--Flaubert being at once the greatest realist and the great anti-realist, the realist who dreamed of abolishing the real, the luxurious stylist who longed to write 'a book about nothing, a book with no external attachment.'" Unless Wood deplores Flaubert for his "luxury," for his effort to transcend mere documentary description, one now wonders why he finds fault with the anti-realists. If they too are among Flaubert's children, then they are only attempting to live up to his ideal of the autonomy and integrity of literary art. They just don't think that realism as he understood it is the only way to accomplish this. Wood says further of Henry James that he "found Flaubert's realism exemplary but lacking, because he felt that it did not extend to a subtle moral scrutiny of the self." If Wood agrees with James, then we have arrived at his real complaint against the

anti-realists: It's not that they fail to recognize the centrality of "realism" (Wood has already defined the term so broadly as to essentially render it meaningless, anyway), it's that they fail to engage in "moral scrutiny." He objects to this group of Flaubert's offspring not on aesthetic but on moral grounds.

6) In his concluding paragraph, Wood asks us to "imagine a world in which the only possible novel available was, say, Pynchon's *Vineland* and books like it. It would be a hysterical and falsifying monotony. By contrast, a world in which the only available novel was, say, *A House for Mr. Biswas* would be a fearfully honest, comic, tragic, compassionate, and above all deeply human place." Now, I happen to like both of these books (*Vineland* less than either *V* or *Gravity's Rainbow*, however). I'm glad we live in a world where both kinds of books are available. It would seem, however, that Wood could be perfectly content in the world occupied only by Naipaul. No variety is necessary because this would be a "deeply human place." (What kind of place would the Pynchon world be? Superficially primatial?) Note as well the way in which this comparison is made in the form of moral judgment. Pynchon is "hysterical" and "falsifying." Naipaul is "honest" and compassionate." James Wood is perfectly entitled to elevate Naipaulian realism and denigrate Pynchonian anti-realism (if that's what he wants to call them--I don't think either term does either writer much justice). I do wish he wouldn't

call those of who like the sort of thing a writer like Pynchon does hysterics and liars.

III Realists

The fiction of Stephen Dixon starkly illustrates the difference between realism as a literary effect and "story" as a structural device, a distinction that is often enough blurred in discussions of conventional storytelling. "Realism" is the attempt to convince readers that the characters and events depicted in a given work are "like life" as most of us experience it, but, as Dixon's stories and novels demonstrate, story or plot conceived as the orderly--or even not so orderly--arrangement of incidents and events for explicitly dramatic purposes need not be present for such an attempt to succeed. Few readers are likely to finish *Phone Rings* (Melville House Publishing) thinking it does not provide a comprehensive and intensely realistic account of its characters and their circumstances, and of the family relationships the novel chronicles, but many if not most will have concluded that fidelity to the stages in Freytag's Triangle has very little to do with its realism.

Which is not to day that *Phone Rings* has no story to impart, only that it is one that emerges in the narrative long run, through the accumulation of episodes and interchanges (in this case, as in Dixon's previous novel, *Old Friends*, interchanges over the telephone), although the episodes themselves retain a

214

kind of narrative autonomy separate from their placement as points on a narrative arc. Ultimately, the whole is more than the sum of its parts, but the relationship between the parts is lateral, not linear, the story an aftereffect of Dixon's relentless layering of these episodic elements. (In some Dixon novels, such as, for example, *Interstate* or *Gould,* the repetitions, reversals, and transformations he effects through such layering <u>become</u> the story, or at least what makes the story memorable and gives these novels their aesthetically distinctive shape.) One could say that Dixon's commitment to realism precludes imposing "story" when doing so would only be a way of distorting reality by imputing to it more order and more direction than it in fact has.

Dixon's strategy of allowing his fiction to register the mundane and the contingent can seem obsessive, even perverse. In section 7 of *Phone Rings,* the novel's protagonist, Stu, makes breakfast for his wife. Through a chain of banal actions, Stu accidentally cuts himself with a bread knife. He serves the breakfast and talks with his wife about the fact that he's just cut himself with a bread knife, then, returning to the kitchen and seeing the knife, he wonders what might have happened if the knife had struck his carotid artery. He returns to his wife, who suggests he put a Band-Aid on the cut. The chapter concludes with Stu going back to the kitchen, where he attempts to recreate the situation that led to the accident:

He went back to the kitchen and got the bread knife and opened the refrigerator and wanted to reproduce the way the knife got stuck in the door, but couldn't find a place where it could have got caught. Just somewhere here, in the top shelf of the door, and then before he could do anything about it the knife, buckling under the pressure and something to do with realizing it was stuck and perhaps overcorrecting the situation by pushing the door too far back, sprung out of whatever it was into his neck. Okay, enough; forget about it as you said.

In section 10, "Brother of a neighbor dies. Stu reads about it in the *Sun*." Stu wonders whether he should send condolences, starts walking up the hill to the neighbor's house, decides not to after all, and returns home. "I'll just send a condolence card. I'll get it at the drugstore and speak to Peter about his brother sometime after," he says to his wife in the section's closing line.

While these set-pieces are loosely connected to the novel's overarching depiction of Stu's grief over the death of his brother, it certainly cannot be said they advance "plot" in any but the most incremental sort of way--they present us with additional scenes from Stu's life, but do not reduce that life to the bare sum of those scenes. Each provides an equally significant account, however brief or however extended, of Stu's experience (just as the telephone conversations that make up a large portion of the novel's "action" remain self-contained exchanges that allow Stu to invoke past experiences), but *Phone Ring*s, like much of Dixon's fiction, encourages us to consider the portrayal of its characters' experiences as an end-in-itself, not as the prop for a conventional narrative structure artificially imposed on these experiences.

However, if *Phone Rings* is a novel of character rather than plot, Dixon doesn't always seem at pains to delineate his characters with the expected kind of specificity. Here is a phone exchange between Stu and his brother Dan:

> . . ."I'm only calling to tell you something that might interest you that happened today. Of course, also to hear how you are. But that, later, for I don't want to lose what I called to say, unless everything with you's not okay," and Dan said, "No, we're fine. What?" "I was going through my top dresser drawer to throw out all the useless papers and single socks and so on, and came across Dad's old business card," and Dan said "Which one? His dental office or the one he used after he lost his license and sold textiles for what was the company called. . .Lakeside?" and he said "Brookhaven. On Seventh Avenue and 38th." "And a third card. In fact, four," and Stu said "This one was for his 40th Street dental office--his last," and Dan said, "That's what I was getting to. First the Delancey

Street office, which he had from 1919 till we moved to the West Side in '37, and he set up his practice there. Then Brookhaven, if you're right, and it sounds right--Brookfield or Brookhaven," and he said "Take my word, Haven". . . ..

It is nearly impossible to distinguish between Stu and Dan based on their speech patterns and characteristics alone--and in this novel they are known primarily through their speech. Both exhibit the same tendency to free association and other kinds of roundabout locutions (perhaps influenced by American Jewish speech patterns), to digressive asides and fragmentary utterances. Moreover, many of the other characters in the novel talk like this as well, as if the novel's primary objective is to project a kind of collective voice or to create out of workaday language itself a collective character that is the ultimate focus of Dixon's interest.

This does not mean that the characters in *Phone Rings* are inadequately rendered or fail to convince as plausibly "real" people. If anything, Dixon's emphasis on the quotidian and the conditional only lends them authenticity--this is the way people actually do talk and act, after all--and his prose style more broadly so insistently restricts itself to the plain narrative essentials, refusing to indulge in figurative embellishments and descriptive decoration (literally sticking to the prosaic) that it might seem these characters are not the creations of writing at all but are merely being caught in the midst of their ongoing, pre-existing lives. Thus, chapters begin like this:

> His younger daughter comes into the bedroom and says, "Phone call for you." He's working at his work table and says, "Darn, I'm right in the middle of something. That's why I turned the ringer off." "Next time tell us to tell callers you're busy and you'll call back," and he says "Next time I will, thanks," and gets up and picks up the phone receiver and says hello. "Uncle Stu, it's Manny.". . .

This goal of representing life as lived (right down to including details and dialogue most other writers would simply eliminate for efficiency's sake) may also be the motive behind Dixon's often excessively long paragraphs. To adjust his prose to the artificial demands of paragraphing would be a false way of representing the flow of experience, and Dixon's method in effect forces the reader to regard experience in this way--one thing after another. His style--and it is such, a deliberate effort to compose a style that seems without style--does produce a flattening effect, by which actions, thoughts and speech seem to occur on the same discursive plane and receive the same degree of emphasis, but this is more fundamentally the consequence of an approach that seeks to make its treatment of reality as material as possible. We don't get "psychological realism" from Stephen Dixon, at least insofar as that term indicates an effort to plumb the depths of consciousness, to approximate the ineffable. His characters think out loud: "He'd never told Dan this. Thought several times to but then thought better. Made Isaac swear not to tell Dan or Zee about it. 'Oh, on second thought, you can tell her,' after Isaac swore he'd never tell either, 'but not Dan. You do, he won't let me take you anywhere for the next few years. I know him. . . .'" What originates in Stu's ruminations becomes just another form of exposition.

I find Dixon's strategies fascinating (he usually manages to extend them just a little bit farther with each book) and his ability to elicit from them compelling and often emotionally affecting fictions impressive indeed. He's one of the few writers to whose work the descriptions "experimental" and "realistic" seem to apply equally, although his inclination to the former is almost always a way of further securing the latter. His relative lack of popularity among even readers of serious literary fiction is both surprising and understandable: Surprising because he's finally such an engrossing and rewarding writer, understandable because his style of realism, shunning as it does the facile resort to "story," calls into question the idea that fiction functions to elucidate life by, figuratively at least, whipping it into shape.

In an otherwise positive review of Dixon's *Meyer* (*Time Out New York*, Sep 20–26, 2007), Craig Morgan Teicher asserts that "While Dixon's jerky prose, often cast in several-page paragraphs, can be slow going, it's impossible to stop reading, in part because Dixon is so amazing at giving the sense of being inside somebody else's head."

I don't agree that Dixon's prose can be "slow going." It's usually demotic, accessible, briskly paced. That Dixon does not use his thoroughly transparent prose style--there's no forced figurative language, no frills, all of its focus is on evoking the realities of a world recognizably our own--to tell a conventionally plotted story with only the dramatic bits (those activities that give the story its proper "arc") included is what might make his fictions slow going for some readers who wonder where all the familiar narrative markers have gone. Dixon's prose doesn't "jerk." It ebbs and flows with the particular, momentary circumstances in which his characters are immersed.

But I especially can't agree with the notion that what Dixon is ultimately after is "the sense of being inside someone else's head." His stories and novels certainly wind themselves around the experience of protagonists, almost always male, usually bearing life stories and characteristics we assume are close to those of Stephen Dixon, whose activities are recounted in rather minute detail, but they do not engage in the usual probing of these characters' minds to create "psychological realism" of the now-customary kind.

Here's the opening of the chapter called "Frog Acts," from Dixon's 1991 novel, *Frog*:

In bed, must be late, no car traffic outside, light coming in, been asleep, up, asleep again, hears a noise in the apartment. He's on his side, front to his wife's back, both no clothes, hand on her thigh. Kids in the bedrooms down the hall. Light noise again. Could be the cat. Whispers "Denise, you hear anything? Denise?" Doesn't say anything, still asleep. He's quiet, holds his breath, listens. Nothing. Lets out his breath, holds it again. Sound of feet. Something. Moving slowly, sliding almost. Sliding, that's the sound. Could be the cat doing something unusual. Slight floorboard squeak. Cat's made that too. Should get up. Scared. Cold feeling in his stomach, on his face. Has to do something, what, scream? It it's someone then that person could in one of the kids' rooms, at one of their doors. Gets on his back, holds his breath. No sound. Lets it out, holds it. Shuffling. Sure of it. Down the hall's wood floor, just a few inches. Shuffling stops, as if he picked up Howard listening. . . .

The first sentence is entirely objective, entirely descriptive, as the narrator (it is a third-person narrator, as in almost all of Dixon's fictions) attempts to orient us to "Frog" orienting himself as he wakes up. It is not a very omniscient narrator (thus the "must be late"), but neither does the narrator/narration simply arise from within the perspective of the character. This outer-oriented narration continues for the next several sentences, although it is interrupted by what could be taken as internal notations of perception--"Light noise again. Could be the cat." Yet these could just as easily be taken as truncated expository signals: "Light noise again" functions simply to tell us that the noise that woke Frog has sounded again. "Could be the cat" does seem to report on Frog's reaction, but it's really a pretty superficial intrusion on his thought process: "'Could be the cat,' he thinks."

A fairly straightforward burst of speech then begins another series of reports on Frog's actions. He hold his breath, listens, hears nothing, breathes again. Then: "Sound of feet. Something. Moving slowly, sliding almost. Sliding, that's the sound. Could be the cat doing something unusual." While this proceeds from Frog's vantage point as the listener, none of it is going on only inside his head. It's still a way of relating (radically reduced as it obviously is) what is happening. Frog hears the sound, determines it must be "sliding." "Sliding, that's the sound" does seem to enter Frog's thought stream more explicitly, as it tells us that something like this articulated thought literally goes through his mind. "Cat's made that too" and "Should get up" also seem to be manifestations of Frog's specific thoughts, although "Scared" is unlikely to have occurred to him so explicitly. It's again the narrator's extremely compacted declaration. The rest of the passage continues with this alternation of condensed exposition and crystallized thought--"Cold feeling in his stomach, on his face. Has to do something, what, scream?"--until the final sentence brings us fully outside Frog's perspective with the registering of his name.

At the most, both the thoughts and the spoken words of Dixon's characters are recorded as if they were part of the scene of action, not as if they constituted a separate realm from the perspective of which the scene, events more broadly, are to be understood. Sometimes, as in his recent novels *Old Friends* and *Phone Rings*, the characters' spoken words are a kind of substitute for thought, a way of externalizing internal states into concrete action. You could call this "psychological realism" of a sort, but usually Dixon finds a way of avoiding the tedious exploration of "Mind" some critics would have us believe is the primary purpose of fiction. Thus Dixon's work <u>does</u> provide us with a vivid rendering of his characters' sense of their immediate surroundings and their ongoing interactions with those surroundings, but not through facilely thrusting us "inside somebody else's head."

Until now the only Russell Banks novel I had resisted reading was *Cloudsplitter*--not because of its length (750 pages) but because it belongs to one of my least favorite genres--the historical novel--and because of all Banks's novels it seemed the most committed to simple realism as an aesthetic strategy.

However, *Cloudsplitter* turned out to be much more interesting than I thought it might be, even if my impression of John Brown, the novel's ostensible protagonist, didn't really change much through reading it. He seemed to me, considered as an historical figure, a pretty one-dimensional character obsessed with religion and what he considered the primary affront to religion in his time, chattel slavery. After reading the novel, he still seems to me a pretty one-dimensional character obsessed with religion, etc. His commitment to the abolition of slavery was all-encompassing, but it amounted to a monomania (certainly the John Brown that emerges from this novel could be described by such a term), and while monomaniacs can be powerful presences in works of fiction--Captain Ahab comes to mind--that power is what makes them memorable, not any complexities of character that might be revealed.

Fortunately, Banks adopts in *Cloudsplitter* a narrative strategy similar to that which Melville uses in *Moby-Dick*, a strategy that takes advantage of the overwhelming personality of John Brown to maintain the narrative's dramatic interest but otherwise focuses much of the novel's attention on the charged relationship between Brown and the narrator of Brown's story, his son Owen. As with Ahab and Ishmael, we encounter John Brown through the entranced observations of Owen, and, like Ishmael, Owen is essentially the last man standing (in Ishmael's case, swimming), surviving the raid on Harper's Ferry to, eventually, tell us the tale of what led up to this singular event. Like *Moby-Dick*, *Cloudsplitter* filters our perceptions of its main character by presenting us with an account composed by a witness to events, in Owen's case someone with intimate knowledge of the personage involved and himself an important influence on those events, but nevertheless an account the fraught nature of which itself provides at least as much dramatic tension as the actions taken by the character motivating the narrative.

As far as I can tell, not that much is really known about Owen Brown, especially the years he spent after the raid on Harpers Ferry (he died in 1889). This gives Banks the opportunity to in essence create a fictional character to both narrate the novel and play an important role in it, allowing some further latitude in the portrayal of John Brown himself. Banks stays faithful to the known facts about Brown and the public events for which he is known, but of course most of the details about his domestic life (especially that part of it spent in North Elba, New York, the relation of which takes up most of *Cloudsplitter)* cannot be known, and Banks focuses his view of Brown and his family on and around these domestic episodes or on the trips Owen takes with his father to Boston and to London. These are the sections of the novel in which we most fully get to know both Owen and John Brown, and they are the elements that most fully redeem the book as "fiction." In comparison, the guerilla campaign waged by the Brown clan in Kansas and the attack on Harpers Ferry seem almost tacked-on, the inherent dramatic action of both de-emphasized and deflected, as if the last 200 pages had to be appended in order to certify *Cloudsplitter* as a proper "historical" novel.

The result, it seems to me, is that *Cloudsplitter*, despite its taking as its main character a "real" person, is not finally much different from *Affliction* in its approach to character and narrative. In each instance, the protagonist makes a forceful impression on the reader, but the effect is due to the manner in which the narrator, in each instance a first-person narrator close to the protagonist, renders not just the actions taken by the protagonist but his own anguished efforts to come to terms with those actions and his part in influencing them. While Rolfe Whitehouse has to do more "research" in order to reconstruct the last days of his brother Wade, Owen has to re-engage his own memories in presenting a narrative of his father's life thirty or more years after the experiences related. Both make good-faith efforts to capture these figures as they "really were," but we can only take them, or should only take them, as projections of the narrators' subjective powers of discernment. This does not mean the depiction of such characters is less truthful; it means the truth that does emerge is the truth involved whenever one human being struggles to understand the motives and the acts of another.

In the case of Owen Brown, the truth is that he never really does understand his father, except in the trivial sense that, given John Brown's consistency of thought and belief, he can usually predict what his father might say or do. As Walter Kirn puts it in the *New York Times Book Review*, "To his children, who follow him through frontier America like a band of nomadic Israelites, John Brown is an unmoved mover. His authority is absolute, and sometimes absolutely maddening" (February 22, 1998). John Brown is, for Owen, a force of nature, and, ultimately, there seems little point in doing other than follow him where he will lead (although it is actually Owen who finally convinces his father to begin inflicting violence on those who would oppose him). Kirn suggests that Owen lives in an "existential funk" that arises from the "chronic shame" of never living up to John Brown's ideals, but I'm not sure this is quite right. Owen isn't so much ashamed of his failure to live up to these ideals as he is baffled by his inability to resist the need to act on them despite the fact he doesn't himself fully share them-- he doesn't share John Brown's religious convictions at all, in fact. It is Owen's open confession of his bafflement, and his honest account of the way in which it informed his involvement with John Brown's self-declared war on evil, that animates this novel and raises it well above mere documentary-style historical fiction.

If the work of Stephen Dixon and Russell Banks shows that it is possible to register in fiction the unfolding immediacy of experience without resorting to facile "psychological realism," Kent Haruf's *Plainsong* demonstrates that fiction can effect a perfectly plausible and convincing rendering of ordinary experience without "getting inside" the heads of its characters at all.

Almost any passage from the novel would do as illustration, since Haruf's approach is remarkably consistent throughout. This is the final paragraph of the first chapter, which is centered on Tom Guthrie, one of the novel's alternating protagonists:

> Downstairs, passing through the house, Guthrie could hear the two boys talking in the kitchen, their voices clear, high-pitched, animated again. He stopped for a minute to listen. Something to do with school. Some boy saying this and this too and another one, the boy, saying it wasn't any of that either, because he knew better, on the gravel playground out back of school. He went outside across the porch and across the drive toward the pickup. A faded red Dodge with a deep dent in the left rear fender. The weather was clear, the day was bright and still early and the air felt fresh and sharp, and Guthrie had a brief feeling of uplift and hopefulness. He took a cigarette from his pocket and lit it and stood for a moment looking at the silver poplar tree. Then he got into the pickup and cranked it and drove out of the drive onto

Railroad Street and headed up the five or six blocks toward Main. Behind him the pickup lifted a powdery plume from the road and the suspended dust shone like bright flecks of gold in the sun.

The point of view here is not quite omniscient, since the third-person narration does cleave to Guthrie's limited perspective ("Something to do with," "Some boy saying this and this too"-- incomplete information because it is incomplete or unclear to Guthrie), at least until the final sentence, when it leaves Guthrie's vantage point to report on the dust left in his wake. But never does it presume to burrow itself beneath Guthrie's conscious awareness, to take us along as well and oblige us to look back out on the world from the subjective set of perceptions roiling around in his mind. Indeed, most of this paragraph consists of a straightforward, externally-based narration of events: "He stopped for a moment to listen"; "He went out across the porch"; "Then he got into the pickup." We're not invited to share Tom's "brief feeling of uplift and hopefulness," not clued in further to the nature of this feeling; we're simply told that he had it.

The rest of the novel proceeds in this way. The things that Tom Guthrie, his children Ike and Bobby, the pregnant teen Victoria Roubideaux, and others do are related to us, but we do not experience these things through them. They just happen, and the characters deal with what happens to them in the best way they can. By the time we've finished reading *Plainsong*, we can't really say we "know" its characters in the way we're encouraged to do so in most narratives steeped in psychological realism. These novels pretend to tell us what's essential about their characters, what literally characterizes them at the "deep" level. They're rung through the rhetorical ringer; very little mystery is left. As a result, in the end, they're boring. The characters in *Plainsong* to an extent remain enigmatic, and they're more convincing as a result.

I didn't really expect to like *Plainsong*. I thought it would be just another exercise in "local color." But Haruf is better than that. His characters seem authentic because they're presented to us with a stark simplicity we assume must be honest. There's no laboring after "vivid" details and colorful tics, no quaint, picturesque descriptions. It's an intensely realistic novel, but after a now decades-long era in which most "literary fiction" has filtered reality through flimsy psychologizing, workshop-derived wrappings of formula, and a gaudy camouflage of superficial surrealism, it's rather nice to encounter it again.

As found in her new book, *The Suburban Swindle*, Jackie Corley's stories would seem to be classifiable as a kind of slice-of-life realism, episodes, some quite circumscribed and plotless, that add a little fictional flesh to bare-bones themes of cultural anomie announced in the first paragraphs of the very first such episode, "Blood in Jersey":

> What are we? What we are is oiled sadness. Dead garden snakes and dried-up slugs. We're what happens when you're bored and scared too long, when you sit in piles in some dude's basement trying to get the guy's white supremacist brother to shut the fuck up for five fucking minutes. You sit in those hordes and some emo kid takes out a bag of clumpy, dried-up weed and shakes it like he's accomplished something.

> What this is is Jersey. This is fear so thick and buried under, you pretend you're not on fire. The boys are brawling on the front lawn and coming back down to the basement with finger-mark welts on their necks and bloody, rubbery scratches on their chests.

But while most of the stories do provide a brief and immediate immersion in the "oiled sadness" of suburban New Jersey youth, the aimlessness and alienation to which we are exposed might seem overly familiar, a little too reminiscent of various movie versions of alienated youth (although I nevertheless do not doubt the accuracy of the portrayal, nor the authenticity of its sources). And if *The Suburban Swindle* was just another depiction of youthful discontent with suburban life, it would not really be able to make much of a claim on our attention. However, the primary appeal of the book, at least for me, lies not in the details of life as endured in New Jersey but in those of its stylistic and formal features already to be perceived in "Blood in Jersey" and its opening paragraphs.

The pruned-back structure of a story like this (admittedly an especially brief one, although all of the stories, even those of a more conventional length, are similarly committed to an overall narrative minimalism) ultimately brings an increased emphasis on the language with which such a lightly plotted story is presented, on the story as the unfolding of its language. Often in this sort of narratively truncated realism "style" is notably de-emphasized, made as "plain" as possible, but here no attempt is being made to conceal the "writing" that, almost literally, turns out to everything in "Blood in Jersey," not just the vehicle for plot and character development. The first several stories in *The Suburban Swindle* likewise deflect the reader's initial interest in storytelling and characterization toward their own verbal flourishes, but even the stories that do introduce incident and more fully sketched-out characters still call attention to the prose with which such elements are deployed more that we might expect in conventional realism.

One might say that the radical exclusion manifest in these stories goes beyond the implicit narrowing of focus to be found in all short stories and extends to the exclusion of any extraneous plot devices and gestures at character "depth" that inhibit immediacy of expression. Of course, one could also suggest that the sparseness in plot and character only reinforces the essential realism of the stories, since the kinds of lives they portray are themselves likely to be rather short on "plot" and psychologically afflicted in generally similar ways. But whether form most often influences content or content determines form, the result in this collection is a kind of fiction in which the form of expression doesn't merely point us to its subject but is dynamically a part of it in a way that I, for one, find impressive:

> The cigarette should burrow through him. It should take his skin to butter and give me a rabbit hole on his skinny, hairless arm. Then I could pull up his shirt sleeve any time I wanted and admire it, that charred empty well. It would always belong to me.

> When I try to bring the coal down in the middle of a lazy map of freckles, he flinches again, laughing. His naked torso folds in on itself, as if he's blocking some probing, tickling hand, and he keeps giggling, high and sloppy and loud. He goes down to the floor, drink still buoyed up in the air by an extended right hand. ("Fine Creatures")

I wouldn't say that *The Suburban Swindle* is a flawless book--sometimes the familiarity of the material does subsume the liveliness of the writing--but it introduces a writer whose approach both to her subject and to the literary presentation it requires certainly makes me curious about what her future work might be like.

Marisa Silver's *The God of War*, on the other hand, is yet another mediocre novel that unaccountably sent reviewers into raptures of praise, larding it with adjectives such as "beautiful," "stunning," and "exquisite." Such praise for a thoroughly drab, utterly undistinguished work of complacent realism, a novel that reinforces the most retrograde notions of what a "serious" novel should be like, leaves one lamenting not just the persistence of the kind of formulaic "literary fiction" this novel represents, but also the inability of so many critics to evaluate this fiction in other than the most vapid, critically submissive terms.

The God of War is essentially a coming-of-age story, perhaps the most frequently invoked subgenre in the history of fiction. In order to justify yet another novel employing this plot convention, one would hope that its author would at least offer something more distinctive in the way of style or voice, something to enliven an otherwise familiar narrative (as done, for example in *The Catcher in the Rye*). But, unfortunately, Silver does not provide such aesthetic compensations. Even though she has chosen to let her protagonist tell his own story, the resulting narrative voice is at best bland and perfunctory. The story is told in retrospect, creating a tone of earnest detachment that fails to engage the reader with the narrator's younger self and makes his story read like an indifferent chronicle of the recent past: Here's what it was like in this small part of the world thirty years ago. When the narrator's language isn't just colorless, it strains after effect in badly wrought figures: "Her cheeks were puffy at the bottom as if she were storing two caramels or some other secrets there"; "The air felt exhausted, as if it had finally given up its day work and had flung its spent self across the land."

About the only plausibly original feature of *The God of War* is its setting on and around California's Salton Sea, a man-made body of water created as an accidental consequence of a water diversion project in the early 20th century. Here, enduring the stench of periodic fish and bird kills, among the detritus of failed efforts to make the area into a resort, and facing what is otherwise an unforgiving desert environment, the adolescent protagonist lives with his mother and his autistic brother. Clearly the elemental bleakness of the setting is meant to reinforce or counterpoint the boy's encounter with the harshness of life, but, considering the indistinct impression we get of the Salton Sea and its environs, the novel could just as well be set in any other struggling, off-the-beaten-track community where young people are forced early to confront adult problems. The peculiarities of the Salton Sea are summoned to provide a kind of exotic backdrop, but since we really learn very little either about it or about the way it has conditioned the lives of those who live near it, it ultimately does not play a very meaningful role in the story. It seems something of a gimmick, a way to differentiate this novel from all the other novels of "local color" competing for attention in the literary marketplace.

The story mostly concerns the narrator's efforts to protect his brother from those whose misperceptions might do him harm, including his own mother, whom the narrator feels never really accepted her autistic son's condition. (In an ironic twist, his younger brother winds up protecting the narrator from danger, although even here the latter finds it necessary to conceal his brother's responsibility for the act of violence involved.) The novel's core situation, single mother barely able to support herself and her two sons, one of whom is severely mentally disabled, provides inherent possibilities for both melodrama and sentimentality, and it doesn't fail to exploit most of them. It especially fails to avoid sentimentality, as almost every time the younger brother figures into a scene the reader's heartstrings get tugged:

> . . .He didn't take his mouth from the straw the entire time he sucked, not even to breathe. There was no end to his appetite. He ate whatever food was offered to him even if he had just finished a huge meal. Laurel and I learned to tell him when he was done eating and we were expert at distracting him so that he could tear his mind away from

the food and land on a new obsession for a while. More than any other of his traits, this hunger upset me, made me feel unaccountably mournful. It filled me with a great nostalgic sadness for lost things, the way a rich person might feel if he had to live as a pauper, always remembering he fancy cars and clothes of a bygone life. . . .

It is perhaps inevitable that such a character will evoke cheap emotion, but Silver does little to mitigate this effect. Indeed, her decision to include such a character in a novel narrated by a family member almost ensures sentimentality, and the final chapter relating the younger brother's premature death in a group home only lays on the sentiment more thickly, suggesting to me a deliberate strategy to create pathos and evoke pity.

In both its conventionality and its sentimentality, *The God of War* is representative of a certain kind of "literary fiction" that mainstream reviewers just can't seem to resist. Realistic, mostly humorless, but full of "human emotion," these novels seem to appeal to critics and some readers as adequately "serious" to be elevated above popular potboilers and genre fiction, without violating the presumed need to be "accessible." They shield these critics and readers from more formally and thematically challenging fiction, which can be safely marginalized, and thus ignored. As long as the "literary" in "literary fiction" continues to be associated with novels like *The God of War*, the word will become only more accurately defined by such other words as "tedium" and "pretense."

PART FIVE

The Elements of Fiction

I Beyond Story

The biggest problem with Julian Evans's "The Return of Story" in the December 2004 *Prospect* is that its central contention, on which the burden of his anti-aesthetic argument is placed, is simply wrong. "In the cinema" Evans writes, "a core of narrative innocence survives across a spectrum of values represented by Spielberg at one end and Abbas Kiarostami at the other. In the novel, however, story has gone down in a blaze of modernist attitudes. . ." Clearly Evans doesn't really read very many of the scores of novels published every year in both Great Britain and the United State. If he did, he would certainly discover that almost all of them--perhaps not exactly 100% of them, but pretty close to that--do indeed tell stories, and almost as many (90%? 95?) tell very traditional stories of a sort Evans's most conventional "storyteller" from the past would immediately recognize and heartily endorse.

(Evans is notably reluctant to name names in his indictment against contemporary novelists for abandoning narrative, but he does cite Martin Amis and Salman Rushdie. Come again? Amis doesn't tell stories? How did I miss that? And Rushdie? *Midnight's Children*? Perhaps one could call this novel "magical realism," but since when has magical realism done anything but tell stories? *One Hundred Years of Solitude*? If

Evans has indeed read these books but still would claim they don't tell stories, he's a pathetically poor reader.)

But Evans gives the game away when he praises Fitzgerald's "The Rich Boy" because it "consists of a linear narrative managed by a modern consciousness." It's not that modern/postmodern novels jettison narrative altogether, it's that they don't stick to <u>linear</u> narrative. One might have thought that the history of fiction in the 20th century had at least demonstrated that stories don't need to be "linear" to be stories or to engage a reader's attention, but apparently not. Apparently most of this fiction is to be dismissed as so many "literary bleeps and squeaks," although Evans is assuredly mistaken if he really thinks fiction will be returning to the practices of the past in some ingenuously earnest kind of way ("down with self-consciousness!") or that the fiction characterized by "modernist attitudes" will just disappear. It prompts one to ask: If Evans really dislikes what fiction has become, why does he bother with it all, even to deplore it? He's stuck with it, so perhaps he should just console himself with the "narrative innocence" of movies. (Except that we all know that "the cinema" at its best lost its narrative innocence a long time ago as well.)

What Evans really dislikes is art itself, at least as far as it has dared to sully the innocence of fiction: "The histories of the novel and of storytelling ran together until the early 20th century; since the 1920s, that history has been one of formal drift, away from the novel as a social form that described how characters live in relation to others. . ." It's telling that, for Evans, any deviation at all from the tradition of "storytelling" must be "drift," almost literally, given the language here, some kind of ethical betrayal. To be a muddle-headed aesthete, even to be interested in the aesthetic qualities of literature at all, has long been anathema to a certain kind of critic, grounds for accusing writers of being morally deficient, but why, for example, would it probably not occur to these critics to declare, say, composers too interested in art, too attentive to the needs of form over those of morality? Even the most conventionally tonal music is by its very nature about form, about the relationships between sounds and the interaction of purely musical qualities. Is fiction not allowed to explore the possibilities of the linguistic medium in something like the way music explores the possibilities of the aural medium? Why when a fiction writer does this is he/she more likely to be considered some kind of malefactor?

Furthermore, Evans is again simply wrong in his assertion that "The histories of the novel and of storytelling ran together until the early 20th century." This is a common, but mistaken, belief about the development of fiction even in the 19th century. Evans cites Henry James as one of his storytelling heroes, but who would say that James's real preoccupation was telling stories? That he wasn't more interested in the "how" of storytelling--point of view, style"--than in the "what"--events, narrative progression, the details of "what happens"? For some reason it is assumed that the great figures of literary realism were also tale-spinners, but who can read Chekhov and say this? His stories are about character, situation, revelatory moments. As far as narrative is concerned, in most of them almost nothing happens. The fact is, the more fiction "drifted" toward realism, the less it focused on story at all--"story" was an artificial construction that was not faithful to the way real people actually experienced their lives.

But for Evans, fiction is not about individuals at all, which is presumably also an ethical breach: "Novelists may want to write narrowly or widely; but the novel remains a social form, and our fiction should communicate that whatever identity we may have is composed not merely of ourselves but of others. The novel, in its fully realized state, exists to reflect on those links between us - on their making and breaking. How can it do that other than through stories?" Evan's assumption couldn't be clearer: novels are not about art, they're sociology. Moreover, they're a particularly smarmy form of sociology, in which we are lectured to about our duties to others. They're a handy form of indoctrination and propaganda. Stories just keep it simple. And Evans's superior insights are apparently not restricted to moral issues: He also knows what novels are <u>really</u> for, has somehow acquired a knowledge of and wisdom about what they should appropriately be like in their "fully realized state."

Robert Douglas-Fairhurst in his essay "Melting Away" (*Telegraph*, November 2, 2004) is really quite thoughtful about "silences" and endings in fiction. For instance:

> . . .writing is always partial: it involves the choice of some words rather than others, and choice requires rejection. As Henry James observed, "Stopping, that's art": the writer must know what to shut out, when to shut up.

> But even stopping need not be an imaginative curb, because alerting us to what is not being said can also remind us of how often life gives words the slip, whether through secrets, reticence or repression.

And:

> Fictional endings are the moments when speech topples over into silence, so they regularly provide concentrated images of the horror of death, from the corpse-strewn scenes that conclude Shakespeare's tragedies, to the newer worry over entropy that filters into a novel such as Forster's *Howards End*, which begins with Mrs Wilcox looking "tired" and ends with Mr Wilcox "Eternally tired".

> But endings can also be more lively and enlivening than this. "Every limit is a beginning as well as an ending": George Eliot's "Finale" to *Middlemarch* points out that it is no easier to tie up all loose ends in a

novel than it is to draw a sharp line between one life and another life.

The insights here about the use of silence in works of serious literature are especially useful. What's not said, of course, is often as important as what is--Beckett, for example, seems to me the writer who has most profoundly understood the literary possibilities of silence, as well as the advantages of saying too little rather than saying too much. Somehow, these seem to me to be the real choices available to serious writers--either refusing to say what readers can be led to hear nevertheless, or saying so much that readers similarly come to understand what words can "say" and what they can't. (In contemporary American fiction, Carver on the one hand, Elkin on the other.) Saying just the right amount seems the most boring approach one can take. And it is the role of literary criticism, one it's no longer much assuming, to help readers prepare themselves to note the silences and make sense of the noise.

But I can't quite accept Douglas-Fairhurst's descriptions of the role of endings. He speaks of them as "stopping," as the final point in the narrative line a novel or play has drawn. This line, he suggests, is extended further by the reader into "life." (The final ending, of course, being the Big Ending awaiting us all.) "Above all," he writes, "good endings take us to the point where we emerge from reading better prepared to meet the challenges of the world." Perhaps some, perhaps many, readers have had this experience in reading narrative literature, but surely this can't be the more immediate purpose of endings in literature. Most writers have no better idea of how "to meet the challenges of the world" than anyone else.

Writers do, however, presumably have a somewhat better idea of how to shape works of fiction into literary art. They know how the ending relates to the other parts of the novel or story. They ought to know how they want the reader to relate the way the story ends to what has come before. In other words, an ending is more like a completion, the final piece of what should be the artistic whole, the last element in the literary design that allows the reader--perhaps forces the reader--to take a figurative step back and perceive that whole as it has now been finally presented. In this respect, it is no more--also no less--important than any of the other parts of the whole.

Douglas-Fairhurst's notion of the function of endings in fiction only reinforces the too widely-held idea that fiction is all about, is only about, "the story." Actually, stories are a dime a dozen. There probably is some inherent fascination with stories hard-wired into the human brain, but most people would rather get their stories from movies and television. Fiction writers aren't going to get anywhere by continuing to compete with these media; the best writers stopped competing long ago. If fiction is going to survive as a vital--although not necessarily "popular"-- literary art, writers will have to turn their attention away from stories in the simplistic sense Douglas-Fairhurst's otherwise intelligent remarks nevertheless still invoke and instead concentrate on the more dynamic possibilities of fiction as a form aside from the requirements of narrative. At the very least, they need to think through unexamined assumptions about how stories work and what they accomplish. ("Dumbing down" complex ideas or dramatizing "issues" just won't do.) Great writers have never been simply great storytellers, although some have indeed been great ones; a story may keep you reading until the end, but if you don't go back and retrace the steps that got you there it may well prove to be an "imaginative curb."

In the May/Summer 2004 issue of *The Writer's Chronicle*, Alice Mattison offers an interesting essay defending the use of coincidence in fiction. Subtitled "An Essay Against Craft," the essay commends the use of coincidence as a way of taking risk, which Mattison feels is discouraged in a literary world dominated by the workshop "rules" implicitly taught in creative writing programs. Writes Mattison: "I don't think directions or rules are available, just terms. . .that undeniably simplify discussions of writing and literature." Such simplification is at times useful, but "the problem arises when we begin to draw conclusions from successful choices, assuming that what works once will work in every instance."

A few paragraphs after the statements just quoted, Mattison is discussing a Charles Baxter essay in which "Baxter glances at the sort [of stories] that were rejected as old-fashioned by the authors who first made stories turn on insight. He characterizes the stories that Henry James and James Joyce rejected as those with 'plot structures tending to require a set of coincidences or connivances of circumstance.'" Mattison comments: "It hadn't occurred to me, before I read Baxter's sentence, that coincidence <u>defines</u> the type of story in which it appears. I hadn't noticed that such stories. . .were helpless without coincidence."

Although Baxter and Mattison don't use the word, what they are both describing is the influence on early novels in English of the "picaresque" narrative. The picaresque story-- derived from the term identifying the protagonist of such stories, the "picaro"--was introduced by Spanish writers of the 16th and 17th centuries, and is essentially a journey narrative in which the picaro, usually a roguish character, embarks on a journey in which, literally, one thing happens after another. There's not really a sense of progression in the picaresque narrative, just a series of episodes, and usually the protagonist remains more or less unchanged, undergoing no transformation or "epiphany." The most famous picaresque novel is undoubtedly *Don Quixote*, in which Cervantes alters the form by making his protagonist a deluded but not antisocial or rascally character.

248

The early British novelists of the 18th century were greatly influenced by the picaresque narrative, especially such writers as Tobias Smollett and Henry Fielding. Fielding's *Tom Jones* is probably the most famous of these British picaresque novels. It adopts the journey conceit, the episodic structure, and adds an element of explicit comedy that exceeds even the kind of doleful humor to be found in *Don Quixote*. (*Tom Jones* remains a tremendously readable book, and I would highly recommend it to anyone who wants to know what the picaresque form can accomplish.) Charles Dickens was in turn profoundly influenced by Smollett and Fielding, and his novels represent a further fashioning of the picaresque into a narrative technique of great flexibility and latent aesthetic potential.

But this was indeed the "old-fashioned" kind of storytelling that came to be rejected by later writers more concerned about the "craft" of fiction. Perhaps the first writer to really move away from the picaresque was Flaubert, and he may be the writer most responsible for converting fiction into a more gracefully "shaped" kind of storytelling, and therefore a form that could be taken seriously as a mode of literary <u>art</u>. Mattison identifies James and Joyce as the writers who came to "shape" their stories around the occurrence of an "epiphany," but it was really Flaubert who showed James and Joyce that such an aesthetically intricate effect could be brought off in fiction.

Since Flaubert, the notion of "story" in fiction is thus usually associated either specifically with the kind of dramatic narrative leading to revelation or epiphany pioneered by James and Joyce or more generally with the kind of carefully structured narrative encapsulated in "Freytag's triangle": exposition, rising action, climax, denouement, etc. Most genre fiction probably uses the latter, most "literary" fiction the former. Most best-selling potboilers are likely to use the Freytag-derived narrative filtered through Hollywood melodrama. In this context, the picaresque story almost doesn't seem like a story at all, since it doesn't arrange itself in some shaped pattern, but is instead just a series of incidents strung together.

I go over all this not to offer some kind of lesson in literary history but ultimately to suggest, with Mattison but more broadly than her advocacy of "coincidence" goes, that the picaresque ought to remain a viable option and can provide an alternative to the workshop-reinforced domination of the revalatory narrative. To some extent the picaresque style was revived by postwar American writers such as John Barth and Thomas Pynchon, but in my opinion it still contains much untapped potential. It can free the writer from the tyranny of story--the creation of narrative tension by which too many stories and novels are reductively judged--but at the same time allows for the depiction of external events, provides an aesthetically justified motive for abjuring the directive to probe the psychological depths, and perhaps most of all makes available all

kind of other effects--satire, subplots, a larger cast of characters--
that the craft-like story discourages. Of course, this is not the
18th century, and writers now would be using the picaresque
form in a much more self-conscious way, but that in itself would
likely give such fictions a "shape" that would rescue them from
mere formlessness. (Although attempting a truly "formless" novel
might be an interesting experiment in itself.)

I am not suggesting that the picaresque narrative is
superior to the more conventionally shaped narrative most novels
employ. The possibilities in "shaping" the latter kind of narrative
have by no means been exhausted, although most published
novels don't seem much interested in exploring these
possibilities. A renewed interest in the picaresque might,
however, help demonstrate that there is more than one way to tell
a story, multiple ways to "shape" a work of fiction, without
sacrificing readability or even fiction's "entertainment" value.
(Both *Don Quixote* and *Tom Jones* are nothing if not
entertaining.) And in the final analysis using such a narrative
strategy wouldn't really involve abandoning "craft"; ideally it
would further demonstrate that craft is just as much involved in
the breaking of convention as in its repetition.

II Narrative Strategies

Selah Saterstrom's *The Meat and Spirit Plan* (Coffee
House Press) and Corrina Wycoff's *O Street* (OV Books) both

depict young women whose experience is partially determined by the unpleasant circumstances in which they are raised. Both are notably honest in their portrayal of the external influences that limit their protagonists' opportunities, but also just as honest in their implicit acknowledgement of the bad choices each has made. But ultimately they are quite different kinds of books both formally and stylistically, and, although I enjoyed reading both of them, that they are so dissimilar in method, only to stand finally as variations on a common theme and mode, seems to me their most noteworthy limitation as works of fiction.

The Meat and Spirit Plan presents us with the first-person narrative of the life of a young southern girl (unnamed) who floats through her school years in a kind of sexualized haze and ultimately winds up in a Scottish university studying in the "Postmodern Seminar for the Study of Interpretive Uses" in the religion department. There she continues to exist in a fog of misdirected energy and generalized excess, culminating in a debilitating illness that forces her to return to the United States. She recovers, and the final pages of the novel suggest she might finally be getting her life into some kind of order.

The narrator's alienation from her enervating surroundings, from the monotonous drift of her own life, is profound if not often explicitly acknowledged. It is, however, unmistakable in the affectless but cumulatively affecting chunks of prose that serially approximate the aimless, one-thing-after-another succession of experiences that make up the narrator's life. These prose pieces ultimately acquire a kind of poetic intensity of effect in their bleak circumscription of the character's experience, although they avoid self-consciously "poetic" devices:

> In a motel room across from the bed I am in is another bed just like it. In it Stripper Stephanie is on top of some guy then the guy I am with pulls me out of the bed we are in. He pushes me in the bathroom, into the shower, and closes the door. Once inside the bathroom he realizes the light is off and he opens the door, turns it on, then closes the door again. I like the lights on, he says. Do it, he says. Do what, I say. It, he says. I do not know what he means. Do it, he says. Standing in the shower I make a face like I'm a girl in a horror movie.

Unfortunately, the novel's ultimate attempt to integrate the narrator's dislocated experiences into a more coherent account of a life gone wrong then recovered, which is ham-handedly reinforced by the explicit revelation that the novel we have just read has literally been written by the narrator as a capstone to that recovery, robs it of some of its accumulated force. It becomes just another version of a bildungsroman, an opportunity for its female author/protagonist to "express" herself and her newly-found sense of direction. What had been a fairly provocative portrayal of dissolution, of a young American woman giving in to her impulses on her picaresque journey into adulthood, becomes a rather conventional story of a young lady learning her lesson.

The conclusion to *O Street* is equally frustrating, but in this case it is not due to a weakening of poetic concentration but a kind of loss of narrative will. The book is a sequence of short stories focusing on the life of Beth Dinard, who at the beginning of the book is an adult literally returning to her hometown in New Jersey at the news of her mother's death but who appears in other stories at various stages in her life. In effect, we return with Beth to revisit her past, which is recounted in a series of discrete stories (some focusing on her mother as well). One could call the book a novel-in-stories of the kind that has become increasingly popular over the last decade or so.

Most of the stories are conventional slices-of-life revealing something essential about Beth's upbringing by a drug-addicted, borderline mentally ill mother, her attempts to cope with the miserable circumstances in which she is forced to live, her escape from those circumstances and subsequent efforts to establish some sense of normalcy for herself, etc. They are generally well done, most culminating in a moment of subtle illumination of the book's predominant themes--the search for security, the persistence of memory, leaving and being left, etc. Only one of the stories, the title story, attempts something different, and it's probably the best in the book. In it, Wycoff effectively uses second-person narration to evoke a former schoolmate of Beth's, who had abandoned the "O Street Girl" as a friend but years later is moved to call Beth on the phone to explain herself. It's a well-executed story in it own right, and it lends the book as a whole a refreshing change of approach and perspective.

Unfortunately the last two stories in the book bring it to an overly safe and predictable conclusion. The final story in particular, about the immediate aftermath of the death of Beth's mother, attempts to explicitly gather the book's otherwise implicit narrative strands but succeeds only in burdening it with too many passages of forced exposition and awkward reflection:

> After she learned of her mother's death--as Beth walked block after block in the oppressively hot Chicago night air--she kept looking in ruts beside curbs, half expecting to see her glasses. Thirteen years ago, she'd fallen into disrepair when she'd thought her mother was dead. Would she do that again? She was thirty-five now, too old to lose everything a second time. She'd been at her job for ten years; she'd finally managed to move back to one of Chicago's more decent neighborhoods where an abundance of grocery stores stayed open all night, and maybe, soon, she would meet a woman to love.

The reader has to wade through too much of this sort of "summing up," and the effect is to make us feel that the author did not have enough confidence in her narrative strategy--

whereby the parts add up to a whole without all connections being made overt--or in her readers' ability to assimilate that strategy so that she could in effect leave it to fend for itself. In the effort to create a novel-in-stories, Wycoff has put too much emphasis on the novelistic, with its more direct demand for coherence and closure, and not enough on the inherent capacity of her individual stories to carry the needed narrative weight.

Both of these books, then, are compelling up to a point, but at that point essentially retreat into overly familiar exercises in composing a "life story." For me, fiction has to be more than an opportunity to recount one's experience with some literary license allowed, even if that experience is rooted in difficult or colorful or unfamiliar circumstances. It has to find an aesthetic strategy that elevates the "story"--which too often is just the same old story novelists have been telling for years, if not centuries-- beyond mere narrative facility through formal ingenuity and/or stylistic resourcefulness. Each of these books demonstrates admirable facility--and Saterstrom shows real skill as a stylist-- but each of them pulls up short of the necessary aesthetic inspiration.

The danger of reading a novel primarily for the opportunity to "identify" with its characters--as well as to interpret their actions by judging them on moral grounds--seems well-illustrated in a review at *The Mumpsimus* of Susann Cokal's

Breath and Bones (Unbridled Books). The reviewer, Catherynne M. Valente, writes of the novel's protagonist:

> Famke is a horrible woman, and despite the narrative's assurances that we *must* love her, the reader cannot identify with such a shallow, idiotic, and careless person. (July 26, 2005)

Even if it were true that this character is "a horrible woman"--deliberately portrayed as such by the author--would this be a good reason to so dislike this novel as to call it "truly, shockingly bad"? (Valente's focus is almost entirely on the moral failings of this character, although she does pause occasionally for an ad hominem comment on the author herself, as when she wonders "if she has had any practical experience with human bodies at all.") Surely we can all think of fiction we've read in which one or more of the main characters are morally dubious, if not just plain repulsive, but which we nevertheless judge to be compelling and aesthetically powerful books. (*Journey to the End of the Night? Naked Lunch?* Much of Flannery O'Connor?) Shouldn't it be a critical rule of thumb that in order to fairly assess a work of literature for what it seems to be offering us we make an effort to put aside moral judgment, especially judgment of fictional characters, until we have honestly determined the role these characters play in the work's aesthetic order and in the context of its broader thematic concerns?

However, it simply is not the case that the protagonist of *Breath and Bones* is the "shallow, idiotic, and careless person" this reviewer takes her to be. Famke Summerfugl (or Ursula Summerfield, or Dante Castle--her identity is as quickly changed as her location as she travels across the western United States) is determined to get what she wants (a reunion with the artist for whom she has served as a model back in her native Denmark), but her very single-mindedness is at least as much the product of an uncertain sense of self as it is a more willful character flaw. Indeed, it is her lack of a truly developed personality, her ability to become the object of others' obsessions, to take on whatever attributes are required to survive in an environment she is in some ways too inexperienced to know is hostile to her presence, that really define her as a character. Famke leaves a fair amount of distress and destruction in her wake, but little of it is due to her "careless" or "idiotic" behavior. If anything she cares too much (especially in comparison to many of the people she encounters, who have more or less acceded to their limited circumstances), as her quest is motivated by her belief in the artistic genius of Albert Castle and in her own role as his inspiration, and she is anything but an idiot. When finally she does reunite with Albert, she has been able to learn enough both about herself and human nature to recognize he's not nearly the man she had in her earlier romantic haze taken him to be.

It might be that Catherynne Valente reacted as she did to Famke because she failed to consider that *Breath and Bones* is essentially a picaresque novel, Famke its picaro. One doesn't normally approach a picaresque novel with an assumption that its protagonist will be a "rounded" character who will provoke either emotional attachment or moral revulsion. Since the root meaning of "picaro" is "rogue," if we were to demand of such a character that he/she be a model of propriety, we would be denying the picaresque form its motivating agency. It's the "adventures" of the picaro that solicit our attention in this kind of fiction, and whatever change or enhancement of character that emerges is secondary to the experiences to which the character is submitted, to the <u>process</u> by which change or growth might (or might not) occur.

Cokal has in this case herself enhanced our perception of the picaresque form by making her protagonist a woman. Famke is neither more nor less "horrible" (or desperate or confused) than most picaresque anti-heroes, but surely one of the problems Catherynne M. Valente has with her is that she's an anti-<u>heroine</u>, a woman taking on the role traditionally associated with misfits and outcasts, one that inherently calls for a certain amount of guile and disregard for moral niceties. One wonders if Valente would express the same contempt for a male character engaged in similarly venturesome conduct as Famke Summerfugl. Is a picaresque narrative acceptable for exploring the moral margins of male behavior, but inappropriate for depicting women who also find themselves caught in marginal circumstances? Are women, even in fiction, to be judged by different standards than men? If we find ourselves having moral qualms about a female character acting in ways that are conventional in a literary mode usually reserved for men, should we be rethinking our expectations of "female behavior" or our assumptions about those conventions? Perhaps these are questions Susann Cokal would like us to ask while reading her book.

(And I certainly don't think that Cokal's narrative insists that "we *must* love" Famke. It seems to me that Cokal has written the kind of novel she's written precisely to induce in us a degree of ambivalence about her main character. To engage in the kind of questioning of literary means and ends I've just outlined almost requires that we feel uneasy about our response to a character like Famke.)

At one point Valente calls *Breath and Bones* "a romance novel that thinks it's too good for the genre" and at another claims it falls into a certain kind of "realist trap," so it's hard to know whether she thinks it strays too far from reality or not far enough. However, it is certainly true that the kind of quest narrative the novel uses allows for a fair amount of exaggeration, coincidence, and melodrama (think of *Tom Jones*, of many of Dickens's novels, or, indeed, of *Huckleberry Finn*.) *Breath and Bones* incorporates its share of all of these, but never to the extent that we begin to disbelieve in its created illusion of an historical time and place. (In this regard, I actually found the historical epigraphs presented at the beginning of chapters completely superfluous.

The novel's success depends on the integrity of its own narrative logic, not on the broader historical picture it presents.) Thus, although B & B is not recognizably "postmodern," it also is not simply a "realist" novel retreating into the past. (And, again, the only reason I can see to call it a "romance novel" is that its protagonist is a woman who believes herself to be in love.)

Finally, Valente says of the style of *Breath and Bones* that "the language of the novel was so simplistic as to give Potter and Co. a run for their broomsticks." She must have in mind a passage such as this, as Albert Castle is working on his pre-Raphaelite portrait of Famke as Nimue:

> . . .He had beautiful fingers, long and bony, with a rainbow of paint always under the nails, and to Famke's mind they produced wonders. They had drawn her as an earthly Valkyrie, in a cloak made of swans' feathers (and nothing else); painted her as a nearly naked Gunnlod, the loveliest of the primordial Norse giants, watching over the three kettles of wisdom in a deep, deep cave (Albert seemed to very fond of caves.) And now this Nimue, a wizard's lover, who could be from icy Scandanavia but would be of great interest to the English critics who could make Albert's fortune. Famke had never heard of Merlin or of Nimue, but Albert was teaching her a great deal about the mythology of her people. He liked to set her

lessons from the traveler's guidebooks scattered over the mantel.

There is a certain ingenuousness to a passage like this (although the novel does not stick exclusively to Famke's implied point of view), but ultimately it works as much to expose the pretensions of Albert Castle ("Albert seemed very fond of caves") as the "simplicity" of Famke's perceptions. And this clash between Famke's innocence and the rather sordid actualities she encounters (both in America and in Denmark) ultimately provides the novel with what might be its most resonant conflict.

Catherynne M. Valente and I seem to have read different books. She read a story motivated by the actions of a morally compromised romantic heroine. I read a well-executed variation on an always-renewable form that if anything explicitly challenges a reflexively "moral" response to works of literature.

In what is unfortunately one of the few available reviews of Rosalind Belben's impressive novel, *Our Horses in Egypt*, Stevie Davies calls it "a radical experiment in narrative." I think this is probably an overstatement, but there is certainly more going on in this novel, both structurally and stylistically, than might at first seem apparent.

Its twinning of narrative strands, one chronicling the experiences of a literal "war horse" conscripted into cavalry service during World War, the other narrating its owner's attempt to track it down in Egypt several years after the war, is not particularly innovative, although it is brought off effectively. And while in effect assigning the role of protagonist to a horse does allow Belben to avoid several worn-out devices still being trotted out (so to speak) in so many contemporary novels, the notion of a story centered on a non-human "character" is also by no means especially "radical." However, Belben's novel does present itself in ways most readers are likely to find distinctive, even if they are otherwise primarily engaged by the emotion-laden story Belben wants to tell.

Most noticeable is Belben's prose style, especially the pervasive, staccato-like dialogue featured in the sections of the novel dedicated to the quest by Griselda Romney, whose own husband was killed in the war, to find Philomena, the horse requisitioned at the beginning of the war who apparently survived it. Here's a representative sample:

> "In the old days, we managed."
>
> "These fellows you found. . ."
>
> "They said they knew what they were about."
>
> "You're so gullible."
>
> "I shan't be again. I had to chloroform myself when Georgie was born."
>
> "It didn't put you down."
>
> "How could it, a whiff or two! I was glad of it."

"Poor Bunny."

"Oh, oh, don't!"

It isn't that this conversation is disconnected or incoherent that makes it seem so elliptical. It undoubtedly makes perfect sense to the speakers, and careful reading can certainly establish the context in which these remarks are being offered, even if such context does become clearer and the subject of conversation somewhat more comprehensible in a retrospective reading of this passage. (In this way, *Our Horses in Egypt* encourages a more attentive and recursive kind of reading, which, in my view, need not be a burden and can ultimately enhance the reading experience.) The cumulative effect of this dialogue is a sense of thoroughgoing fidelity to the speech patterns of these characters as rooted in country, region, class, and time period. It is an actual example of "realism" unencumbered and applied with great rigor, and it is likely to unmoor the assumptions of those readers tied to a more conventionalized, less ascetic understanding of the role of "realistic" dialogue.

The second striking feature of Belben's novel is perhaps best illustrated in the section narrating Philomena's experiences in the Great War. While there is a narration of these events, it also comes shorn of rhetorical embellishment and narrative elaboration:

The Turkish machine-gunners played very freely across the Dorsets' front. Major Sandley wilted in the saddle. The dust raised was shot through with rosy rays of sun. Burgess sailed through the air, and was himself winged like a flapper. Riderless horses heaved themselves up, and thudded on with the rest. Philomena was so distracted (she had a curious view) she didn't hear the whump when, at four hundred yards, the files closed for impact and Corky was hit in the neck. She didn't pay any attention to his snort. But she saw the white of his eye. He was stubborn.

All of the narrative/expository passages in the novel proceed in this way, almost as if story were being built by accretion, storytelling replaced by listing: then this happened, then this, then this. Perhaps because *Our Horses in Egypt* is a historical novel, such a technique seems only the more appropriate, more faithful to the historical "record" (even when incidents and interactions have been imagined) as simply what happened, the essence of the historical past without the unnecessary intrusion of the storytelling gestures so many historical novelists seem to need.

Belben's listing strategy extends even to her sometimes idiosyncratic punctuation:

Nine yeomanry regiments had been withdrawn from Palestine. "The Bull" had lost, also, two infantry divisions; five and a half seige batteries; nine more British battalions and five machine-gun companies. He had been deprived of 60,00 battle-hardend troops. Infantry divisions arrived from Mesopotamia and India; and their transport drivers had to be trained. . . .

The semi-colons here seem to function not as a marker of sentence boundaries but as just one more way to extend the list of details associated with the withdrawal. *Our Horses in Egypt*, no matter how accurate its rendition of the British victory in Palestine, is finally still a rendition, its narrative method as much artifice as any other, but its triumph is perhaps in the way it skillfully employs its artifice while simultaneously appearing to conceal it. History seems to lie before us, however much it has been conjured up by a particular kind of verbal manipulation.

So skillful is this manipulation that, despite the deliberate poverty of means in the novel's construction, *Our Horses in Egypt* still tells an affecting story, both in the half concerning Griselda's finally hopeless effort to bring Philomena back alive and in that focusing on the Palestine campaign. And what could have been a smarmy resolution in which Griselda finally does find Philomena and spirits her back to England to live out her days in tranquility becomes instead a bitterly appropriate portrayal of a Philomena brought to ruin through overwork, beyond rescue and suitable only to be euthanized in a token act of pity. This is a novel that risks sentimentality at every stage in its development but that avoids it through unfaltering artistry.

Most discussion of the work of Israeli novelist Aharon Appelfeld eventually focuses on Appelfeld's status as a "Holocaust writer," even if it is acknowledged that in his novels the deportation of European Jews to the death camps and to their murder there is not directly depicted, nor are the horrors experienced there by those who managed to escape or survive their attempted murder explicitly recalled, rarely even mentioned. The silence about the massacre itself is taken to be a strategic silence, whereby the Holocaust looms even larger for its absence in Appelfeld's narratives.

I don't necessarily disagree that Appelfeld's consistent elision of the Holocaust has the effect of drawing the reader's attention to that elision, but perhaps it would be just as true to Appelfeld's intentions and achievement to regard his subject not as the Holocaust, nor even as the conditions, attitudes, or assumptions that preceded and, to a lesser extent, succeeded the event itself, but more plainly as the lives lived by diasporan European Jews prior to the cultural cataclysm represented by the Holocaust, as well as the subsequent response to the extinction of that way of life by those who remained. Applefeld's fiction seems to me much more concerned with the specific experiences of specific characters in a specific time and place than in subsuming those experiences into some overarching abstraction, even one as potent as the Holocaust has become.

For this reason, I also have trouble reading Appelfeld's novels as allegories, as many other reviewers and critics seem to do, although in their relative brevity and episodic structure they undeniably do seem closer to fabulation than to slice-of-life realism. The two most recent of his novels to be translated into English, *All Whom I Have Loved* and *Laish*, might especially seem to invite allegorical interpretation, but while I would not begrudge readers their attempt to find in these novels the kind of accessible "meaning" usually associated with allegory, assuming that the allegorical content is an adequate measure of what Appelfeld's fiction has to offer seems to me at best mistaken and at worst just a way of assigning it to some manageable category that excuses inattentive reading.

Appelfeld is often enough compared to Kafka, but this comparison in turn generally assumes that Kafka's fiction is allegorical in a more or less overt way. But of course Kafka created narratives that appear to incorporate an allegorical level of meaning only to complicate and ultimately to deny that meaning. Kafka's world purports to be comprehensible, its ultimate sense to be discovered just around the next narrative turn, but it is finally a world of no-sense, or, more accurately, only of the aesthetic sense made through its own impeccable construction. Kafka is at pains to give his inscrutable world as much substance and texture as is necessary to make it. . .real. The point of reading Kafka's fiction is not, it seems to me, to arrive at a conclusion that the world we live in is absurd, or frightening, or grotesque, but that the world Kafka has created is self-sustaining and entirely logical.

If Kafka is a touchstone in understanding the work of Aharon Applefeld, then something like this focus on texture, on the imaginatively concrete, must be true of Appelfeld's fiction as well. Like Kafka, Appelfeld in all of his novels is concerned above all to sustain the integrity of his invoked world, to make the reader's experience of that world as palpable as the more customary world assumed in most novels. Indeed, if part of Appelfeld's ambition as a fiction writer is to recapture the lost world of prewar European Jewry, then insuring that the particulars remain in the foreground of the reader's attention seems all the more necessary, even if those particulars must unavoidably be filtered through fallible and subjective retrospection.

All Whom I Have Loved is a characteristic foray into recollected experience, transformed into a narrative of confusion, loss, and the imminent dissolution of all ties to life as it had been known. The story is narrated by Paul Rosenfeld, another of the fictional stand-ins for the young Aharon Appelfeld that we find in numerous Appelfeld novels, and the experiences he relates again seem variations on the essential core of experience Appelfeld brought with him when he managed to emigrate to Israel a year after the war ended. Paul is separated first from his father, a struggling artist, in an acrimonious divorce from Paul's mother, with whom Paul lives afterwards until he comes to feel neglected by her in her efforts to assimilate into the local community--she ultimately marries a schoolteacher colleague, a gentile--and then goes to live with the penurious father. While still living with his mother, Paul is cared for by Halina, a local peasant girl whom Paul eventually witnesses being murdered by her abusive boyfriend. After going with his father (including on a trip to Bucharest, where the father briefly experiences renewed hope in his artistic career, only to have it come to nothing), Paul learns his mother has become sick with typhus, from which she shortly dies. The narrative concludes with the shooting of Paul's father during an attempted robbery of a Jewish store and with Paul facing an anarchic future.

The bare bones of this story--a young Jewish boy growing up in Eastern Europe with some degree of turmoil and/or premature tragedy afflicting his family while the even greater trauma of persecution is beginning to build--recurs in several of Appelfeld's novels. This makes his body of work as a whole more broadly representative, as a new reader can start with any one of the novels and immediately become acquainted with Appelfeld's persistent themes and methods. Since the quality of the novels is remarkably consistent as well--at least in those that have gotten to us English speakers in translation--such a reader can be fairly well assured he/she is getting an illustrative sample of Applefeld's accomplishments as a writer of fiction. It also makes the "allegorical" element of Appelfeld's fiction a less relevant and less helpful orientation to his work for the already committed reader. The symbolic implications of the setting and events related are already apparent enough, and what keeps one reading Appelfeld is less the payoff in "meaning" than an interest in how he will again reshape a particular set of experiences into an engrossing fiction that draws us deeper into the specificity of its recreated world.

A careful reading of *All Whom I Have Loved* would dwell on a moment such as this:

> The next day I stood by the door and said good-bye to Mother. I did not cry. I felt the anguish of parting later, in the bedroom amidst the rumpled bed and scattered clothes. It was a sunny day, and the yard behind the house was filled with light. We went out, and Halina immediately began to show me her wonders: she walked on her hands and then made noises like the cawing of crows; she imitated sheep and cows, frogs, and cuckoos. And for a moment she seemed to be not a person but an amazing animal that knew how to do everything that animals can do: to climb trees nimbly, to crawl, to leap over fences, and to fly. Halina lost no time in trying to teach me her skills, but I was far from agile and scarcely capable of producing a single whistle.

Then we rolled in the grass. Halina was slender and very nimble. I tried hard to catch her, but she ran fast and could hop like a rabbit. I stared at her and knew: I would never be able to do the same.

Not only is this passage notable for its aptly chosen detail--"in the bedroom amidst the rumpled bed and scattered clothes"--and not only does it provide us with an episode of brightness and joy as a balance to the descending gloom that we readers of Paul's narrative can always sense (and the joy is in this case itself leavened by Paul's underlying sadness at the separation from his mother), but to the extent it invites us to incorporate the scene into the abstract allegorical narrative paralleling the actual narrative of his experiences that Paul relates we should be wary of effacing the latter while agreeing to the former. Paul's "I would never be able to do the same" might point us to the incipient terror of the Holocaust, or more generally Paul's long-term inability to indulge in simple pleasures, but it might also, almost certainly does, refer to his literal inability to "run fast" and "hop like a rabbit," at this specific time and place as well as in the projected future. That Paul is "far from agile" is a simple matter of fact, however much we might want to see it as a symptom of some larger metaphysical condition.

If anything, *Laish* even more obviously seems to court an allegorical interpretation, as it is structured explicitly as a journey, the figurative status of which is further reinforced by the cast of characters and the purpose of their journey: At some unspecified point late in the nineteenth century, an untidy group of Jews is making its way in a caravan across Eastern Europe, its stated mission to reach a point of embarkation to Jerusalem. The group consists of traders, ex-convicts, religious seekers, and various other vulnerable people who have joined up with the caravan over the years. The story of their journey is related by a teenage boy, for whom of course the journey acts as an initiation into the ways of the world but who really acts more as a dispassionate observer of the motley assortment of pilgrims and their interactions with the gentiles they encounter. The caravan more or less falls apart by the time it reaches the port of Galacz, but a few of them do remain, their ultimate fate uncertain as they prepare to board ship and the narrator notes that "It appeared to me that all those who had fled were standing at some distance and staring at us."

It would be easy enough to take this story as "the story" of Modern Jewry prior to the founding of Israel, upon the precipice of which the survivors of the caravan symbolically stand. And to some degree it is that story. But it is hard to believe that Appelfeld wrote the novel merely, or even primarily, to advance such a story through what is finally one of the hoariest of devices, the journey narrative. The variety of characters presented and experiences related presses upon the reader's attention more than the goal of the journey itself, and the effect seems more picaresque than emblematic. If *Laish* does recall Kafka in leaving the caravan and its origins somewhat enigmatic, it also never resolves the enigma into something more readily accessible to interpretation.

Like *All Whom I Have Loved*, *Laish* is composed in short, compact chapters, each relating a brief episode or mini-narrative in Appelfeld's characteristically reticent prose. (At least this is the persistent impression I get from the translations I have read; to examine Appelfeld's prose style more thoroughly would require a facility with Hebrew I don't myself possess.) Even more than in *All Whom I Have Loved*, in *Laish* this manner of writing calls attention less to the narrative as a whole, its forward momentum, and more to the self-sufficiency, both in language and in structure, of these discreet parts. Appelfeld is another of those writers who, for me at least, blurs the line between poetry and fiction, in this case by working against the pull of allegory and preserving space for a quiet autonomy of language. To read *Laish* simply for the meaning conveyed by its plot is to willfully overlook its more impressive effort to find the words that might begin to render experiences that at some point become essentially inexpressible. This is the greater triumph of all of Appelfeld's work.

III Point of View

"Point of view" is an element of fiction that, it seems to me, is often invoked but seldom really appreciated. In our haste to get to the "story," or to ascertain what the work in question has "to say," we acknowledge that the narrative is presented in "third-person" or "first-person," but don't appropriately consider how both of these modes of presentation--as well as their many subtle if less recognized variations--affect the terms of our encounter with both the story told and what is said. This goes well beyond the usual distinctions made between "reliable" and "unreliable" narrators (although this distinction remains important), "omniscience" and "central consciousness," or stories told by the main character and those told by a secondary observer. My reading experiences convince me that point of view is not simply a flourish added to the underlying "content" of fiction, nor a way of establishing "voice," not just a way of providing stability while the story unfolds, but fundamentally conditions our perception of all of the other "elements" of fiction we otherwise might think take precedence: plot, character, setting, etc.

The centrality of point of view in determining the nature of the fictional "world" we are entering in a particular work of fiction became only more obvious to me while reading Jeffrey Eugenides's *The Virgin Suicides*, a novel I had not previously read because I had assumed, mistakenly I must now say, it was written primarily to become a movie, as is the case with so much current "literary fiction." I both admired and enjoyed the novel, and mostly for the same reason. I admired the way in which Eugenides was able to maintain his experiment in first-person plural narration--"we" rather than "I" as the origin of the narrator's voice--and I enjoyed the collective invocation of the Lisbon sisters and the story of their early deaths that the narrative embodies. Much of what I enjoyed in the novel--the detached view of the sisters, the baffled way in which the stand-in narrator attempts to comprehend both the sisters' behavior and the love-trance induced in him and his confederates by their charms, the ultimate mystery of the sisters' decision to do themselves in--have been singled out by some reviewers and commentators as flaws, however, and it does seem to me that this results from an unwillingness to allow the novel's adopted point of view to create the sort of effects it is logically inclined to produce.

It is true that we don't ever really get very close to the Lisbon sisters, so that as characters, indeed, as the ostensible protagonists of the story, they don't quite come into focus as much as we might like. They remain wispy, uncertain figures in a novel that inevitably leads us to seek more definition, more certainty. We are just as bewildered by the Lisbon sisters, and just as unclear about what might be going on in that house across the street--the perspective we are forced to assume--as the narrator, but this is not a problem with "characterization." Since there is no satisfactory answer to the question "Why?"--not even the narrator's assiduous efforts to compile "evidence" and interview the Lisbon parents can provide such an answer--or since Eugenides wants to suggest that getting to "know" the Lisbon sisters by taking us inside their heads will leave us no more enlightened, their role as characters in this novel is necessarily limited to the external observations given. To complain about this is to deny the novel its enabling source of expression in the inquiring "we."

It is tempting to say that the narrator(s) become the main characters, but this isn't quite right either. Only occasionally does one of the boys emerge from behind the verbal curtain to assume an active role vis-a-vis one of the sisters--most notably "Trip Fontane," who attempts to court Lux Lisbon--and the narrator's role ultimately is really to testify to the enduring spell cast by the sisters, to give us access to them through a concerted act of memory from which they have never departed:

> Our own knowledge of Cecilia kept growing after her death, too, with the same unnatural persistence. Though she had spoken only rarely and had had no real friends, everybody possessed his own vivid memories of Cecilia. Some of us had held her for five minutes as a baby while Mrs. Lisbon ran back into the house to get her purse. Some of us had played in the sandbox with her, fighting over a shovel, or had exposed ourselves to her behind the mulberry tree that grew like deformed flesh through the chain link fence. We had stood in line with her for smallpox vaccinations, had held polio sugar cubes under out tongues with her, had taught her to jump rope, to light snakes, had stopped her from picking her scabs on numerous occasions, and had cautioned her against

touching her mouth to the drinking fountain at Three Mile Park. A few of us had fallen in love with her, but had kept it to ourselves, knowing that she was the weird sister.

The Virgin Suicides could thus be called a novel without conventional characters (the closest to a rounded, "sympathetic" character might be Mr. Lisbon, who almost becomes compelling in his cluelessness) and, since the sisters' fate is more or less known from the beginning, not much plot aside from the filling-in of details. If plot and character are what you must have, these no doubt must seem to be irremediable deficiencies, but the narrative method Eugenides employs invites us to cultivate a different relationship with the characters, one that emphasizes wonder over intimacy, and assume a more relaxed attitude toward plot, one that allows for meditation on what happened, not just a serial record of what did happen. The point of view in *The Virgin Suicides* works to shape a particular kind of fictional space, one that accentuates distance and concealment. Narrating it from some other perspective would have produced a wholly different, in my opinion much more ordinary, novel.

Many readers and critics approach *The Virgin Suicides* for its thematic implications, its depiction of stifling suburbia, a morally unhinged middle class, the decline of the industrial Midwest, etc., but I think even these concerns gain the prominence they do because of the way the narrative is related to us. The near-mythic quality the story takes on, its rendition of decline-and-fall, the implication of the whole community in the unfolding of its collective trauma provide the tale of the Lisbon suicides a heightened drama that substitutes for the lesser drama of mere plot and gives the tale a kind of allegorical resonance. A less well-calibrated narrative strategy would not have accomplished the same effect.

Dara Horn's *The World to Come* begins with these two paragraphs:

> There used to be many families like the Ziskinds, families where each person always knew that his life was more than his alone. Families like that still exist, but because there are so few of them, they have become insular, isolated, their sentiment that the family is the center of the universe broadened to imply that nothing outside the family is worth anything. If you are from one of these families, you believe this, and you always will.

> Lately it had begun to seem to Benjamin Ziskind that the entire world was dead, that he was a citizen of a necropolis. While his parents were living, Ben had thought about them only when it made sense to think about them, when he was talking to them, or talking about them, or planning something involving them. But now they were always here, reminding him of their presence at every moment. He saw them in the streets, always from

behind, or turning a corner, his father sitting in the bright yellow taxi next to his, shifting in his seat as the cab screeched away in the opposite direction, his mother-- dead six months now, thought it felt like one long night-- hurrying along the sidewalk on a Sunday morning, turning into a store just when Ben had come close enough to see her face. It was a relief that Ben could close his office door.

No doubt this seems thoroughly unexceptional to most readers of fiction (which is actually one of the problems with Horn's novel), an expository passage that begins to acquaint us with the themes the book will explore and introduces us to the character whose present actions and experiences provide the hinge by which the rest of the novel moves. But that we have become accustomed to this kind of discourse, all but take it for granted, suggests it has hardened into a convention we simply accept as the strategy appropriate for a certain type of third-person narrative, which itself has become more or less a default setting for our sense of what narrative discourse should be like. I would submit that this strategy has outlived its usefulness and often inhibits the discovery of fresh, genre-expanding aesthetic approaches to fiction, even approaches to the representation of consciousness, which in a novel like *The World to Come* is carried out in such a perfunctory way that it becomes harder to appreciate some of the novel's other virtues.

Although the reader's attention is first of all directed by the Tolstoy-like opening to what presumably will be the novel's overarching theme, the encompassing context within which the story (as it turns out, multiple and intertwining stories) will proceed. To me, the real work being done by this paragraph is in the way it settles the reader into the novel's discursively shaped world, begins to evoke a particular kind of relationship between narrator and character. Are these generalizations about "family" being offered by a hovering, all-knowing narrator, or have they been filtered through the consciousness and specific experiences of Benjamin Ziskind? The second paragraph confirms that it is the latter, and we are thereafter comfortably placed as readers inside Benjamin's awareness (and, later, several other characters' awareness) and way of thinking about things.

I say "comfortably" because by now this mode of psychological realism, by which the depicted world in a work of fiction comes to us not through omniscient description but through the perception of that fiction's characters ("Lately it had begun to seem to Benjamin Ziskind that the entire world was dead"), has become so thoroughly familiar that it acts as a kind of narrative machine, spinning out sundry versions of what Henry James called third-person "central consciousness" stories in what has admittedly become a very efficient manner. In order to provide a little variety in what is otherwise a rather uniform approach, one can include multiple or alternating centers of consciousness, as Horn does in *The World to Come*, but even here readers are ultimately encouraged to regard the storytelling as more or less transparent, if anchored in a particular character's version of reality, and the style as unintrusive, if sometimes decorated with a suitable figurative flourish. It is precisely the expectation that the reader will be satisfied with this mechanical, mass-produced variety of storytelling that makes me unable to read a book like *The World to Come* with much enthusiasm, even though I can acknowledge that Dara Horn does have some narrative imagination and that the novel weaves together its various strands--which include both invented characters and real historical figures, occurrences in the present interlaced with episodes from the past--with admirable skill.

In "Finding Traction" (*Agni* 63, 2006) Sven Birkerts describes the mindset with which he approaches the submissions he receives:

> Basically—short version—a work of prose (or poetry) can no longer assume continuity, not as it could in former times. It cannot begin, or unfold, in a way that assumes a basic condition of business as usual. The world is no longer everything we thought was the case, and the writing needs to embody this—through sentence rhythm, tone, camera placement, or some other strategic move that signals that no tired assumptions remain in place. This writing must, in effect, create its own world and terms from the threshold, coming at us from a full creative

effort of imagination and not by using the old world as a prop. Now, this last is a tricky assertion and it will be very hard to make clear, not to mention binding. I don't mean for a moment that the world as we know it cannot be invoked, or used, or dissected. Of course it can. But it cannot be taken simply on faith, as unproblematic, treated as a natural signifier; nor can it be cashed in as if it were a treasury bond from the literature of a former era.

I agree entirely with Birkerts, and if I were an editor beginning to read *The World to Come* for potential publication, I would almost immediately conclude that it "assumes a basic condition of business as usual," that numerous "tired assumptions remain in place," that while the novel does attempt to "create its own world," this attempt comes not from the "threshold," but from a place where fiction is regarded as a set of fixed assumptions and techniques from which is chosen the one that will most efficaciously carry the narrative burden to be placed on it. In this case, Horn doesn't so much lean on the "literature of a former era" (she actually takes this as part of her subject, and her examination of Jewish artistic/literary traditions is one of the more compelling aspects of the novel) as on this set of presently-established conventions, themselves a product of "modern" storytelling practices but, as I have been contending, now urgently in need of reexamination. In invoking the "world to come," Horn's novel is, of course, endeavoring to capture something essential about this world, about our longings and frustrations, but it is impossible to read such passages as the one quoted above without thinking that this is at odds with its very prosaic language and method of character creation, which do depend on customary "props."

As if the author herself recognizes that this method lacks dynamism, especially when confined to a single character over the course of an entire narrative, she presents us with multiple characters and their interconnecting stories and makes of the larger narrative of which these are a part a kind of mystery tale embedded in recent history. These are Dara Horn's efforts to embody a "full creative effort of imagination." The result is entertaining enough, at least when I am able to ignore the listless "sentence rhythms" created by Horn's adherence to the central consciousness-style of narrative exposition. (And all too many other novels require that I similarly put aside any expectation of stylistic vigor, narrative innovation, or formal invention, novels that aren't even going to manifest to me the intelligence and skill with which Dara Horn shuffles around the conventional elements she has chosen to use, or won't manifest anything more than such skill with the conventional.) But, ultimately, I don't want to put these things aside, and I'm increasingly uncertain why so many writers--especially among "emerging writers"--think it's appropriate to ask me to do it. There are far too few original stories and arrestingly portrayed characters around to justify losing interest in new ways of telling them and uncommon means of summoning them up.

I share Scott Esposito's enthusiasm for Heather McGowan's *The Duchess of Nothing*, although I don't exactly agree with his analysis of the novel's narrative strategy:

> The premise of Heather McGowan's "Duchess of Nothing" seemingly is not the most promising material for a novel, yet McGowan has fashioned an engrossing, entertaining book. She accomplishes this not through plot but instead through a stream-of-consciousness narration that beautifully characterizes her unnamed protagonist in in a voice that is by turns tragic, farcical, pathetic, poignant and hilarious. (*San Francisco Chronicle*, April 9, 2006)

Later in his review Scott echoes this claim about "stream-of-consciousness narration," suggesting that McGowan presents us with an "unadorned reality filtered through an unstable mind." But *The Duchess of Nothing* is not really a "stream-of-consciousness" novel, at least not as the term has been used in the critical discussion of this technique that has accumulated since its introduction by novelists such as James Joyce, Virginia Woolf, and Dorothy Richardson. In the work of these writers, stream-of-consciousness is a variant on, an intensification of, <u>third-person</u> narration. It is more or less the culmination of the movement toward psychological realism in fiction, which might be said to have begun--at least in English language fiction--with Henry

James's use of the third-person "central consciousness" approach. James's fiction helped to bring about the transformation of the omniscient narrator--knows all, sees all--into the much more limited narrator essentially restricted to the vantage point of the character whose experience is being related. But the narrator is still of the third-person variety, originating from outside that experience and telling us the story on the characters' behalf.

Stream-of-consciousness takes this a step farther and attempts to provide a window of sorts on a character's experiences as they are being processed through that character's mind. Such narration is frequently fragmentary and discontinuous, in an attempt to mimic the way such processing actually occurs, or at least to mimic it as closely as written language is able to do so--it is, like everything else in fiction, ultimately an illusion created through prose. If reality ultimately exists in the mind of the beholder, then the stream-of-consciousness method is an effort to have fiction reflect what is *really* real.

The Duchess of Nothing is a first-person narrative, so, however much we are made to view the world through the constructions of its protagonist, it can't really be said to consist of her stream of consciousness. While I certainly agree that McGowan portrays this character through "a voice that is by turns tragic, farcical, pathetic, poignant and hilarious," it is a voice, a garrulous and idiosyncratic one, in fact, a voice that in many ways works in a manner that precisely reverses the effect created by the stream-of-consciousness strategy:

> Across the cafe Toby stands at the coffee machine gazing into a silver jug. His lips move, to some terrifying soliloquy, I imagine. Behind him well-dressed citizens sip their coffees, quietly content being Italian. If you could understand the strength it takes to sit here quietly, I tell the boy, If I had the power to describe how it feels to do exactly the opposite of what I'd like. I wish you could see the storm that rages beneath my surface. I was never meant to sit quietly, I tell the boy, This sitting quietly was never my idea. I flick my skirt idly, exposing my knee. It stares up at me, a hilly rebuke. I want to leave everything behind as soon as it is a minute past new. Every night after supper I'd like to drop the plate I'm washing, turn, never see any of it again. And yet I remain. I swallow my coffee, I remain.

Although it is Toby who is described as engaged in "some terrifying soliloquy," *The Duchess of Nothing* itself is an extended soliloquy, its narrator's overflowing monologue interrupted only occasionally by a word or two from "the boy" (her sole companion through most of the book). The narrator may feel there is a storm "raging" inside her, but it's really the storm of words she releases that manifests her inability to "sit quietly," her desire to "leave everything behind as soon as it is a minute past new." Whereas stream-of-consciousness tries to direct our attention to the internal drama unfolding in human consciousness, the narrative strategy in this novel externalizes everything, articulates explicitly in the narrator's own language what in s-o-c would remain half-formed and implicit. It's as if the narrator literally can't resist translating into comprehensible speech every thought that comes into her head.

In his review of the novel, Richard Eder accurately notes the protagonist's "grandiloquent self-proclamation," but I cannot agree with Eder that she is an example of an "unreliable narrator." Eder believes that her reticence in fully disclosing the particulars of her past (or even of her present arrangement with "Edmund," brother of "the boy") creates an incompleteness of context that suggests willful manipulation on the narrator's part (Boston Globe, March 26, 2006). While it is true that the novel is somewhat short on expository detail, I would argue that this is simply the consequence of the narrative method McGowan has chosen and to which she remains faithful: no "infodumps" if that would make the narrative voice ring false. I would argue further that it is this method that otherwise invokes the somewhat misshapen world and off-kilter perspective that, to me, are a large part of this novel's appeal. For the narrator to be "unreliable," we would have to believe she is deliberately presenting us with a false account of herself, her actions, and her background (and that we would be able to tell, ultimately, that the account is false), but that she is in effect working out as she goes what she thinks about her situation does not, in my view, make her unreliable. It makes her, as Scott puts it, "by turns tragic, farcical, pathetic, poignant and hilarious."

Eder is ultimately rather contemptuous of "the woman," as he chooses to call her. She is "pitiable," guilty of "track-covering, the shame that flickers beneath the arrogance." She has a "skewed and inflated vision of herself and her life." She is "cold." And indeed the narrator does seem frustrated with her situation, unable to square her sense of her own worth with the increasingly desperate circumstances in which she finds herself. She is certainly impulsive. More than anything, however, she is instinctively unconventional and incapable of settling for "normality"--confronting the possibility of accepting a normal life at the novel's conclusion, she instead lights out for the territory: "Then I go out once more, slamming the door behind me. I like the sound so much, I open the door and slam it shut several times." I suppose one could feel contempt for a woman who doesn't behave as she ought, who turns her back so decisively on domestic bliss, but I just find her a very interesting character quite unlike most protagonists of most literary fiction. Both she and *The Duchess of Nothing* itself are much more convincingly "transgressive" of established norms--of female behavior and of conventional "psychological realism"--than other novels sometimes accorded that label. In short: Anyone interested in a refreshingly different kind of reading experience should read this book.

After re-reading Jim Thompson's *The Grifters*, it became even more apparent to me that Thompson's novels provide an especially useful illustration of the differences between third- and first-person narration in fiction. I still enjoyed *The Grifters*, which is narrated in the third person, but reading it a second time made me more aware of its limitations, as well as the virtues of the first-person narratives to be found in novels such as *The Killer Inside Me, Pop. 1280*, and *After Dark, My Sweet*.

Here are a few paragraphs near the beginning of *After Dark, My Sweet*. The story is being told by "Kid" Collins, the novel's protagonist, and he has stopped in at a roadhouse for a glass of beer:

> The bartender slopped a beer down in front of me. He scooped up the change I'd laid on the counter, sat down on the stool again, and picked up a newspaper. I said something about it was sure a hot day. He grunted without looking up. I said it was a nice pleasant little place he had there and that he certainly knew how to keep his beer cold. He grunted again.

> I looked down at my beer, feeling the short hairs rising on the back of my neck. I guessed--I knew--that I should never have come in here. I should never go in any place where people might not be nice and polite to me.

That's all they have to do, you know. Just be as nice to me as I am to them. . . .

We then learn that Kid Collins has spent some time in "institutions" (eventually that he has just escaped from one), but we really don't need that information to know that something's not quite right with the Kid. His very need to elicit a response from the bartender and those short hairs rising tell us what we need to know. And we wouldn't know it in the same way if the Kid himself wasn't telling us. The novel immediately plunges us into the world of Kid Collins as he is able to articulate it, and most of its melodramatic punch comes from being jolted by the Kid's direct verbal flourishes. (And he is, it turns out, an ex-boxer.)

The Grifters starts out pretty well, too:

> As Roy Dillon stumbled out of the shop his face was sickish green, and each breath he drew was an incredible agony. A hard blow in the guts can do that to a man, and Dillon had gotten a hard one. Now with a fist, which would have been bad enough, but from the butt-end of a heavy club.
>
> Somehow, he got back to his car and managed to slide into the seat. But that was all he could manage. He moaned as the change in posture cramped his stomach muscles; then, with a strangled gasp, he leaned out the window.

Several cars passed as he spewed vomit into the street, their occupants grinning, frowning sympathetically, or averting their eyes in disgust. . . .

This also steeps us immediately into the world as experienced by Roy Dillon, but in *The Grifters* he shares our narrative attention with his mother Lilly and his girlfriend, Moira Langry, and so the story involving the three of them will have to be told by a third-person narrator who has access to their thoughts and emotions but filters them through his own more distanced narrative voice. It's not quite full-blown "psychological realism," but Thompson nevertheless can achieve his signature hard-boiled, scary/depraved effects only by fishing around in the characters' minds for their perceptions of and reactions to the inevitably untoward situations they encounter. The verbally-constructed "voice" of a character like Kid Collins is lost, and we have to pick our way through such vague verbiage as "incredible agony" and be satisfied that just "somehow" Roy Dillon returned to his car.

Thus, while the novel commences with a typical Thompsonesque bang, it's not long before we get a little bogged down in passages like this:

. . .He had looked around extensively and carefully before choosing Los Angeles as a permanent base of operations, and his capital was now reduced to less than a thousand dollars.

That was a lot of money, of course. Unlike the big-con operator, whose elaborate scene-setting may involve as much as a hundred thousand dollars, the short-con grifter can run on peanuts. But Roy Dillon, while remaining loyal to the short con, was abandoning the normal scheme of things.

At twenty-one, he was weary of the hit-and-get. He knew that the constant "getting"--jumping from one town to another before the heat got too hot--could absorb most of the hits, even of a thrifty man. So that he might work as hard and often as he safely could, and still wind up with the wolf nipping at the seat of his threadbare pants. . . .

In my view, we're being given way too much "information" in a passage like this, information that is perhaps important for us to have but that would be less intrusive if it were parceled out gradually by a first-person narrator or if it was at least provided to us <u>dramatically</u>--through showing rather than telling. It would be better, for example, if we saw Roy Dillon "abandoning the normal scheme of things" rather than being told this was the case through an awkward inventory of the contents of Roy's mind. A secondary effect of this third-person technique is the fuzzy, flabby language: "He had looked around extensively"; "can run on peanuts"; "the wolf nipping at the seat of his threadbare pants". Not only does such writing lean heavily on cliche--which again might be more tolerable if it were issuing from a first-person narrator--but it helps to make passages like this themselves seem like just so much perfunctory "scene-setting."

Perhaps this is why I actually prefer the Stephen Frears movie made from *The Grifters* to the novel, something I would not say of the film adapted from *After Dark, My Sweet*. Frears's film is able to dispense with the third-person narrator and focus on the characters and their overlapping stories in a direct, unmediated way. We get Thompson's lowlife plot without his narrator's sometimes laborious attempts to move it along. It is also probably why I think Thompson's best novels are those related to us by his sublimely scuzzy first-person narrators. It's impossible to reproduce these novels on screen because their narrators are so inseparably a part of their appeal. Such is undoubtedly true of most well-devised first-person narrators, which is one reason I believe this method of storytelling is almost always more promising as a way of creating distinctive, aesthetically pleasing works of fiction than the kind of close-in third-person narration that has in most literary fiction become more or less the only available alternative (and that is probably often used precisely because it does lend itself more easily to screen adaptation.)

It seems to me that almost all of the reviewers who found fault with Jonathan Littell's *The Kindly Ones*--some of them quite harshly--failed to take sufficiently into account the effects and implications of its origin in the first-person narration of its protagonist. They made the mistake of imputing to the author, or to the author's "intentions," ideas that are properly confined to the discourse of the narrator.

The first step in a critically generous assessment of a work of fiction has to be to engage with the work on its own embodied terms, as far as those terms can be apprehended by the discerning critic. When a novel or story is presented as a first-person narrative--related either by the protagonist or some other subsidiary or observing character--this ought to be a sign that the account we are given is rooted in the perceptions, the language, and the assumptions of the narrator. All first-person narrators are to this degree "unreliable," although some third-person narrators might be unreliable as well (if such a narrator hews especially close to the perspective of the characters on whose behalf the narrator essentially speaks) and sometimes reliability is mostly irrelevant. Especially when a character is as self-involved, not to mention self-deceived, as Maximilien Aue, the true-believing Nazi SS officer who narrates his war experiences in *The Kindly Ones*, any critical commentary must acknowledge that "meaning" or "theme" (and even at times "style") are conditioned by the limits of the narrator's perspective.

One has to assume that in creating a narrator with such extreme limitations as Dr. Aue, Littell is fully aware of building in a space for ambiguity and uncertainty, of presenting us with a character whose every utterance has to be considered potentially compromised by context. One might assume further that Littell is posing to readers an explicit challenge precisely to scrutinize the text in this way, not to take it as the author's own account of Nazism or to judge it by standards inappropriate to the kind of work it is. Thus when Laila Lalami complains that the reader of *The Kindly Ones* is not "drawn into the narrative by the beauty of the language, a masterful use of point of view, or an intriguing personal life against which the monstrosity of the main character could be highlighted," she implies the novel would be less objectionable as a portrait of a "monster" if instead of its "plodding style" it employed beautiful language, unified the point of view so that the narrator seemed less dissociated, or made Aue's personal life more "intriguing" and less repellent. She is asking it to be something other than itself, something less troublesome (*Los Angeles Times*, March 15, 2009).

For a text authored by an SS bureaucrat to exhibit "beautiful" language would defy belief even more considerably than does Aue's ability to show up at every important stage of the Final Solution, which Lalami describes as "unrealistic." If ever a novel justifies a "plodding style," *The Kindly Ones* is it, since it so accurately reflects Aue's bureaucratic soul. I confess I do not find this novel lacking "a single narrative consciousness" as Lalami sums up her problem with Littell's handling of point of view, although I agree that Aue's narration does modulate in tone.

This seems to me, however, a consequence of the fact that Aue's "narrative consciousness" inherently veers from "confessional" to "argumentative," etc., not that this fragmentation is a flaw in the use of point of view. Narrative consciousness is finally unified by Aue's particular kind of fragmented consciousness, although even if we found only disunity in the expression of point of view, I'm not sure why that in itself should be regarded as an aesthetic failure. It could be argued that "unity" of consciousness in fiction is actually a false representation of actual human consciousness, which is likely much more disunifed than we want to think.

That Maximilien Aue's "personal life" is so distasteful as to make his story doubly monstrous was a common reaction among reviewers of *The Kindly Ones*. David Gates asserts in his *New York Times Book Review* assessment that "Aue is simply too much of a freak, and his supposed childhood trauma too specialized and contrived, for us to take him seriously" (March 5, 2009) while Michiko Kakutani adds that "Aue is clearly a deranged creature, and his madness turns his story into a voyeuristic spectacle" (*New York Times*, February 23, 2009). Ruth Franklin scoffs that the novel's "utterly persuasive evocation of depravity" could be taken "as a sign of achievement." Franklin's review in particular evoked the critical queasiness stirred up by Littell's novel, with its widely quoted remark that "This is one of the most repugnant books I have ever read." She further contends that "there is something awry in this book's unremitting immersion in Aue's worldview, without any effort--

direct or indirect, latent or manifest, philosophical or artistic--to balance or counteract it in any way" (*The New Republic*, April 1, 2009). Melvin Jules Bukiet claims similarly that it is "not that a reader necessarily seeks a lesson, but fiction and nonfiction ought to approach the subject as more than an opportunity to wallow in the worst humankind has to offer" (*Washington Post*, March 7, 2009), and these two comments most explicitly reveal the incomprehension with which so many American reviewers of *The Kindly Ones* reacted to the narrative constructed by its protagonist.

Both Franklin and Bukiet implicitly testify here to the success with which Littell has given over the novel to his protagonist's *Weltenschauung*, a word Aue himself uses frequently, even if they also find that aesthetic act objectionable. In my opinion, a novel could do worse than engage in an "unremitting immersion" in its character's worldview, or, for that matter, "wallow in the worst humankind has to offer." That the critic found himself wallowing seems an indication that Littell has indeed created a compelling "narrative consciousness" that brings us uncomfortably close to an unsavory character with a repulsive worldview, not to mention overwhelming psychological problems.

Does an author have a responsibility to "balance" a character's unpleasant views or behavior with normative gestures, either "latent or manifest," indicating the author disapproves of the character's opinions and actions? Surely no reader believes that Littell <u>does</u> approve of his character's actions, so the perceived problem here must be that exposure to a character like Maximilien Aue will unduly soil the sensibilities of the reader. But surely no one expects readers to be converted to Nazism or sadomasochism through Aue's account of himself, either, so one must conclude that Franklin's and Bukiet's dislike of an "unremitting immersion in Aue's worldview" has been converted into a general critical requirement that bad people as depicted in fiction must be "counteracted" by a "philosophical or artistic " effort to meliorate their evil. One suspects that, despite his protestation that we don't necessarily need a "lesson" from such a novel as *The Kindly Ones*, Bukiet would prefer that its unmediated access to the point of view of a morally compromised protagonist be placed in a more didactically clear context as a corrective to "wallowing."

What is going to focus our attention on "the worst humankind has to offer" if not, at least occasionally, fiction? Is this a subject that ought to be ignored or forbidden? Why not write (or read) a novel that allows a Nazi SS man to speak of his experiences as witness to and participant in the attempted extermination of Jews and any other undesirable people? For such a novel to be successful it will almost necessarily offend and disturb some readers, but that is the consequence of attempting the work in the first place. Taking offense--or finding the novel "repugnant"--is not a credible aesthetic judgment, and in my opinion most of the negative reviews of *The Kindly Ones* lack credibility because they were either explicit expressions of distaste of this kind or thinly disguised versions of such distaste masquerading as critique of character and plot logic.

The major accomplishment of *The Kindly Ones* is the author's thoroughly successful ventriloquism of Dr. Aue, a performance that requires we abide this character in all of his true-believing, sadomasochistic, murderous horror or else the effort is subsumed into the usual safe moralizing provided by "balance." Balance would only produce a cop show-like view of evil, which is comfortably softened by the presence of reassuring outrage at human perfidy. It could be argued that this sort of easy portrayal of the conflict between decency and depravity is false to the actual content of evil, a sentimentalized response. It seems to me that, precisely to the extent Littell has avoided "balance," he has given us a more persuasive representation of evil, something that we must experience for ourselves in its half banality, half degeneracy through Aue's recitation. Only this "unremitting immersion" gets us anywhere near the reality of evil.

Some reviewers focused their criticism of *The Kindly Ones* more on its deficiencies of plot than on a moral repugnance toward its narrator. Lalami observes that "like Forrest Gump, [Aue] conveniently manages to be wherever the most significant events of the war take place, at the time in which they take place, and to interact with all the relevant figures of

Nazism," a plot progression which Zak M. Salih describes as "a collection of the Nazi regime's greatest hits" (*Baltimore City Paper*, April 8, 2009). Peter Kemp further complains of the "pitiless prolixity" with which Aue tells his story and doubts "Aue's prodigious capacity to recall in profuse, minute detail all that was done and said. . . " (*The Sunday Times*, March 1, 2009). That a fussy bureaucrat like Maximilien Aue would remember his actions in great detail--that he might even have records of them--doesn't seem that far-fetched to me, but the question of whether Aue knows too much brings us back to Aue's status as narrator. Perhaps he does too conveniently recall the details of his wartime experiences. As far as I know, no one has questioned the accuracy of the historical details in which Aue's fictionalized story is embedded, but of course there is no way to "verify" the details of the fictional story. Ultimately, it really makes no difference: these are the things that were "done and said" that Aue wants us to know, and the impression they leave about him is presumably the impression he wants to leave.

The same is true of the plot developments that place Aue at so many of the crucial events of the war's waning years. Perhaps Aue is manipulating the historical record in order to give himself a role in all of these events, but again it doesn't really matter. The self-portrayal that emerges is the one Aue must intend. That this portrayal is a damning one suggests either that Aue is (consciously or subconsciously) submitting himself for judgment or that his particular involvement in the Final Solution is to be taken at face value. The former is not impossible, especially given his willingness to reveal all of his psychosexual problems as well. However, accepting that Aue happened to be in a position to witness so much of Nazi Germany's dissolution, at least for the purposes of the novel his fictional existence makes possible, doesn't seem to me such a difficult concession. His presence at the decisive stages of this process could just be, in fact, the reason he decided to write his memoir, following up on the less comprehensive accounts of other ex-Nazi colleagues.

Whatever degree of artifice Littell has brought to the plot of *The Kindly Ones*--at least that part of the plot devoted to chronicling the extermination program as it leads Aue from the Ukraine to Hitler's bunker--I found it riveting. Unlike some commentators who concluded that through the recounting of these events with their frequent expressions of dismay with the program and its methods, Littell was attempting to "humanize" Dr. Aue, I found the portrait of SS officers manifesting a degree of struggle with the task they'd been assigned a compelling alternative to the usual image of Nazis as unambiguously malevolent. To this extent, a character like Aue is humanized, but this only makes his and his fellow officer's actions more appalling, since they arise from recognizable human beings rather than caricatures. Some of these actions, such as the Babi Yar massacre, are hard to take, but their depiction commands attention.

One element of the novel's narrative structure does threaten to become overly artificial. Overlain on the story of Aue's war journey is a parallel association with Aeschylus's *Oresteia,* featuring Aue as Orestes (a device similar to the "mythic method" of Joyce's *Ulysses*). Ultimately these parallels might be a little too neat. Daniel Mendelsohn does a good job of teasing out the implications of this strategy in his review of *The Kindly Ones* (the title being a direct reference to the "furies" of Aeschylus's play, who are transformed at the end of the play into "kindly ones"), and while I agree with Mendelsohn that Littell employs the strategy skillfully, I can't agree that the problem it causes is that, in portraying Aue as "a sex-crazed, incestuous, homosexual, matricidal coprophage," it works against the historical portrayal of Aue as a "human brother" (*New York Review of Books*, March 26, 2009). I just don't perceive any effort on Littell's effort to affirm Aue as a "human brother," as opposed to simply a "human being," and it does not make him into something other than a human being to imply, metaphorically, that Aue is a man pursued by his own sort of "furies."

What makes me less enamored of the mythic method as employed in *The Kindly Ones* is precisely that it threatens to disrupt our "immersion" in Aue's fictional memoir, that it intrudes on the performance of Aue's narration a different kind of performance, one that makes us too conscious of the author-- Jonathan Littell--as the puppeteer pulling Aue's strings. For an exercise in point of view like *The Kindly Ones* to work most efficaciously, it ought to commit itself fully to the discourse of the narrator, and in my opinion the narrative doubling introduced by the Orestes story detracts from that commitment.

Unless. In his review of the novel, Paul La Farge comments that "If it were only Aue making himself out to be Orestes, you'd dismiss the gesture as an unjustified but understandable bid for sympathy, but it's Littell who puts Aue through Orestes's paces, as if to give credence to Aue's assertion that 'in this [life] I never had a choice,' that his free will was curtailed by 'the weight of fate'" (*The Believer*, May 2009). Of course it is finally Littell "who puts Aue through Orestes's paces" in that Aue is the narrator of the novel Littell has written. In this sense, Littell puts Aue through all of his "paces." But there's nothing really to prevent us from attributing most, if not all, of the allusions to the *Oresteia* to Aue himself, either through the many direct references he makes or through both the additions and omissions (such as the episode in which he kills his mother and her husband, which he subsequently can't remember) he brings to bear on the story he wants to tell. If Aue attempts a play on our sympathy through these allusions--"I never had a choice"-- we can accept it as such without believing his resort to this grandiosity actually absolves him of blame.

I'm not really sure I fully embrace this interpretation. The heavy-handed allusiveness may just be an aesthetic mistake, a secondary flaw we have to countenance while otherwise acknowledging the narrative power of the novel as a whole. *The Kindly Ones* rather early on overwhelmed my own general disdain for history-based fiction not by "bringing history to life" but by bringing life to history.

IV Style

In a post at his weblog *sIngularity* (October 29, 2004), Trent Walters objects to the paucity of compelling characters in the horror fiction he's been reading for review. He then goes on to speculate about how "character" in fiction is created.

> There are two obvious extremes of characterization (obvious because of their extremity) that help writers to quickly sketch a vividly realized character. One is the crazy or really weird character common to the literary story. Writers do this often to get noticed by a literary magazine, to do something that hasn't been seen. The other is the object or affectation of the character's that distinguishes this character from the others. He's the thin man, the fat man, the girl with the bone through her nose, the three-legged dog, the boy who stutters.

> But neither rendering has much to do with character except that they both quickly sketch what a character appears to be, but appearances don't capture the reality of a character. Actions characterize the character (or, in the case of Hamlet, inaction, which is still an act). . . .

It may be true that in some fiction--perhaps in horror fiction more than most, although I have my doubts about this--character emerges mostly from "action," but I would propose that in the very best fiction, genre or otherwise, character is actually just an illusion created by the use of language in a particular way--by a writer's style, although the illusion thus created may be more or less a conscious act, may in fact be simply an artifact of the stylistic choices the writer has made to begin with.

It is sometimes said that among the first "realistic" characters in works of fiction are those to be found in the novels of Jane Austen. They seem quite firmly rooted to the soil of real life, restrained in their actions and words in comparison to most of the fiction of the 18th century, where realism tends to be sacrificed in favor of color and narrative dynamism. But isn't this a consequence of Austen's style, which is itself quite understated and restrained? To the extent a character like Elizabeth Bennet seems to us a very levelheaded and quietly witty woman, isn't this because Jane Austen is a very calm and quietly witty writer? What else do we need to know about Jane and Elizabeth Bennet beyond what we learn from this brief exchange early on in *Pride and Prejudice* about Mr. Bingley: "'He is just what a young man ought to be,' said [Jane], 'sensible, good-humored, lively; and I never saw such happy manners!--so much ease, with such perfect good breeding!' 'He is also handsome,' replied Elizabeth, 'which a young man ought likewise to be, if he possibly can. His character is thereby complete.'" How much of the effect on our perception of character comes from the revelations of "speech" in the ordinary sense, and how much from the fact Jane Austen is a master at composing very sly and exquisitely worded dialogue?

Likewise, Dickens's characters are usually described as outsized and vigorous (and they are), but how often do we pause to consider how outsized and vigorous Dicken's own style actually is? Don't his characters come across to us in the way they do because of that style? Even the minor characters in Dickens are always vivid, partly because of Dickens's strategy of picking out one or two habits or features and exaggerating them, but also simply through Dicken's forceful and distinctive way of writing, as in this brief account of "Mr. Fang," from *Oliver Twist*:

> Mr. Fang was a lean, long-backed, stiff-necked, middle-sized man, with no great quality of hair, and what he had, growing on the back and sides of his head. His face was stern, and much flushed. If he were really not in the habit of drinking rather more than was exactly good for him, he might have brought an action against his countenance for libel, and have recovered heavy damages.

It could be said that the effect of a passage such as this comes more from what is usually called "voice" rather than style per se, but what else is voice in writing but the concrete effect created on the printed page by an appropriate arrangement of words and sentences and paragraphs? Dickens's style, garrulous but pointed, seemingly ingenuous but actually quite caustic at times ("brought an action against his countenance for libel, and have recovered heavy damages" seems a delicate way to put it, but is really very cutting), might be called "theatrical," but so might all of his characters, their theatricality a reflection of the language used to create them.

Similarly, the characters in Henry James's fiction, which most readers find quite convincing even when the fictions themselves are judged to be somewhat short on dramatic action, share the obsessed and ratiocinative qualities of James's style. When James Joyce or Virginia Woolf create character through the use of the stream-of-consciousness technique, the characters that emerge, Leopold Bloom or Mrs. Dalloway, aren't compelling because of the "content" of their thinking or even because we're given a glimpse into the way they think, but because of the manipulations of language and expected novelistic discourse that each author performs. Literally, it's the strange way in which the words--broken up, rearranged, discontinuous--are put down on the page. "Character" in *Ulysses* or *Mrs. Dalloway* can't be separated from these purposeful arrangements of words.

To use an example from genre fiction: How much more do we ever really learn about Chandler's Philip Marlowe than we do from the very first paragraph of *The Big Sleep*, as Marlowe stands before the Sternwood house?:

It was about eleven o'clock in the morning, mid-October, with the sun not shining and a look of hard wet rain in the clearness of the foothills. I was wearing my powder-blue suit, with dark blue shirt, tie and display handkerchief, black brogues, black wool socks with dark blue clocks on them. I was neat, clean, shaved and sober, and I didn't care who knew it. I was everything the well-dressed private detective ought to be. I was calling on four million dollars.

Everything we associate with Marlowe is here, manifested in this brief but punchy paragraph: his powers of observation, his self-deprecating, wiseass attitude, accomplished through a demotic yet also eloquent style. And in this case it is specifically a <u>writing</u> style, as Marlowe is the narrator of his own adventures, which ultimately makes it impossible for us to separate Marlowe the writer from Marlowe the "character." The "action" in which Marlowe always becomes embroiled is fun to read, perhaps even keeps us reading, but for me such action adds little to my perception of him as a character, which is also always being reinforced by the way in which he describes this action to us.

First-person narration makes it most apparent that it is style--voice, if you wish--that evokes character, not action, certainly not the quirks or affectations that some writers try to use to force characters into being "vivid," to return to the comments quoted above. Not only is the narrator's own character what we discern through his/her style, but all the other characters about whom such a narrator might speak clearly enough are what they are because of the way this narrator speaks about them. But good writers approach third-person narration in the same way they would a first-person narrator. It is itself a character, a voice, with his/her/its own distinctive way of summoning a fictive world through writing. Perhaps at his point you have to say that character and style are indivisible, but this is where "the reality of a character" has to start.

There are some writers for whom style supersedes character, for whom the "authorial" character is the main character, and their fiction doesn't suffer in the least from it. Stanley Elkin is such a writer. His characters are believable enough, vivid certainly, but their vividness comes not from any externally imposed "features," fastened onto the characters like artificial limbs. It comes from Elkin's inimitable and inexhaustibly inventive style. Here is a third-person account of Ben Flesh, protagonist of *The Franchiser*:

> *Forbes* would not have heard of him. *Fortune* wouldn't. There would be no color photographs of him, sharp as holograph, in high-backed executive leathers, his hand a fist on wide mahogany plateaus of desk, his collar white as an admiral's against his dark, timeless suits. There would be no tall columns of beautifully justified

print apposite full-page ads for spanking new business machines with their queer space-age vintages, their coded analogues to the minting of postage, say, or money--the TermiNet 1200, the Reliant 700, Canon's L-1610, the NCR 399-- numbers like license plates on federal limousines or the markings on aircraft.

Though he actually used some of this stuff. G.E. had an answer for his costly data volume traffic; Kodak had found a practical alternative to his paper filing. He had discussed his microform housing needs with Ring King Visibles. He had come into the clean, bright world of Kalvar. A special card turned even a telephone booth into a WATS line. Still, *Fortune* would do no profile. *Signature*, the Diners Club magazine, had never shown an interest; TWA's *Ambassador* hadn't. There was no color portrait of him next to the mail-order double knits and shoes.

(It's worth noting how Elkin here describes Flesh by what he's *not*; all the clutter of detail only produces a stereotype that Ben Flesh mercifully avoids.)

Here's a first-person narrator, from *The Bailbondsman*:

So I'm Alexander Main, the Phoenician Bailbondsman, other men's difficulties my heritage. Alexander Main the Ba'albondsman, doing his duty by the generations and loving it, thriving on the idea of freedom which is my money in the bank, which is my element as the sand was my ancestors'.

So give the Phoenician your murderer, your rapist, your petty thief yearning to breathe free. Give him your stickup guy and embezzler, your juvenile delinquent and car robber. Give him you subversives and menslaughterers. I *like* dealing with the public.

Pretty clearly both Ben Flesh and Alexander Main are really Stanley Elkin. Or "Stanley Elkin," the manufactured authorial presence. In many ways, all of Elkin's characters seem just like all the others, are versions of this most important character, the writer. No one who loves Stanley Elkin's work, as I do, could want it any other way. Who needs characters when you can be carried along by writing like this?

The Mumpsimus (May 15, 2004) points us to an essay on Angela Carter in which Carter is quoted as saying "I've got nothing against realism. . .[b]ut there is realism and realism. I mean, the questions that I ask myself, I think they are very much to do with reality. I would like, I would really like to have had the guts and the energy and so on to be able to write about, you know, people having battles with the DHSS, but I, I haven't. I've done other things. I mean, I'm an arty person, ok, I write overblown, purple, self-indulgent prose - so fucking what?"

The defensiveness with which Carter speaks here is well-justified. Not only was she accused of being un-British in her choice of subjects and her prose style, but writers like Carter, who willingly employ an "overblown, purple, self-indulgent prose" are frequently treated not like they are in some way bad writers but are actually bad people. I am frequently amazed at the vehemence with which some reviewers and readers react against stories or novels that are unconventional or stylistically "excessive." The authors of such works are regarded as deviant, hostile to "ordinary" readers, just plain contemptuous of good order in matters of storytelling and style. (Even a writer as conventional as John Updike is sometimes attacked for these sins.) And woe indeed to the writer who, like Carter, combines an extra-realistic approach and a "purple" prose.

An essay in the Spring 2004 issue of *Raritan* reprises these once-infamous remarks by Philip Roth:

> . . .I set myself the goal of becoming the writer some Jewish critics had been telling me I was all along: irresponsible, conscienceless, <u>unserious</u>. A quotation from Melville began to intrigue me, from a letter he had sent to Hawthorne upon completing *Moby Dick*. . ."I have written a wicked book and feel spotless as a lamb." Now I knew

that no matter hard I tried I could never really hope to be wicked; but perhaps if I worked long and hard and diligently, I could be frivolous.

And indeed from *Portnoy's Complaint* on, Roth produced numerous books that were "frivolous" in comparison to his earlier work, that went beyond the bounds of decorum in structure and good taste in style, that were "excessive" in many, many ways, but . . .so fucking what? They are also books that will continue to stand as among the best American novels written in the latter part of the twentieth century. They are all clearly the consequence of "hard and long and diligent" work, and in their very excesses and frivolity are as serious as anything written by more obviously earnest writers of the time, including Roth's colleague Saul Bellow.

Yet there are still readers who can only see the frivolity-- that is the comedy, as savage as it can sometimes become--and the excesses--Roth's frequently freewheeling style--and who regard books like *Sabbath's Theater* and *Operation Shylock* as fundamentally not serious, as irresponsible treatments of subjects that ought to be treated in a grim and sober way. They welcomed, on the other hand, *American Pastoral*, because it seemed closer to this more earnest approach. I think Roth would probably agree with Carter in every particular of her statement, and both of these writers could serve as models of the sort of writers willing to endure the charges that their writing is an example of moral failure, as long as it is ultimately seen, rightly, as an aesthetic triumph.

Whenever I hear or read someone urging writers to be "clear," to "communicate," to avoid "trickery," I can only take it as an exhortation to be good. Not to offend official sensibilities or imply that many readers are too timid in their willingness to take risks. In the name of literary decency not to engage in "too much writing." Perhaps in the long run these stylistic gatekeepers can be persuaded that literary form and style have nothing to do with morality, but most of them probably don't really much like literature, anyway, if "literature" is more than just an opportunity to assert your own virtue.

According to Zadie Smith, in a 2007 *Guardian* essay showered with much praise for its "honesty:

> . . .writers do have a different kind of knowledge than either professors or critics. Occasionally it's worth listening to. The insight of the practitioner is, for better or worse, unique. It's what you find in the criticism of Virginia Woolf, of Iris Murdoch, of Roland Barthes. What unites those very different critics is the confidence with which they made the connection between personality and prose. To be clear: theirs was neither strictly biographical criticism nor prescriptively moral criticism, and nothing they wrote was reducible to the childish

formulations "only good men write good books" or "one must know a man's life to understand his work". But neither did they think of a writer's personality as an irrelevance. They understood style precisely as an expression of personality, in its widest sense. A writer's personality is his manner of being in the world: his writing style is the unavoidable trace of that manner. When you understand style in these terms, you don't think of it as merely a matter of fanciful syntax, or as the flamboyant icing atop a plain literary cake, nor as the uncontrollable result of some mysterious velocity coiled within language itself. Rather, you see style as a personal necessity, as the only possible expression of a particular human consciousness. Style is a writer's way of telling the truth. Literary success or failure, by this measure, depends not only on the refinement of words on a page, but in the refinement of a consciousness, what Aristotle called the education of the emotions.

Style is "an expression of personality" It's also a mark of the writer's "manner of being in the world." It's also "a personal necessity. . .the only possible expression of a particular human consciousness." It's also "a writer's way of telling the truth." It's also "the refinement of a consciousness." And it's also the "education of the emotions."

That's an awful lot of weight to heap on words and sentences and paragraphs, especially in fiction, which, except in the hands of narcissists and pseudo-philosophers, is not a medium for the "expression" of anything, but the attempt to convince your readers that words on a page evoke a "world," and to make something aesthetically pleasing out of prose. If you can do this, then all of the handwringing about "human consciousness" and "telling the truth" and educating emotions is just so much pomp and circumstance.

Frankly, I really don't know what any of the declarations made in the above-quoted passage are even supposed to mean. How am I to know anything about the writer's "personality" from reading his novel? I don't care about his personality in the first place; I want to know what he can do with words. He can take his "personality" to his therapist. "A writer's personality is his manner of being in the world: his writing style is the unavoidable trace of that manner." Is this like "grace under pressure"? The writer goes around perfecting his "manner" and then transfers his concocted "lifestyle" to the printed page?

There's no way that fiction can embody the writer's personality. Personality is itself a fiction that we use to make overgeneralizations about ourselves and other people. At best, a work of fiction might create what seems to be a personality "behind" the work, but this doesn't happen with all fiction (and T. S. Eliot was right in suggesting that good writers try to avoid it, anyway) and to equate that personality with the "real" personality of the writer is only a mark of bad reading. Neither of these personalities exist in the first place.

I suppose style could be "the expression of a particular human consciousness" if the writer's "consciousness" was itself the subject being explored. That is, if the writer was writing some kind of psychological memoir rather than fiction. But I don't see how consciousness in this pretentious way of speaking about it is even at issue in the writing of fiction, and I certainly don't see how style has anything to do with getting it expressed. A good writer's style does exhibit certain continuities and characteristics over time, but is this an effect of "consciousness"? Isn't it just a function of that writer's particular way of living with language? (Perhaps in alluding to the expression of "consciousness," Smith is actually referring to the creation of consciousness in fictional characters, the pursuit of "psychological realism," but this is not how I read the passage in question.)

Similarly, style as a way of "telling the truth" might be plausible if by this we mean that the writer has found the right style--the right words and sentences and paragraphs--to evoke the fictional world he/she is after. If it means "telling the truth" about the characters and events portrayed <u>in the fiction</u>. If it means telling the truth in some more metaphysical sense, telling the truth about The Way Things Really Are, to me such pronouncements are just cant.

Smith makes her essentially anti-style view of style most explicit when she concludes that style has something to do with "the refinement of a consciousness" rather than refinement of "words on a page." "Style" in art and literature is a material characteristic, an identifiable, distinctive arrangement and rearrangement of the elements of the medium, whether that be language, paint, musical sound, etc. It is not some ineffable, mystical quality, a "personal necessity," something these people have but those do not. Literary style is the means by which accomplished writers manipulate language for aesthetic effect. You can educate your emotions all you'd like, but if you haven't created something aesthetically pleasing with your words, you haven't succeeded as a writer of fiction.

In her own response to Smith's essay, Jenny Davidson carries the argument to its unfortunate conclusion: "I find in particular as a reader that my doubts about a particular writer's style (his/her sentences, say) can rarely be expressed in strictly aesthetic terms, it always shades into questions of character--it is good to see Zadie Smith saying that so clearly here" (*Light Reading*, January 12, 2007). Here we return to the notion of "style as moral failure." The inevitable consequence of associating a writer's "sentences" with "questions of character" (with the "expression" of character) is to confuse a response to writing as a response to the writer. A failure of art becomes a moral defect. Conversely, an artistic success becomes a vindication of "character," the experience of art reduced to the degree of one's sympathy with the artist, however much a figment of the imagination he/she turns out to be. Compared to these "refinements of consciousness" the writer makes available, all discussion of the skill with which he/she organizes "words on a page" is, of course, "merely literary."

When I read *On the Road* for the first time, I didn't care for it much. I didn't exactly hate it, but I was disappointed. I had not at that time developed the suspicion of writers and novels alleged to be "saying something" that I now have, but I do recall being puzzled by the reputation--conveyed to me by fellow graduate students, I must say--this novel had of being a radical statement of postwar restlessness, or disaffected youth, or spiritual exhaltation, or whatever other urgent "content" *On the Road* was supposed to offer. I couldn't find any statements at all in it, although the characters certainly seemed restless, occasionally expressed disaffection (but not with the government or what could be conveniently labeled "the culture"), and at times appeared to be in a state of exhaltation (frequently drug- or alcohol-induced, but not always). The novel's style, as well, though obviously unconventional, did not at the time fulfill my expectations of what a transgressive style might accomplish.

In short, *On the Road* seemed rather tame to me, its rebellion more ingenuously earnest than hard-edged, and I read no further Kerouac for many years. Not too long ago, I decided to try reading *On the Road* again, expecting that I would quickly enough find it the same tepid experience as the first time around, that I would in fact probably stop reading it fairly early on and consign Kerouac permanently to the category of literary disappointments. However, although I can't say I immediately became entranced by it, I did not stop reading it. I did almost immediately judge the novel's protagonist, Sal Paradise, to be a more interesting character than I had previously, when he seemed to be mostly a cipher. Now I saw his restlessness as a genuine craving for experience, not affectation or pretense. At the same time, I found Dean Moriarty a less annoying character than I had the first time around, although I still wouldn't identify his appearances in the novel as necessarily among its highlights. I suspect that the reputation as an "outlaw" text to which I responded impatiently in my initial reading of *On the Road* originates in an over-identification with Moriarty, who some readers took to be the novel's most important character. I think Sal Paradise is obviously the main character, and while Moriarty has his role to play in the intensification of Sal Paradise's immersion in experience, he <u>does</u> still too often come off as affected and pretentious, and future critics and scholars would do the novel a service by focusing more on the way his character reinforces the novel's formal and stylistic ambitions and less on his dubious deeds and spurious words of wisdom.

It was precisely the formal and stylistic qualities of *On the Road* that I eventually found myself appreciating more charitably on this second read. I think I originally experienced *On the Road* as essentially formless, even though I understood it was very loosely structured as a "picaresqe" narrative ("very loosely" being the characteristic I noticed most). What now seems clearer to me is the strategy by which Kerouac both enlists the picaresque strategy--which is often thought of as a kind of denial of form, although it really isn't--and fractures it even further to convey an impression of "spontaneous" action that the novel merely chronicles. *On the Road* invokes the journey motif associated with picaresque, but where most classic picaresque narratives present the journey as a serial, unbroken series of episodes that lead directly to journey's end, *On the Road* fragments the journey, leaves it off only to pick it up again, the episodes united by the participation of Sal Paradise, who meets up with and then departs from the various characters who contribute to his effort of "going West to see the country," as he puts it in the novel's first paragraph. The novel thus can be taken as an experiment with the picaresque form specifically, but also as an effective application of "form" more generally.

I never really agreed with the criticism that as a stylist Kerouac at best exhibits a "plain" style or that, at worst, in his dependence on the declarative mode his is essentially a style without style. He <u>does</u> frequently employ the declarative mode, but this approach also prompts Kerouac to long, cumulative sentences that invoke a kind of lyricism:

In Newburgh it had stopped raining. I walked down to the river, and I had to ride back to New York in a bus coming back from a weekend in the mountains-- chatter-chatter, blah-blah, and me swearing for all the time and the money I'd wasted, and telling myself, I wanted to go west and here I've been all day and into the night going up and down, north and south, like something that can't get started. And I swore I'd be in Chicago tomorrow, and made sure of that, taking a bus to Chicago, spending most of my money, and didn't give a damn, just as long as I'd be in Chicago tomorrow.

It's true that Kerouac's prose does not much incorporate traditional figurative language--more of which may be what I was looking for in my initial reading of *On The Road*--but sentence length and structure are as much a part of "style" as metaphor or simile, and Kerouac's style is not just dedicated to moving the story along. This passage doesn't so much move forward as it does spin in circles once the essential action--getting on the bus-- is established. It might seem that Sal Paradise is impatient to get beyond the usual recording of scene--"chatter-chatter, blah-blah"- -but Kerouac uses that impatience to motivate Sal's creation of an alternative way of writing that mostly avoids fancy phrasing and obligatory dialogue (although Kerouac's novels have plenty of dialogue--it's just not of the ornamental variety) without sacrificing an attention to language to the exigencies of plot. An examination of a passage such as this one also shows that

Kerouac was not oblivious to the effects of pace, rhythm, and variety: the short first sentence of the paragraph sets up the expansive second sentence, which is followed by the still-lengthy but more an afterthought final sentence.

Kerouac famously described his method of composition as "spontaneous prose," designed to mimic the spontaneity of jazz musicians. I take Kerouac to be sincere in his description of the aims and nature of this method, and it seems to capture the real achievement of Kerouac's fiction. It is dangerous to impute "development" in Kerouac's work, since the publication dates and the dates of composition of his books are so much at variance. (*On the Road* was written in the late 40s, while the published follow-up, *The Dharma Bums*, was written in 1957, *after* many of the subsequently published novels.) However, it does seem to me that in reading Kerouac's novels in the order of their publication it is in *The Subterraneans* (published 1958) that we really see a more radical version of spontaneous prose. We can see it as early as the novel's second paragraph:

> . . .I was coming down the street with Larry O'Hara old drinking buddy of mine from all the times in San Francisco in my long and nervous and mad careers I've gotten drunk and in fact cadged drinks off friends with such "genial" regularity nobody really cared to notice or announce that I am developing or was developing, in my youth, such bad freeloading habits though of course they

did not notice but liked me and as Sam said "Everybody comes to you for your gasoline boy, that's some filling station you got there" or say words to that effect--old Larry O'Hara always nice to me, a crazy Irish young businessman of San Francisco with Balzacian backroom in his bookstore where they'd smoke tea and talk of the old days of the great Basie band or the days of the great Chu Berry--of whom more anon since she got involved with him too as she had to get involved with everyone because of knowing me who am nervous and many leveled and not in the least one-souled--not a piece of my pain has showed yet--or suffering--Angels, bear with me, I'm not even looking at the page but straight ahead into the sadglint of my wallroom and at a Sarah Vaughan Gerry Mulligan KROW show on the desk in the form of a radio, in other words, they were sitting on the fender of the car in front of the Black Mask bar on Montgomery Street, Julien Alexander the Christlike unshaved thin youthful quiet strange almost as you or as Adam might say apocalyptic angel or saint of the subterraneans certainly star (now), and she, Mardou Fox, whose face when I first saw it in Dante's bar around the corner made me think, "By God, I've got to get involved with that little woman" and maybe too because she was Negro. . . .

The free-flowing disregard for sentence boundaries is very pronounced here, but this of course does not mean the passage lacks all structure or does not bear up under analysis. The fused clauses and phrases set up their own kind of rhythm, which can be heard if one reads the passage with care. The first three lines encourage us to read without pausing but the forced pause created by the quotation marks around "genial" allow us to catch our breath before moving on through the next two lines and arriving at the inserted nonrestrictive "in my youth." Since Kerouac otherwise so insistently abandons the comma in such a passage, we must assume that the commas here are quite intentional, a way of creating musical effect, a staccato-like phrase that lead to the different kind of variation provided by the quoted words from "Sam." Similar effects are created in the rest of the passage through the use of dashes, which also introduces digressions that reinforce the analogy with jazz improvisation, and additional inserted commas, parentheses, and quotation.

This stylistic strategy seems to me a genuine contribution to literary stylistics specifically and to American literature more generally. It also makes The *Subterrraneans* itself an important text both in postwar American fiction and American literature as a whole. Combined with the novel's relative brevity (in my copy, 111 pages), the "bop prosody" of *The Subterraneans* makes it a work at least as close to poetry as to "fiction" equated in the modern era with "storytelling," in which "style" is often enough just another element of "craft" when it isn't disregarded altogether. *The Subterraneans* is probably just as revelatory of the "underground" culture of the 1950s as anything else written during the era, but it is less likely to be regarded as a work whose documentary value exceeds its literary merit. *On the Road* will no doubt continue to be taken as Kerouac's signature work, but I now think *The Subterraneans* will be more highly regarded by future readers as an innovative work of prose.

The criticism frequently leveled at *The Subterraneans*, that it offers, through the character of Mardou Fox, a severely limited portrayal both of women and African-Americans will probably linger into the future as well, but while it is true enough that the novel's narrator, Leo Percepied, has a view of women and African-Americans constricted by his background and the era in which he lives, his affair with Mardou is inextricably linked to his desire for experience (a trait he shares with all of Kerouac's protagonists), which in this novel means an affinity with the "subterraneans" of the title and an immediate curiosity about Mardou, who most strongly evokes the "Other" for Percepied. The limitations of Percepied's assumptions about gender or race have to be balanced against his acceptance of a way of life not much in accord with the cultural norms his background and the era would have him affirm. I think most readers are/will be able to strike this balance.

One could argue that Mardou isn't really much developed as a character at all, as neither are any of the other characters in this novel, even, to some extent, Percepied. Our sense of knowing them only incompletely, however, is probably an unavoidable consequence of Kerouac's method in *The Subterraneans*. It is a novel less concerned with the delineation of character than with it narrator's response to his experience and its delineation in language.

PART SIX

Saying Something

I Critiquing American Society

In an essay about the "feud" between the critic Irving Howe and the novelist Ralph Ellison about the role of "protest" in fiction, Darryl Lorenzo Wellington observes:

. . .Whereas Ellison saw a danger in collective generalizations, Howe was attuned to the perils of erasing society. In his autobiography, *A Margin of Hope*, Howe asks, "Since language has unbreakable ties to possible events in experience, can the meaning or value of a work be apprehended without some resort—be it as subtle and indirect as you wish—to social and moral categories?" The quote is taken from a passage on Howe's student days, studying the tenets of the New Critics and their aspiration to substitute close analysis of a text for the study of background historical forces. Typically for projects this high-minded, the New Critics failed to see that "the evaluative terms offered by New Criticism— terms like coherence and complexity—were heavily freighted with associations drawn from history, psychology, morality. Is there any evaluative term not so freighted, and must not any attempt to find purely 'intrinsic' values wither into sterility?" (*Dissent*, Summer 2005)

Howe's contention that because "language has unbreakable ties to possible events in experience" criticism must attend to "social and moral categories" is an argument that is very frequently made by those who believe that literature transcends mere "art." It is these "unbreakable ties" between language and the reality it represents that make literature different than, say, painting or music. These forms are freer to "be themselves"--to create a closed-off space where aesthetic qualities are allowed a degree of autonomy--than literature because the latter occurs in language and language is the means by which we conduct our everyday affairs and through which we make the world meaningful.

In my opinion, however, it is precisely because literature is made from a medium so thoroughly tied to modes of conventional discourse and ordinary communication that the creation of genuine art using such a medium should especially be acknowledged and allowed a certain degree of independence from the kind of "social and moral" criticism favored by Irving Howe and his current epigones. Creating literary art is very hard to do, and writers have had to resort to increasingly radical strategies (hence both modernism and postmodernism) to wrest it away from the moral inspectors.

Nothing we do, of course, is entirely beyond the reach of "social and moral categories" if we choose to employ them. But why must we always do so? Why is it necessary to subject that human activity we call "art" to relentless political and cultural analysis even when the artists themselves reject such an analysis as a willful distortion of the purpose of their work? Because we can? Can we not also choose to preserve an aesthetic space for works of literature? Besides, if you really are most interested in sociopolitical or moral interrogation in the first place, why spend your time trying to whip poems and novels into some suitably discursive shape?

Thus, for Howe to say that the kinds of critical terminology associated with New Critical formalism are "heavily freighted with associations drawn from history, psychology, morality" is to say something not very interesting or very useful. That human beings forge their conceptual and critical tools from various sources of human activity is not a very startling revelation. Where else could we get them? No one who ever believed in the efficacy of such terms as "coherence" or "complexity" ever believed they were "intrinsic values" separated from historical forces and derivations. They were just terms that served nicely, right now, to describe the aesthetic goals much of modern literature had set for itself. For me, it is those who cite the historical contingency of everything, as if this were urgent news, who betray a residual longing for absolutes and essences. How awful we don't have them!

Wellington admonishes Ellison for "brandish[ing] a vision of Art with a capital A," for encouraging a fruitless debate that just goes "round and round." But the argument is not circular.

The dispute between the view that art is "truth telling" and the view that art is art could be settled if the parties agreed that "Art with a capital A" can exist if we allow it to (that it has its own kind of value if we allow ourselves to find it), but that this doesn't foreclose the possibility that "truth" will emerge for some readers as well (perhaps not so forcefully for others). Those of us who agree with Ellison simply don't want to rush quite so quickly from the immediacy of art to its supplementary implications.

Although Michael Collins describes his ambitions perhaps somewhat more boldly than most, these remarks illustrate a common enough view of the ultimate purpose of fiction:

> "After I was shortlisted for the Booker, I learned that no one reads literary fiction any more. . .That's because the action--the novel's crises--are all in a character's head, not in on-page action. So I got to thinking about using crime to critique American society, perhaps a dismemberment murder mystery to echo the dismantling of the U.S. middle class." (Quoted *in Macleans*, Oct 25, 2004)

Never mind the distinction between "literary fiction" and genre fiction. As far as I can tell, Collins himself has never written the kind of literary fiction he describes, but clearly he thinks of his work as serious nevertheless; even if he did prefer fiction in which the "action" is "all in a character's head," this doesn't preclude the larger goal of critiquing society. Indeed, writers of literary fiction are more likely to think in such terms than those who work in the genres, where in many cases--especially science fiction or detective/crime fiction--some sort of implicit examination of "society" is built into the very nature of the genre, almost hard to avoid.

Those listening to Collins make this remark did not seem to object to the idea that writers might want to "critique society," merely to Collins's further theories about "the peculiar suitability" of the United States to this kind of crime fiction: "Europeans, he said, tend to visit only coastal America, and have no idea of the bizarre religious beliefs and brooding violence exhibited by the mad inhabitants of the territory between New York City and San Francisco." What the author of this *Macleans* article calls "Collins' naked ambition and political paranoia" apparently did not appeal to this audience, but they surely would not have taken exception to a writer's claim to be "critiquing" society, since the notion that this is what fiction does, at some fundamental level, is very widespread.

This kind of social commentary, if not exactly political propaganda, is certainly "political" in that it values social or cultural change as the potentially most salutary benefit of writing and reading fiction. Like satire, it seeks "correction" of the flaws and mistaken beliefs it portrays. Such a conception of literature's relevance to its readers views political change and the consideration of essentially political issues to be the most important, if not the only, way for literature to be serious in the first place. Aesthetic achievement is not dismissed altogether, but it becomes at best a trick used by the skillful writer to draw the reader's attention to those sociopolitical concerns that are really what have motivated the writer to begin with.

How many works of literature from the past have survived because what they provide is deemed to be social commentary, offering insight into the cultural mechanisms and assumptions of a particular time and place? Hardly any. It is sometimes said that, for example, Dickens gives us this kind of window onto the social landscape of his time, but to the extent this is true--and it is partly true--it is a consequence of Dickens's much broader aesthetic ambition to build a whole fictional world, related to the concrete realities of Victorian England, but thoroughly transformed, out of the socially determined materials he had to work with. (And he had no other materials; he lived in Victorian England and not somewhere else.) Works of literature, especially fiction, can always be used by the cultural historian as the source from which to dredge up "information." But a novel or poem or play that can only be used as such a source has already been judged no longer worth reading.

As I mentioned earlier, it hardly seems necessary to insist that a genre like crime fiction should seek to "critique" society. Given the various conventions of the genre--the focus on law enforcement (or on the attempt more broadly to redress lawless acts), the inherent need to "investigate" a particular social mileu, the search for an explanation, to the extent it can be found, for what motivates people to violate social and cultural norms--a critique of sorts will almost always arise from a crime or detective novel. The hard part for a crime novelist (at least it seems to me) is to find suitable ways of making this intrinsic kind of commentary aesthetically satisfying as the subject of a work of fiction. Literary novelists have on the one hand an easier job-- they don't have to fulfill these generic expectations (at least not these particular ones) and ought to be less constrained in the attempt to find aesthetically satisfying forms--and an even harder one--to find such forms absent the inherent interest-value these embedded conventions additionally provide. Perhaps this makes it all the more tempting simply to fall back on "commentary" as fiction's ultimate justification.

It is not, I hope, simply contrarian to suggest that politics is not the most important, certainly not the only important, endeavor with which a serious-minded person might want to occupy him/herself. Nor is it necessary that he/she engage in social commentary in order to be discharging the duties supposedly assigned to the writer of fiction. If this were the case, it would be much easier, and ultimately more useful, to forego fiction altogether and write political speeches or make documentary films. (There seems to be more money in the latter as well.) It may or may not be true that "no one reads literary fiction any more," although I myself think such a claim is unsupportable. There are, in sheer numbers, many more readers of serious fiction than there "used to be," given the vast increases in population just over the past half-century. Probably the percentage of serious readers within these populations isn't significantly lower, either. Even if fewer people do want to read "literary fiction," it's precisely because it has increasingly become reduced to an attempt to "critique American society," through the combined efforts of certain so-called literary journalists, by academics, and by the editors of prominent book reviews.

Given a choice between such lugubrious stuff--at least in the way it is presented--and more artfully done "entertainment," some readers have understandably gone for the latter. (One wonders how popular Michael Collins will be among such readers.) As well: If I have to choose between the social critic and the artist, my vote goes to the artist.

II Subversive

This is a common defense of "political fiction":

Imaginative writing can be both literary and political simultaneously, and inevitably is, to varying degrees. In its own way, fiction can accomplish something similar to what Noam Chomsky and many other progressive workers try to accomplish through non-fiction: the creation of works that clarify and better the world socially, politically, culturally. . . . (Socialit.org)

Right down to the invocation of Chomsky, this is the sort of thing I object to when I hear talk about political fiction. Notice how this very definition actually erases itself: How can fiction "be both literary and political simultaneously" if it is attempting to do what "many other progressive workers try to accomplish through non-fiction"? If the goal is so resolutely political, it can't also be literary, or the two terms are simply washed of their meaning. Further, since the goal, to the extent it can be reached, is going to be reached more readily through non-fiction (why bother with the artsy stuff?), why not just stick to nonfiction? Is it somehow not glamorous enough? Needs to be gussied up with some "literature"?

Perhaps when some people speak of the "political" impact of fiction, they really just mean that works of fiction "reflect" the society that produces them, or that some readers might find what they read in a work of fiction to have some sort of broader, social relevance. But this is then made out to be something with much more significance than it really has. How can a work of literature not reflect the social forces that have made themselves felt to the writer, since the writer belongs to his/her society and unavoidably responds to such forces? Readers may indeed find a particular novel or poem to have social implications, but this does not mean that the work was written to have this effect. Certainly such implications can be a salubrious side-benefit to an otherwise attentive reading experience, but surely few writers really want these particular implications to be the only ones their work might have. I don't want to close off the possible meanings a work of literature might have for an individual reader, but to value fiction or poetry primarily for its social commentary is not really to give your full attention to what literature has to offer.

Sometimes, especially among academics, the "political" value of literature is identified more specifically as its capacity to be "subversive" or "transgressive." As M. Keith Booker puts it in his book *Techniques of Subversion in Modern Literature*, "After all, even the most transgressive works of literature do not in general immediately send their readers into the streets carrying banners and shouting slogans. Transgressive literature works more subtly, by chipping away at certain modes of thinking that contribute to the perpetuation of oppressive political structures." To the extent that literature professors still put any value at all on literature itself, it is usually through this construct of the subversive. Not all works of literature finally measure up, of course--some are simply hopeless in this context, and since for such critics there is no other context, they are better consigned to the trash heap of literary history--but even those that don't seem to hold out much promise of being transgressive in any obvious way can be shown to have their transgressive moments if the critic digs hard enough and misreads strenuously enough. Booker, for example, finds Gilbert Sorrentino hopeless, his "mere rule breaking for the sake of rule breaking" insufficiently "transgressive in a genuine political sense, i.e. challenging existing dominant ideologies in a way that contributes to the process of social change." On the other hand, the fiction of Monique Wittig " [harnesses] the transgressive techniques that are inherent in sexuality not in the service of subjectivized experience but of a socialized and communal political statement." Beware of those "subjectivized experiences."

So-called "conservative" defenders of art or literature are finally no better, even though they frequently claim to be "depoliticizing" the arts. In an interview, Roger Kimball says of academic criticism in general that "One common ingredient is an impatience with the idea of intrinsic merit or intrinsic worth: a poem, a novel, a 'text' of any sort never means what it appears to say but is always an essentially subversive document whose aim is to undermine established values" (*Front Page*, December 16, 2004). One might think this is a defense of the aesthetic in art, but it's really just another version of politics. "Intrinsic merit" is itself a political tool; as Kimball also puts it in the same interview: "The great enemy of the totalitarian impulse, in intellectual life as well as in politics, is the idea of intrinsic worth." Putting aside the unexamined metaphysical assumptions informing the notion of "intrinsic worth," what Kimball really wants to recover is not art itself but "the traditional fabric of manners and morals that stands behind the work of art." For someone like Roger Kimball, art is no more to be valued for its real aesthetic qualities (which do often indeed rip at the "traditional fabric" he wants to preserve), but for the way in which it can be enlisted to enforce a "traditional" social order. In the end, people like Roger Kimball and M. Keith Booker are dancing a kind of vicious dance together, each partner despising the other but unable to let go.

Do I then think literature is <u>merely</u> a "subjective experience" or, even worse, just "entertainment"? Absolutely not, although it is those things first and foremost. A "subjective experience" of art or literature can indeed be a very profound one, even transforming the way the subject thinks about him/herself as well as the social world into which the reader must inevitably return. I might even say that such an experience can ultimately prove "subversive" in its effects, as long as the word is used in something like the sense conveyed by the poet Stephen Dunn:

> No, I don't think [artists] have a moral obligation, except maybe to be interesting. Or, if they do, it's to subvert the status quo by resisting official versions of it, then reconstructing it so others can see it anew. Not with an agenda in mind, but through simply trying to find the right language for what is elusive. . . (*Poets and Writers*, August 19, 2004)

"Official versions" of the status quo are not just political. Such versions can be imposed by family or by our own incuriosity, or by society and culture more broadly. They are all "official" versions of the way things are that we have simply come to accept and haven't questioned much. Works of literature can provoke us into questioning them by showing us that there are always alternative versions, that descriptions of reality are only tentative and that a final understanding of the way things are isn't going to be possible. (Art that suggests there can be a final understanding isn't really art.) Literature does this both through its content--the alternative versions we're presented with--and through form--the way in which the perceived world is "reconstructed," to use Dunn's word. Literature in its aesthetic dimension--literally, the "art" by which it is made--displays to us the imagination at work, reminds us that there are effectively no limits to the human imagination.

To me, this is all indeed powerfully subversive. Through art we become aware that the world can always be remade. Art is the enemy of all certainties and settled doctrines. This is not likely to be acceptable to political critics of either the left or the right, the Bookers or the Kimballs, which is why I would say that in the final analysis such critics don't really much like art at all. They literally don't have any use for it, unless it can be distorted to suit their own ideological predispositions. As Stephen Dunn says, poets and fiction writers are "trying to find the right language for what is elusive." And afterwards, it remains elusive. In my opinion, the only way that literature can "clarify and better the world socially, politically, culturally" is by revealing to us, perhaps to our dismay, that this is a fact.

I read Mary Gaitskill's *Veronica* hoping to have confirmed the judgment that she is "one of the most transgressive American writers working today," as one review put it (*Flakmagazine*, November 29, 2005). I should have known better. Words like "transgressive" and "subversive" are used so promiscuously to describe any fiction that threatens to "critique" reigning norms, just as "innovative" is used reflexively to describe any work that doesn't obediently proceed in the narrative direction prescribed by Freytag's Triangle, that normally I just disregard their invocation as so much boilerplate. Having read in a number of places, however, that Gaitskill was a truly transgressive and unconventional writer, I decided to see what *Veronica* had to offer.

No doubt I should not take out on Gaitskill my impatience with such critical inflation, but I don't think she's done much to discourage the idea she's a "daring" writer. As it turns out, the attempted transgressions in this novel are entirely transgressions of sexual morality or propriety. In the milieu in which its characters move--the fashion industry, AIDS-frightened New York City in the 1980s--there's lots of sex, much of it exploitative and unhealthy. Apparently we're to be taken aback by passages such as this one:

> . . . Alain looked up and smiled. "Do you like [the haircut]?" I asked. He stood and said of course he liked it, it had been his idea. Then he jumped on me.

I say "jumped" because he was quick, but he wasn't rough. He was strong and excessive, like certain sweet tastes--like grocery pie. But he was also precise. It was so good that when it was over, I felt torn open. Being torn open felt like love to me; I thought it must have felt the same to him. I knew he had a girlfriend and that he lived with her. But I was still shocked when he kissed me and sent me home. . . .

Frankly, the idea that the fashion world is full of sexual predators and encourages a sadomasochistic attitude toward sex doesn't come as much of a shock to me. If you really want a disturbing portrayal of the way in which women are inculcated into a kind of reflexive sadomasochism, read Elfriede Jelinek, whose fiction truly transgresses modern myths about sex and romantic love without relying on the superficial adornments of the sociological "expose." Ultimately, all of the characters in *Veronica* (maybe especially the title character, who is not the novel's protagonist but whose fate is a sort of cautionary supplement to the protagonist's story) seem to have been assigned their roles in a kind of retrospective account of the hedonistic 1980s, but none of them rise above the highly schematic requirements of these roles. They're types, duly chosen to represent various attitudes and excesses of the era:

I wanted something to happen, but I didn't know what. I didn't have the ambition to be an important person or a star. My ambition was to live like music. I didn't think of it that way, but that's what I wanted; it seemed like that's what everybody wanted. I remember people walking around like they were wrapped in an invisible gauze of songs, one running into the next--songs about sex, pain, injustice, love, triumph, each song bursting with ideal characters that popped out and fell back as the person walked down the street or rode the bus.

In his review of the novel, Benjamin Strong writes that "If *Veronica* has a weakness, it's that it sometimes feels more like a document of the last decade than the current one" (*Village Voice*, Oct 11 2005). Frankly, I'd have just as much trouble with a novel that seems to be a "document" of the current moment as with one that "documents" a previous epoch, but Strong does make a relevant point: *Veronica*, published in 2005, already seems dated, an evocation of a period and of characters that come off as mere historical curiosities. Francine Prose also describes *Veronica* as essentially a period piece--"Gaitskill may be, among contemporary authors, the one best-suited to capture, on the page, a period when the marriage of sex and death was such an extraordinarily close one"--but claims to have found reading the book unsettling, "like biting into a nightmare-inducing, virally loaded madeleine. Halfway through, you may find yourself remembering things you'd forgotten about a moment in time when half your friends were dying young, and when you feared that anyone who had ever had sex (including, of course, yourself) was doomed to a premature and hideous demise" (*Slate*, October 10, 2005).

It's telling that for Prose what is "nightmarish" about reading *Veronica* involves "remembering things you'd forgotten about a moment in time. . . ." What the novel offers is an opportunity to "remember," to recollect from a perspective of relative safety a "moment in time," even if the memories are full of doom and foreboding. But the memories themselves, the effect of being transported back to this time when one realized sex and death could be so nearly aligned, are what is "nightmare-inducing" about the book. Neither its prose, its formal ingenuity, nor even its specific imagery is responsible for its allegedly profound impact. Its status as "document," as a reminder of how traumatic the "AIDS era" was for those who lived through it, remains its primary virtue.

Gaitskill is not a bad writer, but her occasional stylistic flourishes ("her eyes gave off the cold glow of an eel whipping through water") cannot bring its first-person narrator Alison to life as anything other than a stock figure (the unlucky victim of her times) or compensate for the ultimately bland and unengaging memoir-like structure Gaitskill employs as a way of narrating Alison's life and times. Prose claims that *Veronica* "places no. . .strain on our memory. It creates an atmosphere, provokes a response, and suffuses us with an emotion that we can easily, all too easily, summon up." She means this as a compliment and apparently believes this makes the novel "unconventional," since we are not required to revisit the narrative, "searching for some forgotten plot turn, some event or aspect of character." I don't myself find this strategy very unconventional; if anything, it's just a way of reinforcing the cheap appeal to established iconographic images, our cultural memory of the 80s. At best, it's the kind of "newness" that is more interested in the sociopolitical than the literary.

III The Big Dialogue

Horace Engdahl of the Nobel committee has notoriously claimed that "Europe still is the center of the literary world" when it comes to the awarding of the Nobel Prize, that "the U.S. is too isolated, too insular," doesn't "translate enough" and doesn't "really participate in the big dialogue of literature," and that American writers are "too sensitive to trends in their own mass culture" (Associated Press).

On the one hand, it seems likely that Engdahl's remarks were motivated by a non-literary (and entirely justified) dissatisfaction with American political and military actions over the last eight years, a dissatisfaction widely shared across all of Europe these days. Engdahl assumes, wrongly, that American writers, American "culture" more generally, are somehow complicit with these actions or at least haven't done enough to express their solidarity with European critics of American hubris as embodied by George W. Bush and Dick Cheney. To this extent, one might grant Engdahl some forbearance, since his attitude probably reflects a momentary unhappiness with the United States that will surely abate with the passing of the Bush administration.

But on the other hand, Engdahl's comments do reflect some underlying assumptions about both American literature and the role of literature more generally that certainly warrant scrutiny. For one thing, while I suppose it is possible for writers to become "too sensitive to trends in their own mass culture" (especially if we take "mass culture" to be something other than "culture" itself, a separate realm driven by the same mindless forces that drive the American government), most depictions of "mass culture" in American fiction tend to be critical of that culture, often directly satirizing it. Insofar as Engdahl has read much contemporary American fiction, it would seem he hasn't read it very well. Especially among those writers who might be seriously considered for the Nobel Prize--Roth or Pynchon or Barth--"mass culture" is an object of concern and ridicule, not something these writers seek to reinforce. That Engdahl would think otherwise does call his qualifications for the job of awarding a literary prize--the most esteemed literary prize of them all--into question.

One would have to presume that Europe remains "the center of the literary world" because its writers do not have such an unseemly obsession with their own nations' culture, but of course this hardly seems credible. However, since Engdahl provides no additional enlightenment about what it actually means to be the world's literary center, an alternative presumption would seem to be that Europe is central because, well, the Nobel committee most often awards the prize to European writers. I admit both a professional and personal bias toward American fiction in my own reading habits, but to the extent Engdahl is claiming the greatest contemporary writers are to be found on the continent of Europe, I must further admit I find the notion thoroughly unsupportable. There are certainly some very fine writers in Great Britain, but most of them are undoubtedly obscure to someone like Horace Engdahl (writers such as Tom McCarthy and Rosalind Belben), and among them are decidedly not the "name" writers Engdahl probably does have in mind-- Martin Amis or Ian McEwan. There are also excellent writers in France and the German-speaking countries, and I have recently found myself particularly taken by several Eastern European writers whose work I had not previously read, but again the notion that any of these writers are "greater" than Roth, Pynchon, Coover, or Stephen Dixon seems to me palpably absurd. And that such now deceased postwar American writers as John Hawkes or Stanley Elkin or Gilbert Sorrentino were never even remotely considered for the Nobel Prize only highlights the essential cluelessness of those at the "center" of the European literary world.

The comments that have received the most attention in the print media and on literary blogs are Engdahl's suggestions that American writers are "too insular" and "don't really participate in the big dialogue of literature." Most people have interpreted this to be a criticism of American writers for not reading enough translated work or for focusing on domestic "issues," but I find the claims as worded to be virtually incoherent. Either Engdahl is asserting that not enough American writers are contributing to some ongoing "dialogue" about literature separate from their own writing, or the allegation is that they don't conceive of their writing as a contribution to "the big dialogue of literature." As far as I'm concerned, both notions are equally preposterous. The first requires that we think of world literature as some kind of super seminar in which writers are the invited panelists and collegiality the expected behavior. It seems to substitute "dialogue" among writers for literary criticism.

Most likely, of course, Engdahl means something like the second. American writers are too "insular" in that they don't offer their work as part of a cross-cultural discourse that Engdahl is defining as "literature." They are too "isolated" to see the value of this discourse. But literature isn't a "dialogue" monitored by self-appointed arbiters who decide what part of the conversation deserves a prize for its insight. It isn't an attempt to "say" anything, except circuitously or by accident. I'm tempted to construe Engdahl's scolding of American writers for their insularity as just another expression of impatience with the "merely literary," with writing that isn't morally or politically useful, but I doubt he really meant to go quite that far. He is simply reiterating a commonly-held, if implicit rather than thought-out, view that literature is more about dialogue and discussion and nicely articulated platitudes. less about art and aesthetic consummation, which indeed often occurs in isolation and, in literature, as a "dialogue" only between the author and his/her text.

One reason that poets are so infrequently awarded the Nobel Prize has to be that it is much harder to value poetry primarily for its relevance to "the big dialogue." Poetry more clearly foregrounds the aesthetic ambitions of literature, and even those who read novels for the "something said" are often willing to concede that this model is overly reductive as applied to poetry (when such readers even admit to reading poetry--many simply confess they don't "get" it). But since the Nobel Prize seems to be decided according to the criterion that a writer "say" things (that, and the implicit requirement that the prestige of the prize be spread around a little--every once in a while a Chinese or Arabic writer--to enlarge the "dialogue"), poetry, or, God forbid, experimental writing, is nevertheless going to be left at the door. Such exclusion of writing that in its necessary inwardness doesn't meet the blandly humanitarian standards of the Nobel committee is just one of the reasons why this literary prize, the biggest, is also the most idiotic.

On the other hand, David Biespiel is convinced that "America's poets are uniquely qualified to speak openly in the public square among diverse or divisive communities," despite their current "intractable and often disdainful disinterest in participating in the public political arena outside the realm of poetry" (Poetry Foundation, April 30, 2010). Although he assures us he agrees that "a poet must make his way in the world as best fits his vision for himself as an artist," nevertheless his essay is so filled with apocalyptic urgency about the need for poets to reclaim a role in "civic discourse" it clearly implies that those who settle for "quiet rooms of contemplation" are neglecting their responsibilities both to democracy and to poetry.

Biespiel wants to maintain a distinction between poets writing a deliberately "civic" poetry and using the "gravitas" that comes from being a poet simply to speak out on public affairs, but ultimately he really can't keep his frustration with the "cliquish" and "self-reflexive" nature of contemporary poetry from condemning it outright, not just for its civic derelictions but for its retreat into "art-affirming debates over poetics and styles." In other words, poetry has become satisfied with the "merely literary."

To an extent, Biespiel's essay seems to me an effort to shame poets into entering public debates by comparing their retreat into insular "coteries" to the larger retreat of Americans generally, who are "self-sorting into homogeneous enclaves," becoming "a collection of increasingly specialized interests":

> Like Americans everywhere, America's poets have turned insular and clustered in communities of aesthetic sameness, communicating only among those with similar literary heroes, beliefs, values, and poetics. Enter any regional poetry scene in any American metropolis or college town, and you will find the same cliquey village mentality with the same stylistic breakdowns.

Surely poets don't want to be like those huddled suburbanites in their gated communities, damaging the public weal in their very tendency to huddle. "Aesthetic sameness" must surely be avoided in poetry as in lawn care. What good is poetry if it gives us only "stylistic breakdowns"?

Biespiel's call for poet-sages to emerge is predicated on the belief that "Poets are actually uniquely suited and retain a special cultural gravitas to speak publicly and morally about human aspirations." This seems to be an assumption shared by all those who would have both poets and novelists "engage" with the public sphere, but it's a claim that cannot be sustained if what Biespiel means is that poets have some special ability not just to speak "publicly and morally about human aspirations" but to speak more intelligently or more persuasively about "human aspirations" than anyone else.

Certainly the examples Biespiel provides to support his assertion do little to give it credibility: Allen Ginsburg certainly had plenty to "say" in the public realm, but who doesn't think that a good deal of what he said now seems--probably seemed at the time--rather embarrassing in its simple-mindedness? Adrienne Rich may have spoken up from a feminist perspective, but what kind of public impact did it really make, as opposed to the statements of non-poet feminists such as Gloria Steinem and Betty Friedan? Robert Bly is a crank, Dana Gioia a conservative shil, and I'm not sure what Gary Snyder, Wendell Berry, or Charles Simic have ever said that has reached anyone other than their devoted readers who already agree with them.

Biespiel's argument essentially rests on the notion that poets have "the ability. . .to write poems that penetrate differences and discover connection" and partake of poetry's "ancient predisposition for moral persuasion." One could argue that what distinguishes the poet is not primarily his/her ability to "penetrate differences" but to put words together in aesthetically provocative ways and that the connections made are connections between poetry as it has been and poetry as it might be, not between competing "communities," but even if we were to accept Biespiel's amorphous formulation it does not follow that this ability is readily transferable from page to public square. It especially does not follow that whatever "predisposition for moral persuasion" has been attributed to poets over time so naturally manifests itself in modern poets, to most of whom the title "poet" applies in a much more restricted way than it did to Dante or Milton, who did not limit themselves to the lyric mode and who saw fewer differences between poetry and other forms of moral or religious discourse. If most poets now cultivate their own lyrical gardens, it is because that is seen as the appropriate task for the poet, not "moral persuasion."

Even more dubious is Biespiel's accompanying proposition that "when more poets participate in the public sphere of democratic discourse and even politics, then I've little doubt that one consequence will be greater public enthusiasm for the private revelations of our sonnets, odes, and elegies." Exactly why the heretofore unenthusiastic public would suddenly find an interest in sonnets after sampling the poet's political discourse is left unexplored, unless those sonnets turn out to be about "issues" after all--a list of those the "citizen-poet" might take up include "cultural fragmentation, national health care, decrepit infrastructure, threats of terrorism, energy consumption, climate change, nuclear proliferation, warfare, poverty, crime, immigration, and civil rights"--and are not really separable from his/her civic pronouncements. It's hard to know otherwise what would lead people indifferent to poetry to seek it out, so wide is the gap between private and public, at least according to Biespiel in the rest of his analysis. If the sonnets, odes, and elegies are primarily concerned with "memory, private reclamation, and linguistic chop-chop," as Biespiel has it, why would a public yearning for "moral persuasion" bother with it?

I don't want to suggest that poets, or any other writer, or any other citizen, should not enter into "civic discourse." As concerned human beings, of course they should take whatever actions, rhetorical or literal, they think they must. I suppose that the residual esteem still attached to the vocation of "poet" does even give their public words some additional weight, and if particular poets exploit the opportunity given to speak wisely or act courageously on matters of public importance they perform a commendable service. Such a public intervention is only tangentially, even accidentally, related to their work as poets, however, and to laud them for doing it (or condemning them for not) while ignoring the work devalues poetry rather than saving it. It suggests that poetry is mostly good *for something else*, something other than being itself. Why must the value of poetry be judged by its potential to be a good tune-up for speaking out on more important matters?

IV Very Funny

In "Divine Comedy" (*Prospect*, May 26, 2007), Julian Gough lucidly describes the kind of comedy he traces back to the Greeks and that the Russian linguist/theorist/philosopher M.M. Bakhtin called "carnivalesque." In this tradition of comedy, the comedic text (or performance) presents a thoroughly undeceived view of human life, responding to "our endless and repetitive cycle of suffering, our horror of it, our inability to escape it," with unremitting laughter. Although Gough doesn't use the term in his essay, Bakhtin further called such an attitude toward human affairs "radical skepticism." No authority is spared the corrosive perspective afforded by this sort of laughter, no conduct or discourse presented with "straightforward seriousness" can finally be taken seriously.

Such later European writers as Rabelais and Swift were literary comedians of the radically skeptical kind, but, as Gough also emphasizes, it was the development of the novel as a literary form that really gave writers the opportunity to exploit this comedy to its full potential. Gough includes Swift and Rabelais as "novelists," but even though *Gargantua and Pantagruel* and *Gulliver's Travels* could be called proto-novels, the tradition of carnivalesque comedy in the English novel would include some of the very first writers to produce what we now agree are novels: Fielding, Smollett, Sterne, as well as their greatest disciple, Charles Dickens. Bahktin admired all of these writers, and the broad, thoroughgoing comedy they practiced--separate from whatever "happy ending" their books supplied--is what Gough seems to have in mind when he writes of the novelist as one "who did not have a holy book. The novelist was on his own. Sometimes he's even a she. There were no rules. The chaos of carnival had found its form. The fool's sermon could be published, could live on."

Gough is right to assert that

The novel, when done right—when done to the best of the novelist's abilities, talent at full stretch—is always greater than the novelist. It is more intelligent. It is more vast.

This is especially true of comic novels, or at least those novels that are truly "comic" in the Bakhtinian sense and not just "satirical." Satire has traditionally been corrective, a way of using laughter to mock attitudes and behaviors the author wishes to reform. In other words, satire is usually another way of "saying something." It is not radically skeptical because it holds out one source of authority--the writer him/herself--as immune from such skepticism. The author's ultimate goal, cloaked in humor, is to be <u>serious</u> about the errors both individuals and society are prone to. He has a point to make, and the point exceeds the reach of comedy. The satirist doesn't willingly satirize himself.

Perhaps this is one reason why, after Dickens, comedy in fiction--satirical or otherwise--recedes in importance, replaced by realism and naturalism, both of which assume the structure of tragedy and essentially express the tragic view of life. This is, of course, "straightforward seriousness" of the highest order, and, as Gough points out, to be taken as a "serious" novelist required privileging tragedy over comedy:

> . . .western culture since the middle ages has overvalued the tragic and undervalued the comic. We think of tragedy as major, and comedy as minor. . .

The fault is in the culture. But it is also internalised in the writers, who self-limit and self-censor. If the subject is big, difficult and serious, the writer tends to believe the treatment must be in the tragic mode. . . .

With the occasional exceptions Gough notes--Evelyn Waugh, Flann O'Brien--comedy essentially disappears from fiction, or at least so Gough appears to believe. He certainly does imply that little noteworthy comic fiction has appeared since Waugh, especially in the United States. Through the professionalization of fiction writing via creative writing programs, he writes:

> . . .The last 30 years have seen the effects of turning novel writing into an academic profession with a career path. As they became professional, writers began to write about writers. As they became academicised, writers began to write about writing.
>
> And the language of the American literary novel began to drift away from anything used by human beings anywhere on earth. Thirty years of the feedback loop have led to a kind of generic American literary prose, instantly recognisable, but not as instantly comprehensible. Professions generate private languages designed to keep others out. This is irritating when done by architects. But it is a catastrophe for novelists, and the novel.

Here, I'm afraid, Gough really misses the boat. Comedy in fiction--comedy as Bakhtin would recognize it--has flourished in

American fiction since at least the 1960s. One of the few postwar American novels Gough mentions is John Kennedy Toole's *A Confederacy of Dunces*. This is a fine book, but it is far from the only "carnivalesque" novel to be found in postwar fiction. (And I'm not sure I would finally identify it as truly carnivalesque, at least not insofar as this kind of comedy requires "radical skepticism." Ignatius J. Reilly is surely a Rabelaisian character who rejects the authority of everything associated with the "modern," but his own superior status--despite his vices--as one who sees through it all is never really questioned, nor is the authority of his anti-modern views, which have been especially lauded by contemporary conservatives who see Reilly as a kind of moral hero.) Perhaps the finest postwar American writer (in my view) is Stanley Elkin, whose work is relentlessly comic in an almost vaudevillian way, and which implicitly includes within its comic purview Elkin's own hyperactive, gloriously excessive style, it's at times ridiculously extended tropes and setpieces offered up as the focus of laughter in and of themselves. Gilbert Sorrentino takes fiction itself as a subject of merciless laughter, in novels such as *Mulligan Stew* submitting all of its assumptions and devices to his inspired mockery. Novels such as *Catch-22*, *Portnoy's Complaint,* Gravity's Rainbow, and *The Public Burning* stretch satire almost to the breaking point, using comedy to deflate even the most "profound" of subjects--war, sex, democracy--and reveal them to be laughing matters like anything else.

Furthermore, despite Gough's quick dismissal of writers "who began to write about writing," this particular mode of postwar American fiction--metafiction--is actually the most radically comic writing yet produced in American or English fiction (with the possible exception of Sterne's *Tristram Shandy*, which was uproariously metafictional before its time). The fiction of writers like Donald Barthelme, John Barth, Robert Coover, as well as Sorrentino, through its self-reflexivity, its insistence that readers be aware of writing <u>as</u> writing, exposes the act of writing, of fiction-making, to a kind of ridicule. These are the calculations that writers make? Here's how a "story" gets strung together? This is what writers do? In the end, the grand pretensions of fiction are shown to be very artificial indeed, novels and short stories unmistakably disclosed as only words. These writers have been accused of frivolity, of--wittingly or unwittingly--undermining their own craft. But that is the very goal of this kind of comedy. Only by stripping even literature itself of its dignity, of its pretensions to "signify," can fiction keep faith with what I agree with Gough is its real mission: "The task of the novelist is. . .not to fake a coherence that does not exist, but to capture the chaos that does. And in so doing, perhaps we shall discover that chaos and permanence are not, in fact, opposed. The novel, self-renewing, self-destroying, always the same, always new, always... novel... is the art of permanent chaos."

I also agree with Gough that the academization of fiction through creative writing programs has probably discouraged writers from further exploring the possibilities of Bakhtinian comedy. It probably has contributed to the creation of "a kind of generic American literary prose." But I can't agree that it has done so by valorizing metafiction. The problem is not that there's too much postmodernism floating around; it's that there's not enough of it. In my view, only someone who's willfully misreading American postmodernism--the most indispensable ingredient in which is laughter--would say that "Since Joyce and Woolf (and Eliot), the novel's wheels have spun in the sand." Postmodern comedy has taken the anarchic comedy implicit in Joyce and made it explicit. It's the rejection of this liberating anarchy by "professional" Creative Writing that has stultified "literary prose," not the acceptance of a "private language" too influenced by postmodernism. If Gough wants American writers to again see the virtues of his "divine comedy," he could start by urging them to read carefully the very postmodernism he for some reason wants them to think "never happened."

PART SEVEN

The Profession of Literature

I Literary Study

Judith Halberstam thinks the Department of English needs to go:

> I propose that the discipline is dead, that we willingly killed it and that we now decide as serious scholars and committed intellectuals what should replace it in this new world of anti-intellectual backlash and religious fundamentalism. While we may all continue doing what we do — reading closely, looking for patterns and disturbances of patterns within cultural manifestations, determining the complex and fractal relations between cultural production and hegemonies — once we call it something other than "English," (like cultural studies, critical theory, theory and culture, etc.) it will neither look the same nor mean the same thing and nor will it occupy the same place in relation to   the humanities in general, or within administrative plans for down-sizing; it will also, I propose, be better equipped to meet the inevitable demands (which already began to surface after the last election) for an end to liberal bias on college campuses and so on. ("The Death of English," *Inside Higher Education*, May 9, 2005)

I heartily endorse this idea. By all means, let Halberstam and her confreres establish a new Department of Patterns and Disturbances of Patterns Within Cultural Manifestations. This would allow them to do what they most dearly wish to do-- distance themselves from the study of mere literature--and would further allow whatever renegade elements there are within the existing English department who still find themselves interested in the "merely literary" either to reclaim "English" as the name for what they study or perhaps to join in on the makeover fun and establish a Department of Literary Study, in which what actually goes on is the study of literature. The latter could perhaps be done by incorporating extant creative writing programs, and such a department would probably continue to offer traditional composition and linguistics courses. (Surely administrators would not want to entrust such courses to a department that otherwise focuses on "the complex and fractal relations between cultural production and hegemonies." This very phrasing suggests that professors in the new department would not be the logical choice to teach courses the goal of which is to teach students to write.)

I believe that such a bifurcation of English would turn out to be a swell deal for us renegades. Given a choice between the PDPWCM department and its ersatz sociology and a Literary Study department honestly devoted to studying literature, I predict that many undergraduate students would turn to the latter. After all, most English majors have traditionally been drawn to the discipline simply because they like to read. If departments of English and comparative literature are currently suffering "massive declines in enrollment," as Halberstam herself allows they are, I'd suggest that one of the reasons is that what students find when they get there--and what they would continue to find in the PDPWCM department--is a pedantic, turgid, supercilious, and utterly joyless approach to reading. Should the new department of Literary Study reemphasize some of the pleasures of reading, and some of the delight of discovery in the study of literature, it would do just fine in a competition to avoid "down-sizing."

Michael Berube doesn't much care for Halberstam's proposal, for reasons that aren't very clear. "[No] kind of renaming or reorganizing is going to make English a coherent, tidy discipline," he writes. "It would be hard enough to make it coherent if it were devoted solely to literature. . ." (michaelberube.com, June 29, 2005). Berube doesn't seem to understand: Halberstam is advocating that those very tendencies in academic criticism that make English as it now stands incoherent be transferred to the PDPWCM department. The English department left behind would be entirely coherent, despite Berube's doubts. Without those scholars more interested in "cultural production" and "hegemonies" than in works of fiction or poetry or drama, other scholars and critics who think studying such works as forms of literary art is a perfectly nice thing to do would be left alone to get on with the task. Berube continues: "literature, as even the most hidebound traditionalists ought to admit one of these days, is a terribly amorphous thing that touches on every conceivable facet of the known world— and, as if this weren't enough, many facets of worlds yet unknown as well. . . ." I'm not a hidebound traditionalist--in my version of a Department of Literary Study, periodization and other manifestations of curricular slicing would be absent; professors would be free to teach what they want to teach, as long as the ultimate goal was to understand the literary qualities of literature--but in my experience literature is a perfectly morphous subject. Individual works of literature certainly do explore "every conceivable facet of the known world," but the study of literature concentrates on delineating the way they do this, not on using literature as an excuse to pronounce on such "facets" oneself.

What Halberstam and Berube share, ultimately, is a plain impatience with if not disdain for trifling old literature. Halberstam sneers at the notion of "aesthetic complexity," notes approvingly the way "queer theory, visual culture, visual anthropology, feminist theory, literary theory began to nudge the survey courses, the single-author studies and the prosody classes aside," recommends that the study of Victorian literature be replaced with "studies of 'Empire and Culture,' romanticism with "the poetries of industrialization." Berube wants to preserve close reading as "our distinct product line," as "what we sell people" (so much for resisting the corporatization of academe), but reduces such readings to "skills in advanced literacy," something that promotes students' "own symbolic economy." Besides, "you don't have to confine yourself to literary works, either. You can go right ahead and do close readings of any kind of 'text' whatsoever, in the most expansive sense of that most expansive word." Berube forgets that "close reading" was developed specifically as a method of reading literary works, which required close reading because they don't give up their intended meanings so easily, are not storage centers of "meaning" at all but occasions for a reading experience of a distinctive kind. His appropriation of "close reading" is really just a theft of the term for purposes to which true close reading is simply not applicable. (But of course the New Critics have become the collective bogeymen of contemporary literary study, returning now and then from their repressed state to scare the children. They and their appalling practices must be warded off.)

Really and truly, the best thing that could happen to literature would be, once the Department of Patterns and Disturbances of Patterns Within Cultural Manifestations (or some equally dreary equivalent) was actually created, for it to disappear from academic curricula altogether. After eighty years of experimenting with the study of literature as an academic subject, those carrying it out (myself included) have made a complete hash of it. Literature itself is held in contempt not just by the majority of ordinary people but by those professing to teach it. "Literature Professor" has become a near-synonym of "lunatic." That literary study would come to such an end was probably inevitable, since the primary imperative of academe--to create "new" knowledge--is finally inimical to something so difficult to dress up in fashionable critical clothes as serious works of fiction or poetry. Once it was perceived that "aesthetic complexity" was a spent force (at least as the means for producing new monographs and journal articles), approaches to literature that essentially abandoned its consideration as an art form were practically certain to follow. If Judith Halberstam is proposing that, in this context, everyone should acknowledge that the experiment failed, she's performing a useful service. Give literature back to the amateurs.

When I began to pursue a career as a "scholar," my assumption was that literary scholarship and literary criticism were just two different but complementary activities undertaken within the shared space of literary study. There were those who were truly scholars in the traditional sense--text editors, literary historians, etc.--and those who although they called themselves "scholars" were really literary critics concerned with the explication/critical analysis of works of literature as a whole. Eventually I came to understand that the very act of calling oneself a scholar was increasingly a way of actually distancing oneself from mere "criticism," especially criticism of a formalist or aesthetic variety.

Those who helped to install literature as a respectable subject of academic study--and this did not happen until at the earliest the 1920s and 1930s, and probably not completely until after World War II--were not innocent themselves of elevating the "academic" and the "scholarly" over the merely literary. Critical method was almost always more important than a mere "appreciation" of literature. I hate to quote myself, but I have written a "scholarly" essay on this subject (*College English*, January 2001) in which I maintain that "in the battle over the English curriculum between the partisans of cultural studies and the partisans of literary study the latter are in no position to charge that cultural studies relegates literature to a supporting role secondary to the promulgation of a particular critical method. The notion that as a discipline English has ever been, or even could be, essentially a preservation society dedicated to the inherent virtues of literature is mostly unsupportable." Even New Criticism, the critical approach most dedicated to these "inherent virtues" wound up advocating the values of the academy more than the values of literary criticism itself.

However, the earlier proponents of academic criticism were more focused in their efforts on the inherent value of works of literature--on the "literary" as that could be determined. This kind of criticism has been entirely rejected by the present generation of academic critics as "soft," politically incorrect, outmoded, as thoroughly beneath them as "scholars." Academic scholars have a great need to feel superior to the mass of unenlightened and uncredentialed readers--I will foreswear the temptation to speculate on why this is the case--and increasingly academic literary scholars found it necessary to consider themselves superior even to the writers and the literary texts they ostensibly study. For this reason it is likely that scholars will never be persuaded to turn their attention back to the good faith study of works of literature for what they have to offer, and to the extent that academic "scholarship" eventually finds its way into an academic version of the blogosphere, such a practice is not likely to be very interesting to anyone other than academics--and many of them will lose patience with it as well, as battles over critical turf just get transferred to a different arena.

Literary criticism, on the other hand, to the extent it remains such, must apply itself to the sorting out of the claims that various works of literature have on our attention as readers. In short, it must help keep the possibility of reading literature in intelligent but also appreciative ways alive. The academy at present is only helping to kill this possibility. And to the extent that "literary scholarship" actually subsumed the very idea of literary criticism to itself--for a very long time criticism has really only been practiced by those with ties to the academy--it will be necessary, at the very least, for those still within the academy who nevertheless want to study literature to renounce the models of cultural study and critical theory now ascendant as the acceptable methods of what is misleadingly still called "literary study." If some of these folks were to see blogs as a way of returning to real literary criticism, this kind of blogging might actually succeed.

Some of the literary critics I greatly esteem--Harold Bloom, Stanley Fish, Marjorie Perloff, Helen Vendler, Henry Louis Gates--do have ties to the academy, are in most ways "academics." Many of them are also derided as old-fashioned or too eager to engage in merely "popular" criticism by the guardians of the currently established "advanced" practices of academic criticism. My own field of scholarly study, postwar or "contemporary" American literature, has been ruined by these practices, except for the few "scholars" who continue to consider the great writers who have demonstrably emerged from this period and to monitor the developments initiated by current writers. There really aren't many who do this sort of thing without falling prey to the formulas and vapid pronouncements that characterize academic criticism in general. In many ways, unfortunately, it could be said that it was the scholars of contemporary literature who introduced these approaches to literature in the first place.

Literary webloggers would be well-advised to run away from the products of present literary scholarship as if from a plague. If academic bloggers deprecate the lit blogs as lacking substance or rigor, litbloggers should take this as the snobbishness and unearned elitism that it is. The academy is increasingly proving itself to be the funeral home of literature-- one presided over by the academic critic-embalmers themselves. A revived literary criticism, perhaps aided if not spearheaded by literary weblogs, might not be able to rescue all that has been consigned to the tender graces of these critics, but surely something can be saved.

There are a great many older works of literary criticism, written at a time when criticism was being, or had been, largely incorporated into the academy, that are increasingly neglected but still have a great deal of value. One of these books would have to be F. O. Matthiessen's *American Renaissance*, which I recently re-read. I don't know that I would recommend this book to non-academic readers, but for reasons that have nothing to do with its quality. It is in fact, a book of great erudition and discernment, and is probably more responsible for the very concept of the "American Renaissance," and thus for the multitude of survey courses on this period that followed in the wake of the book's publication (1941) for at least the next fifty years than any other single work of literary criticism or scholarship. It may even be said to have provided the model for this kind of "periodization" in academic literary study in the first place.

Furthermore, the book clearly has played a large role in the way its five chosen writers--Emerson, Thoreau, Hawthorne, Melville, and Whitman--are understood by subsequent readers interested in the period. I think Matthiessen undervalues Emerson, overvalues Thoreau, and exaggerates the degree to which Hawthorne was simply trying to provide a more sober view of human nature than was implied in the transcendental assumptions of Emerson and Thoreau. However, I also think the chapters in *American Renaissance* on Melville and Whitman are just about the best things I've ever read about those two writers. At any rate, the overall picture that emerges from this book of the literary goals and accomplishments of each writer is probably the starting-point from which different pictures might ultimately be made.

But ultimately its impressive learning and lengthy explications are, paradoxically perhaps, the very reasons I probably would not recommend the book to readers without an existing interest in these writers and this period or who would rather read the writers themselves than such an extended work of critical commentary. Matthiessen's approach is essentially historical (in the "undertheorized" way of scholars from this generation more interested in literary history than in "subverting" this history), although Matthiessen also states that his primary interest lies "with what these books were as works of art, with evaluating their fusions of form and content." In essence, he wants to understand what these writers thought they were doing, how each of them in turn influenced what the others were trying to do, to let them as much as possible speak for themselves through judicious analysis of selected texts and passages, ultimately to help readers understand why these were and are writers worth reading and taking seriously. What a concept!

However, this has become in so many ways such an alien concept that many readers of *American Renaissance* might think it quaint, even a little bizarre. Why would someone so obviously spend so much time reading Emerson, Thoreau, Hawthorne, Melville, and Whitman so thoroughly, so clearly attempt to think through the implications of why and what they wrote, so patiently take the reader through their essays, fictions, and poems and invite this reader to think further about it all him/herself? Where's the attitude, the jargon, the theoretical superstructure, the knowing superiority to the writers being examined? Matthiessen barely mentions Whitman's homosexuality (or Melville's suspected same-sex orientation), isn't much interested in gender (although is plenty interested in class), only touches on these writers' attitudes toward race, doesn't seem concerned to pivot his analysis in an appropriately progressive political direction, actually thinks the writers he discusses ought to be read on their own terms. In some cases, these omissions are indeed problematic (the omission of race particularly), but more to the point, the book's overall focus on those qualities in these writers that make them important writers in and of themselves just isn't done any more.

And *American Renaissance* is admittedly somewhat digressive, moving ahead or backward from one writer to the other seemingly in midstream, breaking off for a discussion of the painter Thomas Eakins before returning to the homologies between Eakins and Whitman, etc. Its very breadth of knowledge can be intimidating if not irritating--it isn't always clear why we need to know quite so much just to appreciate Hawthorne's stories or *Leaves of Grass*--and its footnotes frequently insert what just seems superfluous information. It's a book for readers of its five chosen writers who are already convinced of their centrality--at least it is for readers now--and who would like to know more about why they wrote what they wrote when they wrote it.

Which is finally why it probably wouldn't be of interest to those who wouldn't already describe themselves as readers of this sort. Anyone who really wants to know what the "American Renaissance" was all about and what these five writers contributed to it couldn't really claim to have this knowledge without reading F.O. Matthiessen, but I fear there aren't many people around anymore who want to know these things. Maybe they shouldn't. Maybe books like Matthiessen's were written according to a "scholarly" model that is ultimately inappropriate for the appreciation of literature. I sometimes think this myself. But I'm glad to have read *American Renaissance* (twice), and my subsequent readings of Emerson, Thoreau, Hawthorne, Melville, and Whitman will be richer and more informed because I have.

II The "Book Business"

Articles purporting to give young writers advice about a writing career and the realities of the book business abound. I would like to offer some alternative "advice" about both "career" and "business" in the life of writers.

The best writers don't have "careers." If they do, it's usually an accident, a byproduct of the happenstance of actually writing a good book, even an important book, and miraculously acquiring readers, in some cases enough readers to make it financially feasible to do nothing but write more books. Such writers certainly aspire to write well, to produce worthy fiction and poetry on a more or less long-term basis, but if they had simply set out to have writing careers, they almost certainly would not have written the important books in the first place. Third- and fourth-rate writers settle for careers.

The "book business" is something to avoid. What has the book business ever done for American literature? Earlier incarnations of the book business (now the "industry") overlooked Hawthorne, neglected Melville, probably helped to kill E.A. Poe, sneered at Mark Twain, ran Henry James off to Europe, couldn't at first have cared less about Faulkner. Even now some of the best American writers--Gaddis, Gilbert Sorrentino, James Purdy, John Hawkes, numerous others--have been and still are cast aside by the "industry," obliged to supplement their "careers" through teaching, or advertising, or not at all and forced to just scrape by. Most of these writers thought the "book business" their enemy.

Of course one could say that all of these writers might have avoided their fates had they simply shaped up and written proper books of the sort the book "audience" wants to read--and thus provided themselves with "careers"--but of course that is just the point, isn't it? They wanted to go their own way and write the books they thought could be written, not the books that needed to be written to support the "book business." They paid the price for it, and perhaps that is how it should be. (I doubt any of them ultimately thought it too high a price, all things considered.) Some of them (Twain, at least) even wound up finding themselves "popular," if not necessarily for the right reasons.

So one could set out as a "bright young thing" to be "successfully published," and one could accomplish this goal. One could have a long and happy "career." But if you think the "book business" will respect you for your talent and originality, assuming you have them, you might come to be bitterly disillusioned.

One might also take into account Kassia Krozser's lament that she is

> baffled and amazed by authors who do not see marketing as part of their jobs. First off, is there really a job description for authors? If so, please forward to me as I have a few holes in my resume and I'm too lazy to do the work myself. Second, what planet are you living on? Very, very few authors have the luxury of not engaging in

marketing. And even they have to do talk show appearances or "Wait, Wait, Don't Tell Me". (*Booksquare*, May 12, 2008)

Why should this be baffling? If writers wanted to be marketers, presumably they would have become. . .marketers. Instead they chose to be writers, presuming that marketing was the job of publishers. Admittedly, publishers now do a terrible job, not just of marketing, but of judging talent, editing, and nourishing careers. Indeed, they're terrible at all the jobs writers once thought defined the very word, "publisher." That writers ceded editorial control to the publishers was the devil's bargain they had to strike with modern capitalism, something they had to exchange in order to get matters of business taken care of. I suppose that, in the wake of the violation of this deal on the part of publishers, writers who still want the benefits accompanying the bargain--placement in bookstores, reviews in important newspapers, etc.--might be forced to do both the writing and the selling, but I don't see why they should have known this would be part of their job, and I certainly don't know why they would continue to regard mainstream publishers as the arbiters of "success." If these publishers are not publishing their books with any care, if they're dropping them after the first book flops (due mostly to the publisher's own incompetence), and if they're going to force writers to do all the grunt work, anyway, what earthly reason do writers have to endure the situation and submit themselves to such humiliations?

I believe that Krozser has the best interests of writers in mind. And I also know that if the publishing of fiction were to move farther toward self-publishing as a viable mode, the need for writers to become marketers and promoters would no doubt become even more acute. But it's the publishers themselves who have brought things to this pass, and it won't do to let them off the hook by claiming they're "book-focused" rather than "author-focused" and noting they're "juggling hundreds, maybe thousands of authors." If they've let their business practices spiral out of control, whose fault is that, exactly? Should we really compound this failure by now chastising those writers who haven't yet gotten with the new program and become their own publicists? The "marketing" crisis is a failure of capitalism, yet another example of its increasingly crude, bottom-line mentality, with the marketing of books now being outsourced to the writers themselves. Should we cheerfully give in to this?

Krozser concludes by urging us to accept the new paradigm in which "the author as a business" holds equal place with "the writer as a creative being." Given we live in a culture that post-Reagan capitalism has transformed into one that is "all-business, all-the-time," acceding to the new paradigm might be inevitable, resisting it futile. Acquiescing to the notion that "Marketing might be a distraction for a writer, but. . .essential if you're an author" may well be necessary to "succeed" in the brave new world avaricious publishers have created, but one might still hope that some people will choose to be writers nevertheless, and let the authors be damned.

According to Sarah Weinman

the publishing world, at least in my estimation, works just like any kind of corporation, any kind of workplace. In other words, landing a book deal is no different than landing the job of your dreams. So a lot of the same skills that apply in the job hunt should be transferable to getting published.

What's the top piece of advice for those on the job market? Make use of any and all contacts. Anyone, be it a friend, neighbor, family member, former boss, people you've worked with on a project, is a contact. Ask advice, get feedback, meet with your contacts on occasion, follow up and above all, be professional. And don't abuse your contact base either, because they are people with valuable time who don't like to be hit up sporadically because you want something.

What gets you an interview? A CV or resume that is polished and stands out, but doesn't stand out too much. Throw in something extra like a letter of reference or two.

What gets an agent to read the first 50 pages? A kickass query letter that is polished and stands out, but doesn't oversell the product, and maybe some choice blurbs from the right people from your contact base. (*Confessions of an Idiosyncratic Mind*, June 3, 2004)

This may or may not be good advice for those seeking entry to the "book industry"--I assume it is--but that it might be accurate is itself enough to make me want to boycott every piece of product to roll off of its assembly line. (If I did that, I know I'd miss a number of actually good books, but if by taking what I can from this assembly line I was only helping to perpetuate it, I'd almost rather do without them.) I understand that book publishing is a business, but it has always been among the least business-like of businesses. If it really was "only a business," only a way to amass capital for owners and stockholders, then almost <u>no</u> "literary" fiction would ever get published, since very little of it ever contributes to the financial stockpile. A truly efficient business would publish only what it considered to be potentially profitable, the more blockbusterish the better. If book publishing had always followed a sound business plan, only Clancy and Grisham and company would be available in your neighborhood bookstore.

So surely book publishing doesn't really work "just like any kind of corporation." I fear that descriptions like this only encourage people to think of it as such, only reinforces the behavior inside the book business that has created a situation in which many perfectly good writers see it as a "closed shop"-- closed to all but the insiders who think they know how to make a buck. If we concede that publishing books ought to be a business like any other, the current trends taking it in that direction will only accelerate. I've recently been reminded by a writer whom I respect that there are people in and around the book "industry" who do care about good writing and only want to facilitate getting such writing into the hands of readers. I don't doubt it. But if book publishers finally do become "just like any kind of corporation," these people will become as obsolete as the books on whose behalf they now advocate.

I've been involved in job searches, from both sides, and I think I know what contacts and connections amount to. A "connection" means the fix is in, the "merits" of the candidate (or the book) no longer count for much, greasing the wheels that move the system becomes the end and not the means. Unless, of course, you're competing with someone with even better connections. Besides, if you succeed in getting the job or getting your book published through contacts with people who may or may not know anything substantial about you or your work, what's the accomplishment? Your work still hasn't been acknowledged for what it may be worth.

"What gets an agent to read the first 50 pages?" How about 50 pages that are good? Agents don't have time to sit around and read 50 pages of a manuscript? They have to be queried and blurbed? They have to be sold on the manuscript based on activities that have nothing to do with the manuscript beyond hyping it? Then what are agents for? It's a pretty sad state of affairs when editors can't edit and agents can't facilitate because they can't find the time to read. Or want to avoid it if they can.

Sarah Weinman's real love is crime fiction, perhaps a field of publishing in which the behavior she advises seems less exceptionable. At the same time, I find it hard to believe that the great crime writers of the past, among them Raymond Chandler, James M. Cain, Jim Thompson, would have been willing to jump through all of the hoops the publishing world now dangles in front of writers and would-be writers. Most of them, in fact, settled for publication in the pulpiest of magazines and the most obscure presses, in the off-chance their work might still attract readers sympathetic to what they were trying to do with it. And indeed in the long run that work continues to attract readers, even more than such writers could probably have imagined, partly because they managed to maintain their literary integrity despite the vagaries of the book business.

Perhaps the most dispiriting comment in Weinman's post is this:

If you get turned down by a job you want, it sucks—believe me, it does—but there are all sorts of reasons which may or may not have anything to do with your ability to do the job. But it's nothing personal. When it comes to a book, yes, it's your baby, you've slaved all your life, you want the rest of the world to love it—and you—as well. But if the book is turned down, well guess what: it sucks, oh yes, but there are all sorts of reasons which may or may not have anything to do with your abilities as a writer. And those reasons, too, aren't usually personal ones.

The reasons likely are not personal, but I confess I find it almost incomprehensible that good work could be refused for reasons that "may not have anything to do with your abilities as a writer," even though I know that good work is rejected because of various and sundry "editorial" decisions. Not everyone can be published, at least not immediately, there are indeed constraints on time and money, sometimes fiction submitted for publication (both to book publishers and to magazines) ought to be rejected, and judgments about such things are always unavoidably subjective. But how often are good writers rejected because more time and effort needs to be expended on writers whose work just isn't as good, but is more clearly commercial, or more appropriately "connected"? To accept such a thing as simply part of doing business might be necessary, but it's a dubious business, nevertheless.

Richard Curtis enthuses over the possibilities of Amazon's BookSurge:

> I pondered – why would Amazon buy a print on demand press? I didn't have to wait long for the answer. A few months ago, they launched a service aimed at helping publishers keep their books in print. When the stock of a book runs low, Amazon takes the publisher's file and reprints the book at Amazon's own plant and fulfills back-orders. How do publishers feel about outsourcing their printing and fulfillment? What's not to be thrilled about? They're making money at no cost to themselves whatsoever. It's all done virtually, and everybody makes money, including you the author. (*Publisher's Weekly*,   August 2005)

Curtis thinks the logic behind this service is unavoidable, and might ultimately result in making Amazon itself obsolete:

> . . .Right now, in order to satisfy those subscription orders on Amazon, Random House has to print five thousand copies at its printing plant and, ship them to Amazon's warehouse. Well, that's perfectly fine if you're in the twentieth century. But this is the 21st, and publishing is

becoming virtual. How about this alternative: Amazon prints all five thousand copies at its BookSurge plant in Charleston, South Carolina. Booksurge then ships the books directly to the customers who pre-ordered them months ago.

Pretty sexy, yes? Neither Random House nor Amazon are out of pocket for the printing cost, because it's covered by the price of the book; nor is there any shipping cost to the publisher, because shipping is paid by the customer. Nor is there any warehouse cost, because there are no warehouses! I used the term "virtual;" we know that in a digital world, all middlemen become impediments. I say unto you categorically that direct bookselling to the consumer, with no middlemen, is the way of the future. And here's something more to think about: as stupendous as Amazon is, it is only a middleman for book publishers. Is there any reason why publishers have to outsource their fulfillment to Amazon? None that I can think of. Once the Random Houses of the world see the profitability inherent in the subscription print-on-demand model, if they're smart--a condition we cannot always take for granted--but if they're smart, they'll realize they can do it themselves.

According to Curtis, this do-it-yourself approach will come to dominate bookselling because cutting out the middlemen and "selling directly to customers is the only way that the book industry will find its way back to profitability."

I certainly agree that the middlemen are "impediments" in the process of getting books into the hands of readers, and that their tentacles have enwrapped the "book business" so thoroughly that debacles like the disastrous 2007 bankruptcy of book distributor Publishers Group West will only become increasingly common.

But I'm afraid the warehousers and the sales people and the "distribution groups" aren't the only middlemen. And it's not only Amazon that will become unnecessary for publishers to "outsource their fulfillment." Bookstores, while in some instances providing a relaxing enough way to spend a Saturday afternoon, aren't really necessary if my primary goal is to purchase the book I've been reading about on the litblogs, and the days when my choices are limited by the tastes of bookstore owners and the limited storage space they have available are of course long over. Even the Borders and Barnes and Noble megastores (maybe especially them, since their inventory is now almost completely determined by big sales and quick turnarounds) cannot supply the diversity of selection now possible online, except at their own online sites. Nostalgia for the old-time bohemian bookstores will linger for a while--and such nostalgia is not altogether misguided--but the bricks-and-mortar bookstore will eventually disappear, as, literally, few people will have much use for them.

Agents are of course the most conspicuous middlemen in today's book business. Like all other agents in our entertainment-industrial complex, they exist to keep the industrial cogs running smoothly and to siphon off as much profit for themselves as possible. But then agents are really the middlemen for the next level of middlemen, the editors. The problem with editors is not that they edit--some writers need editing--but that they mostly don't. (Reportedly, much of the hands-on editing is being sloughed off on the agents. That they must take on this burden in order to maintain their place in the pecking order has to be very frustrating to them.) Instead they indulge in their own delusions of grandeur, masquerading as "gatekeeping," or else they see the writing and reading of books as an opportunity to stamp the process with their own exquisite sensibilities, as demonstrated by editor Juliet Ulman:

> With a book that is clearly well-constructed and interesting but leaves me with no inclination to acquire it, I can see on paper why it works--and often even anticipate that it will be very successful--but I just don't feel particularly enthusiastic about it. . .a really "me" book feels like an intense crush, illuminating and electric -- like it was written just for me. I become infatuated. I have butterflies in my stomach, and I want to tell all of my friends about it. I can hardly think straight until I have

acquired it. (Or at least tried to!) (*Fantasy Magazine* blog,
December 11, 2006)

How darling. Books as boyfriends.

Apparently this is the philosophy behind book acquisition
in our time (aside from chasing after the next blockbuster and
wasting all the marketing money on it, before discovering the
public thinks what you're promoting is just so last year.) All the
editors gather together their "me" books, and everyone's ego is
suitably gratified. Who needs "well-constructed and interesting"
when you can pretend to have half-written this other swell book
just by discovering it?

However, even the editors are just the stand-ins for the
most imposingly intermediate of middlemen, the publishers
themselves. Curtis proclaims that POD will "save the publishing
industry" because it can peddle its wares directly to consumers. It
doesn't occur to him that the efficiency made possible by print-
on-demand will almost inevitably make publishing companies as
we know them obsolete as well. Why entrust the downloading of
your book to self-described publishers when you can send it
straight to your readers yourself? Yes, some services will still be
provided by ostensible middlemen in this new process (some of
them perhaps still operating as "small" presses), but I can't
imagine that, eventually, the technology involved won't be

sufficiently streamlined as to make "self-publishing" effectively the only kind of publishing a writer would desire.

Ultimately, Curtis's shot across the publishing bow is no doubt just a warning to the "book business" that it needs to reconstitute itself to accommodate New Media. He comes to salvage third-party book publishing, not bury it. But if his mission were really to ensure that "books of lasting cultural value" continue to be written and read, he'd acknowledge that publishing as it has existed for the last 50 years is the biggest obstacle to that goal and he'd assist in digging its grave.

Sarah Glazer's essay, "How to Be Your Own Publisher," in the April 24, 2005 *New York Times Book Review*, seems to mark another step forward in the acceptance of self-publishing:

> For the first time, print-on-demand companies are successfully positioning themselves as respectable alternatives to mainstream publishing and erasing the stigma of the old-fashioned vanity press. Some even make a case that they give authors an advantage--from total control over the design, editing and publicity to a bigger share of the profits.

Although it is unfortunate that the essay focuses so much on the new "book" by Amy Fisher, that the NYTBR would devote so much space to the discussion of self-publishing suggests that there is enough potential in it that other book reviews might eventually pay attention to self-published books, if the form does indeed come to attract talented writers of real books.

What John Feldcamp, founder of Xlibris, says about the future of self-publishing is probably correct:

> "Publishing has been an arcane specialist skill under the control of a guild of people that are unique and different from anyone else. . .Those skills have been so complicated they haven't been accessible to normal human beings. What's happening is all the technologies of publishing are becoming increasingly cheap and accessible". . . .

Not only has the technology of publishing been under the control of a "guild," but I would argue that the same thing is true of the editorial side of publishing. Who can honestly say that the decisions made by most mainstream publishers are being made according to some deep-seated love of good writing rather than the financial bottom line? That those in control of the publishing process have this control because they are uniquely qualified to make judgments about the literary merit of what they publish? That their judgments are so obviously sound that we can be confident the books they choose are the best they could find and the books they decline are not worthy of publication?

Writers continue to seek publication through this process because of the lingering distinction that still glimmers faintly from some of the "name" publishing houses and because of the implicit flattery involved in having one's book chosen by people who are supposed to know what they're doing. But today's "book business" only offers most writers frustration on two fronts: Publishers who put most of their emphasis on big-name writers and blockbuster titles, and who while doing so still manage to lose money and fail to bring attention to the writers they do publish.

Akashic Books publisher Johnny Temple in my opinion only lends support to the notion that writers might be just as well off to publish themselves. Although publishers like Akashic are taking up some of the slack in publishing worthwhile books, Temple still calls on writers to themselves do more of the "promotional 'dirty work'" in getting their books noticed. "The ideal, of course, is to collaborate with an attentive and zealous publisher," he writes, "but the reality for most artists in any medium is that little is guaranteed beyond one's own efforts" (*AlterNet*, April 22, 2005). If writers are increasingly being required to fend for themselves once their books are published, is it really such a big leap to doing everything oneself, including getting the book into print in the first place?

Temple comments further:

Once the pitfalls of today's publishing terrain are understood, writers can readjust their expectations. Start with a basic truth that is rarely presented in MFA programs and writers conferences: 5,000 copies sold is a *fantastic* number, particularly for a first-time author. This goes for books published by either indies or majors. (A quick probe of BookScan will show how few books pass this threshold.). . . .

The truth is, most literary fiction is going to appeal to a relatively small, self-selected audience. If writing well and cultivating one's art is what's most important to the serious writer, I don't see why this should be debilitating. Audiences for good work grow over time, but even if they don't, it doesn't seem so tragic for a writer to reach those readers most likely to appreciate what he/she is trying to do. Furthermore, if your book is going to sell only a few thousand copies even if it's published by a New York publisher, surely a self-published book effectively publicized by its author is going to have a chance of equaling this number, at least, especially if the author is able to take advantage of the increasing influence the literary blogosphere seems to be having. (Either by starting up a blog or by appealing to those maintaining existing blogs.) Other ways of marketing one's work on the internet are surely going to develop as well.

Glazer cites several examples of self-published books that have sold many more than 5,000 copies. Most of these are nonfiction books, to be sure, books that fit into what one quoted publisher calls "microniches." But since it is literary fiction that tends to be worst-served by the publishing business, I don't see what writers of such fiction have to lose by going the self-publishing route. If the book business continues to be operated as incompetently as it has been lately, they may eventually have no other choice. I think it's quite possible that some very talented or very brave writer will sometime relatively soon decide to self-publish and will be successful at it. Once it's been established that one can self-publish and still maintain one's dignity (and maybe sell some copies as well), other writers will follow. Being able to efficiently get one's book into the hands of interested readers ought to make up for any "prestige" lost through bypassing the conventional publishers, who are increasingly proving unworthy of the job of gatekeeping for both serious writers and readers.

I do not want to suggest I don't respect the efforts being made by what Temple calls "indie publishing." I do. But I also think self-publishing could simply be another way of going "indie."

PART EIGHT

Art and Culture

I Audience

According to Michael Blowhard:

> . . .the interest most people have in most fiction depends on story, hook, subject matter, and character. Without the chance to relate to and enjoy these elements, 90% of people would lose their interest in fiction. They'd turn elsewhere for story-and-character satisfactions: to history, to journalism, to gossip, even to reality television. (Hey, a lot of people have already turned away from respectable fiction to these other media for their story pleasures. You don't think there's a connection, do you?) But we aren't going to live life without enjoying stories and characters, that's for sure.
>
> Another way of putting it: while the occasional individual work of fiction may fare well enough without much in the way of story, the well-being of fiction generally depends on a shared interest (on the part of readers and writers) in characters, stories, hooks, and subject matter. (*Two Blowhards*, May 16, 2005)

In fact, I do believe there's a connection between the popularity of such things as reality television and the relative non-popularity of literary fiction: "most people" have no interest, have never had any interest, in the sorts of things serious art and literature have to offer. For whatever reason, "most people" are incapable of paying attention to the formal and stylistic qualities that most artists seek to embody in their work, the qualities that make art art. In the case of literature, "most people" pay no attention to the "writin'" (as MB puts it) because "most people" are barely capable of using the language well enough just to get by in their own daily lives, never mind being able to appreciate the skill with which some poets and novelists can make the language say things it's never said before.

These are not "elitist" observations. They are simply facts. It is also a fact that literature has never been something of interest to "most people." But why should it be? MB seems to think he's punctured literary fiction's pretensions by asserting that "90% of people would lose their interest in fiction" if it didn't include "hooks" and other mindless devices, but why would writers want to solicit the attention of people who are more interested in *Wife Swap* to begin with? I don't know if 90% of us are this shallow or not, but even granting the claim, what's the problem with appealing to the 10% who want more, who are capable of paying attention? Why not just leave the "fancypants" writers to the fancypants readers and otherwise ignore them? Why MB's apparent need to denigrate the tastes of these readers even though by his own admission he has the vast majority of non-readers on his side anyway?

To be somewhat more charitable, MB apparently believes that the "well-being of fiction" can only be assured if it competes with other forms of narrative entertainment. But why should this be the case? Why should the measure of the accomplishments of literary fiction--of any form of art--be the degree to which it has appealed to a mass audience? MB clearly enough shares the tastes of this audience himself, but surely even he doesn't think that sheer popularity confers artistic success. I don't myself necessarily think it is the function of serious literature to deliberately reject success in the marketplace or to brandish its unpopularity like a rebel's sword. I think serious writers ought merely to ignore marketplace imperatives when those imperatives are at odds with their artistic integrity. If some readers find this elitist and alienating, so be it. In my opinion, it's better to have readers in sympathy with one's goals, even if this means having fewer readers, than to court readers who can't bother to question their reflexive demand for "story."

MB allows that "writers can (and will) do as they please. Of course, readers can (and will) read to please themselves too." But he can't resist adding that "it's idiotic to think that the fundamentals of most people's interest in fiction will ever extend too far beyond storytelling, subject matter, hook, and character." Again back to "most people." As far as I'm concerned "most people" can "read to please themselves" as well. (Actually, I'm pretty sure "most people" don't read at all.) But I don't really spend that much time obsessing over their reading habits, or putting up lengthy posts explaining why they're so misguided.

William Gaddis scholar Steven Moore says of populist attacks on experimental writers that

> "Of course you don't have to like Joyce (or Pynchon or Gaddis), they're certainly not for everyone, but to dismiss them as pretentious frauds and to glorify simpler, more traditional fiction struck me as an example of the growing anti-intellectualism in our country, right in step with schools mandating that evolution was just a "theory" and that creationism should be taught alongside it in science classes."

> "I couldn't help but detect some laziness as well; some people don't want to "work" at reading a novel (or listening to a complex opera, or watching a film with subtitles, etc). I said earlier I liked a challenge; many people obviously don't, or not when it comes to novels. I got the sense from these critics that they feel the novel is a democratic, middle-class genre that anyone should be able to enjoy, and that these experimentalists were betraying the novel (and their readers) by trying to turn it into something (high art) it was never intended to be. . . . . "
> (*Splice Today*, June 10, 2008)

I don't think I'd call the American impatience with aesthetically complex fiction "anti-intellectualism." Plenty of intellectuals themselves express the same disdain for writers like Pynchon and Gaddis, whose work can't be reduced to sociological observation or political agitation. It's more a resentment of complex art, a disinclination to give such art the sustained attention it requires. It's less "laziness" than it is a fundamental suspicion of anything that isn't useful in a readily apparent way. Critics want novels to be useful as tools of cultural analysis, while ordinary readers want novels to be entertaining, an escape from their own everyday reality.

Nor do I think that this impatience is necessarily "in step" with right-wing cultural values. The radical left can be just as impatient with art that isn't useful to their political battles as the radical right. In fact, the political left is probably more hostile to the "merely aesthetic," which is taken to be an expression of bad faith when it isn't being deconstructed and shown to be ideologically complicit with the political right. It isn't necessary to associate resistance to challenging art with politically conservative attitudes in order to account for its existence.

What may account for it, however, is precisely the assumption Moore detects in many readers and critics that "the novel is a democratic, middle-class genre that anyone should be able to enjoy, and that these experimentalists were betraying the novel." This is an assumption held not just by critics and readers, but by some writers as well, writers who shape their work so that "anyone should be able to enjoy" it, who count themselves failures if their work doesn't reach the broadest audience possible, who are willing to take on themselves the roles of marketer and publicist in order to accomplish this task. It is an assumption that counts novels as just another transitory amusement in competition for the entertainment dollar.

In his book *The Rise of the Novel*, Ian Watt convincingly establishes that the rise of the novel and the rise of the middle class were parallel developments and that this correlation was not just incidental. Novels did pose an opportunity for this now literate social class to exercise its newly-acquired skill. But to insist that novels should (or could, considering the other entertainment options now available) continue to perform this same function 200 years later, after Flaubert, after Henry James, and after all the other writers in their wake who saw that the novel could indeed be "high art," can only be an effort to put the genie back in the bottle. To this extent, the distinction between "popular fiction" and "literary fiction" is quite sensible. Let those who prefer a "democratic" form of mass entertainment stay with the kind of books that dominate the best seller lists. Let those who prefer "challenging" fiction with claims to high art stay with the comparatively few such works that manage to get published. The two groups don't have to intermingle at all.

I don't really mind being identified with the "elitist" group. Nor do I mind that the larger group wants fiction without artistic pretensions. I only mind when writers or readers want it both ways, when they want their books to be "good reads" but also want them to be taken seriously as works of literary art. This usually involves dismissing "high art" standards as "narrow" and elevating popular standards to a place higher than high art. *Ulysses*, *The Recognitions*, and *Gravity's Rainbow* don't "betray" the novel. They confirm its possibilities. To deny that the novel has such possibilities is the real betrayal.

According to Lionel Shriver:

Literature is not very popular these days, to put it mildly. According to the National Endowment for the Arts, nearly half of Americans do not read books at all, and those who do average a mere six a year. You'd think literary writers would be bending over backwards to ingratiate themselves to readers--to make their work maximally accessible, straightforward and inviting. But no. (*Wall Street Journal*, October 25, 2008)

But why in the world would anyone think that writers should be "bending over backwards" to appeal to people who have no interest in reading? What bizarre conception of literature would have it intended primarily for nonreaders? The mangled logic of this view, which perversely seems to be widely shared by many who <u>do</u> read, seems to me so far removed from any plausible assessment of the place of "literature" in our culture as to be pretty close to insane. That "literature is not very popular" at a time when the most potent measure of popularity is *American Idol* ought to be seen as a sign it still offers some hope of resistance to the values of commercial culture. Most of all it should be seen precisely as an opportunity to experiment with aesthetic strategies that challenge audiences rather than giving in to the inexorable pressure to "dumb down."

Since when have serious writers sought to be "maximally accessible, straightforward and inviting" above all? Until the 19th century, "literature" (or what was then simply considered "poetry") could only appeal to that minority of the population who literally could read, and most writers wanted to be "maximally accessible" not to contemporaneous audiences so much as to posterity, where the final verdict on literary greatness would be rendered. It's doubtful that Spenser or Milton thought that this audience would consist of readers for whom they needed to slavishly "ingratiate" themselves in advance. Some like to point out that Shakespeare in his time appealed to a relatively popular audience, but who could carefully examine Shakespeare's texts and conclude other than that the "accessibility" of his language comes not from any attempt to be more "straightforward" but from an assumption that his audience had sufficient listening skills to invite themselves into his imaginative world?

"Literature" of course is itself a concept that develops during the 19th century and after as an umbrella term that attempts to gather "poetry" together again with its now renegade forms, fiction and drama, precisely in order to make them available to the newly literate middle class as "good for" such readers. However, even this dilution of literary value--by which literature becomes valuable not in and for itself but as a tool of education and emergent nationalism--assumed that the appreciation of works of literature was something to aspire to, that "great books" required an elevation of taste and skill, although "common readers" could indeed reach this higher level. We now appear to have reached the point where literature can be relevant only if it turns itself into just another "inviting" mass entertainment.

The larger point of Shriver's essay, about the use of quotation marks, is just puerile: "By putting the onus on the reader to determine which lines are spoken and which not, the quoteless fad feeds the widespread conviction that popular fiction is fun while literature is arduous." Forget that the "quoteless fad" has been around since at least James Joyce and William Gaddis. Forget that not just quotation marks but dialogue itself are optional in fiction--who said that novels should record speech in this way at all? Heaven forbid that any "onus" be put on the reader to recognize that fiction isn't just a prosy version of a tv drama, with some written-out bits to supplement the talking. If Lionel Shriver's version of "literature" is what it takes to move the average books read per year from six to seven, writers ought to preserve their backs and refrain from bending over too frequently.

Apparently the scandal over James Frey's fictional embellishments of his memoirs has not had much of a dampening effect on the production of memoirs:

> Literary agents say they're seeing more memoir manuscripts and proposals than ever. Lee Gutkind, founder of the literary journal *Creative Nonfiction* and a professor of English at the University of Pittsburgh, says he gets 300-400 memoir submissions each month unsolicited, for his publication, which comes out three times a year. This reflects a change in the whole publishing climate, Mr. Gutkind says. In the past, writers would break into the business with autobiographical novels, and move on to other sorts of fiction. Now, "the novel's not hot anymore, and the autobiographical novel has been replaced by the memoir." Memoirs have become "the new door opening for first-time writers, young and old," he says. . . . (*Wall Street Journal*, April 14, 2006)

Gutkind's comment (and the article as a whole) does perhaps help explain the popularity of memoir. It appeals to the sort of reader and, more importantly, the sort of writer for whom writing is primarily a mode of "expression," a way to affirm the self, draw attention to one's own "life story." (Which is not to say that the memoir is inherently an inferior form or to deny that some writers have produced very fine books using the form.) For those perhaps too modest to push themselves onto tv directly (the WSJ article associates the popularity of memoirs with "the public's continuing fascination with reality TV"), memoir is perhaps a somewhat more respectable substitute. And if in addition it lands you an appearance on Oprah, all the better.

That "in the past, writers would break into the business with autobiographical novels" is undoubtedly an accurate statement (especially if your goal is to "break into the business," rather than, say, create an accomplished work of fiction), and further reminds us that even among those authors ostensibly writing fiction, depicting one's life story has always been perhaps the most immediate impulse motivating many, if not most, "first-time writers." An interest in peeking in on such stories is probably the motivating impulse for most readers of fiction as well (at least those readers interested in what is called "literary fiction"). Except now they have books that can satisfy that interest more directly, without the intervening demands of fiction (although apparently these books can make a few things up), and undoubtedly such books will continue to attract readers, as well as writers, for whom emotional directness (through vicarious drama) is the preeminent value, while those of us more interested in fiction as aesthetic invention will watch as books written to embody this value go on losing their market share.

Which might not be such a bad thing. Readers who want their books to be continuous with their television habits will get what they want and will presumably put less pressure on fiction writers to obsess over personal dramas. Writers who feel the need to "express themselves" can do so without restraint; those who really are interested in fiction as a literary form that transcends preoccupation with self and provides a kind of pleasure separate from the voyeurism encouraged by memoir might be able to pursue this interest with a clearer sense of their actual audience. In other words, those of us who prefer serious fiction, tiny remnant though we might be, would be able to indulge our vice without all of the interference and distraction brought to bear by the "book business."

II Affirmation

In an essay in the December 2005 issue of *The New Criterion*, Roger Kimball offers a laudatory account of *Art in Crisis*, written by the Austrian art historian (and Nazi party member) Hans Sedlmayr. "Autonomous man," according to Sedlymayer, "does not and cannot exist—any more than can autonomous art, architecture, painting and so on. It is of the essence of man that he should be both natural and supernatural ... . Man is fully human only in so far as he is a repository of the divine spirit."

Kimball shares Sedlymayer's contempt for the notion that art might have autonomous value:

One need not, I think, share Sedlmayr's theological convictions in order to appreciate the power of his strictures about the search for autonomy. "The fact is," he argues, "that art cannot be assessed by a measure that is purely artistic and nothing else. Indeed, such a purely artistic measure, which ignored the human element, the element which alone gives art its justification, would actually not be an artistic measure at all. It would merely be an aesthetic, and actually the application of purely aesthetic standards is one of the peculiarly inhuman features of the age, for it proclaims by implication the autonomy of the work of art, an autonomy that has no regard to men—the principle of l'art pour l'art." Art has its own aesthetic canons of legitimacy and achievement; but those canons are themselves nugatory unless grounded in a measure beyond art. That is the ultimate, indispensable, lesson of *Art in Crisis*.

One hears this sort of thing all the time, and not just from conservatives such as Kimball. Art that is "purely artistic" (itself such a logically dissonant notion--what proportion of art should be something other than artistic? 5%? 50%?--as to make all accounts of art proceeding from this assumption inherently absurd) lacks the "human element," privileges the autonomy of art over "regard to men." Art needs to accommodate itself (or be made to accommodate) some larger, more important conceptual order: if not religion, then politics, history, ethics, or "culture" regarded as a kind of substitute for "theological convictions."

But, since art is made by human beings for the consideration of other human beings, I just find it puzzling what it means to say that some art might be "inhuman." Is the "human element" in art something mystical to be intuited from the work, or is it stirred in like the secret ingredient in the spaghetti sauce? (Of course, in the case of the Nazi Sedylmayer, we can make a pretty good guess about who and what is being identified in his use of the word "inhuman.") What, finally, can be more "human" than to exercise the imagination in such a thoroughgoing and transformative way as to create a poem, painting, or musical composition that seems so self-sufficient that we want call it "autonomous"? What's inhuman about admiring such an effort to the extent of creating a vocabulary to describe its effects? In my opinion, people who opine about the "merely aesthetic," who find aesthetic values "nugatory" unless they are subservient to a higher principle of judgment, manifestly disdain art except as an illustrative aid, a utilitarian convenience.

It has always been relatively clear (at least to me) that Roger Kimball's protestations against the coarsening of art and the study of art have always been hollow, at best a rhetorical expedient in the broader struggle against liberalism, in the "arts" branch of which Kimball has been one of the most prominent combatants. But it is additionally illuminating to find him admitting that aesthetics mean little to him. (Although it is a little surprising that he would explicitly cite the anti-modernist ravings of a fascist art historian to support his position.) The view of art Kimball expresses here is in many ways representative of the long-standing conservative belief that art should serve simply as one of the props of culture (as it also explains the reflexive horror with which many conservative commentators recoil from unconventional or transgressive art), but the essay should also be a useful reminder the next time Kimball--or one of his like-minded colleagues--rails against the latest outrage among artists or literary critics that artistic accomplishment is really the least of his concerns.

Surprisingly enough (to me), Kimball and I seem to agree at least on one subject:

> "The issue, it is worth stressing, is not the orientation of the politics–Left vs. Right–it is rather the politicization of intellectual life tout court. That is, the task is not to replace or balance the left-wing orientation of academic life with a right-wing ideology but rather to de-politicize academic, i.e., to champion intellectual, not political, standards." (*Ignatius Insights*, August 2005)

If I thought Kimball truly believed this, I'd say that the "conservative" critique of the humanities as they are now taught in American universities would be worth taking seriously. Unfortunately I just can't accept that he does, largely for reasons that are implicit in some of Kimball's additional comments in this interview:

> "I believe that the arts provide a good barometer of cultural health. They reflect the fears, obsessions, aspirations, and ambitions of a culture. It tells us a great deal, I think, that terms like "transgressive" and "challenging" have emerged as among the highest words of praise in the critical lexicon. It tells us, among other things, that much art today is less affirmative than corrosive, that it places itself in an adversarial attitude toward the traditional moral, aesthetic, and cultural ambitions of our culture."

I would agree that the arts are a good indicator of "cultural health," if by this we meant that a healthy culture manifests a great deal of artistic activity--that it produces a significant number of people who value art enough to want to create it. But of course this is not what Kimball means. He means that art is directly reflective of a culture's "health" in moral and spiritual terms. He means that art is valuable primarily if not exclusively to the extent it works to foster such health, ideally to "affirm" traditional assumptions and practices.

A culture doesn't have "fears, obsessions, aspirations, and ambitions." Only people have these things, individual people. Ultimately a critic like Roger Kimball doesn't have much use for individual artists, individual readers or viewers or listeners. Art is not about heightened experience or even simple pleasure; it's about "culture," about the social norms that art can help to reinforce, the ideological "ambitions" it exists to define. Even when Kimball speaks of the "silence" great art can provoke, he's really talking about the silence enforced by the cultural authority which can be conferred upon art (by people like Kimball), which demands recovery of "a sense of the unfailing pertinence of our cultural inheritance." It's the "inheritance" that matters, not the particularity of works of art, nor the distinctive kind of experience (which can indeed involve "silence") that they afford.

Kimball's insistence on the cultural relevance of art is finally not that different from the similar insistence by current academic criticism that art is most useful as an object of "cultural study." Both look past the aesthetic properties of art in order to examine its purported efficacy as a cultural force or its illustrative value as a cultural "symptom." The biggest difference between conservative critics such as Kimball and most academic critics is that for Kimball art should be "affirmative," while for the academic critics--and Kimball is correct about this--it is precisely the transgressive and corrosive qualities of art that are most highly prized. I believe that art at its best is indeed "subversive," but not in the narrow political sense of the term presently conveyed by academic criticism. As I have put it elsewhere in this book, "Through art we become aware that the world can always be remade. Art is the enemy of all certainties and settled doctrines. This is not likely to be acceptable to political critics of either the left or the right. . ." Which is why Roger Kimball probably will never really advocate for the "de-politicization" of art or of academic study. His view of what art is good for is always already intensely political.

When reading Roger Scruton, one can always be sure that the ideas and sentiments expressed are being offered with utter sincerity. The extent to which he is willing to defend a view of the world and the place of humans in it that seems not simply conservative but thoroughly antique can be astonishing, but he does defend it, seriously and systematically. As a philosopher, Scruton sticks to the most fundamental questions of social and cultural value, in many instances raising questions long assumed satisfactorily answered and renewing conservative objections to the direction taken by much of modern culture.

Those who might rebut Scruton's case against modern art and popular culture are perhaps tempted to simply dismiss his invocations of such seemingly agreeable concepts as "order" and "beauty" as so much opportunistic cant. This would be a mistake, not merely because Scruton makes his arguments in an intellectually honest way but because the role of order or beauty in art ought not be denied outright. Scruton is not wrong to consider "beauty" a relevant consideration in the assessment of art. He is wrong in his conception of beauty as it manifests itself in works of art.

In a recent essay, "Beauty and Desecration," Scruton asserts that "the sacred task of art. . .is to magnify life as it is and to reveal its beauty." Since the era of modernism, however, deliberate ugliness has usurped the place of beauty and "[a]rt increasingly aimed to disturb, subvert, or transgress moral certainties, and it was not beauty but originality—however achieved and at whatever moral cost—that won the prizes" (*City Journal*, Spring 2009).

Note that is the transgression not of aesthetic standards but of "moral certainties" to which Scruton objects. Scruton rightly notes that in the 20th/21st centuries "expression" has become the underpinning of most movements in and commentary on "new" art, but rather than examine the specifically aesthetic flaws in an approach anchored in "expression," Scruton instead recoils from the moral anarchy unleashed by the modern Romantic rebel: "This emphasis on expression was a legacy of the Romantic movement; but now it was joined by the conviction that the artist is outside bourgeois society, defined in opposition to it, so that artistic self-expression is at the same time a transgression of ordinary moral norms."

Scruton uses as an example the widespread habit in productions of opera to alter the staging and the dramatic vision to produce a "modernized" version. He cites a particular production of Mozart's *The Abduction From the Seraglio* set "in a Berlin brothel, with Selim as pimp and Konstanze one of the prostitutes. Even during the most tender music, copulating couples littered the stage, and every opportunity for violence, with or without a sexual climax, was taken. . .The words and the music speak of love and compassion, but their message is drowned out by the scenes of desecration, murder, and narcissistic sex."

Even if we accept that Scruton's description of the staging of this opera is true to its director's intent--and I would guess that many others in the audience that night did not see it in this way-- his outrage is directed at its moral implications. It is "an example of something familiar in every aspect of our contemporary culture. It is not merely that artists, directors, musicians, and others connected with the arts are in flight from beauty. Wherever beauty lies in wait for us, there arises a desire to preempt its appeal, to smother it with scenes of destruction." Scruton manages to connect this sort of "re-visioning" in the high arts to the music video, which "is often devoted to concentrating into the time span of a pop song some startling new account of moral chaos."

Scruton cannot appreciate that the operatic production he attended committed an <u>aesthetic</u> offense, not a moral one. I am quite willing to believe that those responsible for it thought it a clever idea to "set the opera in a Berlin brothel, with Selim as pimp and Konstanze one of the prostitutes," but ultimately this is just an aesthetically vacuous attempt to "update" Mozart, to run roughshod over Mozart's original vision of his opera and establish their own overwhelmingly lame one in its place. It is a practice to be found not only in opera but in theater in general, whereby directors and producers with the aesthetic sensibilities of lizards attempt to keep the great works "relevant." One could, I suppose, call this artistic cluelessness a "moral" problem, but most of what Scruton sees as the unleashing of "moral chaos" is finally just the consequence of the aesthetic incompetence of some those entrusted with the job of re-presenting the theatrical art of the past.

I suspect that Scruton does not want to examine the art he despises for its specific aesthetic failings because the very introduction of the "aesthetic" leads for him to the moral decadence he fears. "Beauty" is not to be found in the creations of artists separated from the moral universe to which they must conform:

> We can wander through this world, alienated, resentful, full of suspicion and distrust. Or we can find our home here, coming to rest in harmony with others and with ourselves. The experience of beauty guides us along this second path: it tells us that we are at home in the world, that the world is already ordered in our perceptions as a place fit for the lives of beings like us.

In this view, beauty is not even a "creation" of artists. It is a discovery by artists of "harmony," of the "order" that is "already" there "in our perceptions." Artists, such as the great landscape painters, are, if they are to be artists at all, "devoted to moralizing nature and showing the place of human freedom in the scheme of things."

This harmony and order--a moralized nature--is what Scruton means by the "sacred," the capturing of which is the duty of artists. Modern art is engaged in desecration--the inversion of the sacred. In suggesting that human beings are other than "at home in the world" or that the world itself is not always "fit," modern artists mock and undermine the moral order that art should be celebrating and supporting. It is time, according to Scruton, to recover the sacred, "to rediscover the affirmation and the truth to life without which artistic beauty cannot be realized."

Scruton's is an entirely coherent argument if you accept the underlying world view according to which the role of art is to "affirm" the deep, if not always completely visible, truth in "the scheme of things" that manifests itself in beauty. If you believe, however, that the world at times betrays an order that isn't necessarily beneficent, or that as Scruton puts it in his repugnance at another kind of "truthful" art, a human being can be reduced by life to "a lump of suffering flesh made pitiful, helpless, and disgusting," you might find Scruton's "truth" to be partial indeed. You might, in fact, find it a delusion and the idea that a great artist can't redeem "suffering flesh made pitiful" by an act of imagination (or, as Susan Sontag would have it, "will") anything but an affirmation of life.

III Canonical

Richard Jenkyns believes that, although a "canon" of literary works is necessary in providing us with a stock of appropriate "shared references," such a canon does not have to be exclusively "high cultural."

> It is surely vain to suppose that poorly educated and disaffected young Asians can be brought to a stronger sense of belonging in Britain by a diet of Hamlet, Middlemarch and the Psalms. The truth is that shared references and resonances mostly need to evolve naturally, that most of them derive from popular culture, and that many of them are like family jokes. Television has had enormous power as a unifier; this power is now declining with the proliferation of channels and new media, but in their time Morecambe and Wise did more than Milton and Wordsworth to make us feel one people. (*Prospect*, December 22, 2007)

The obvious flaw in this argument comes from that "in their time." The accomplishments of Morecambe and Wise notwithstanding, the ultimate point of a canon is that it includes "shared references" that are <u>timeless,</u> not merely of unifying value in a particular historical era. Unless future generations will likely value Morecambe and Wise as much as those "in their time" did (although, who knows, maybe they will), there seems little point in enshrining them in a "canon," which will only come to seem as much an imposition on the tastes of those later generations as Milton and Wordsworth.

(I'd love to see *Monty Python's Flying Circus* become canonical, but something tells me that 50 years from now not everyone will find the show quite as bracingly funny as I did when first exposed to it in the mid-1970s. To in effect insist that it is that funny by enshrining it in a canon would not accomplish much.)

Jenkyns correctly locates the origin of our notions of a canon in the deliberations of the Church over which Biblical texts deserved its official sanction, but he doesn't really much discuss the two primary purposes for which the concept of the canon has been adapted to secular culture: to help enhance "national greatness" and to create academic curricula. (Sometimes the two projects overlap.) A canon of great writers focuses attention on the cultural accomplishments a country can claim, the contributions it has made to "culture" and "literature" on a broader, global scale. (Thus, say, Great Britain can claim that "its" poetry is perhaps the greatest any nation has produced.) It also allows the academic study of literature to claim for itself a "subject" of study. "Literature" as a disembodied category of "great writing" is unsustainable as the foundation of a curriculum of study; a semi-official list of sufficiently great writers and texts to justify their inclusion in a prescribed set of courses is needed to give literary studies the status of a "discipline," the core elements of which students will be expected to master.

Because I've never been able to accept the assumptions behind either of these impulses to canon-building, I've never invested much energy in defending the canon against its supposed enemies, those identified by Harold Bloom as the "School of Resentment." Although I agree with Bloom that much of the hostility directed at canonical writers is misplaced and counterproductive, I can't see that preserving the canon in its pre-Theory/Cultural Studies form is either possible or desirable. I have enough regard for most of the texts usually invoked as canonical that I think they will continue to attract readers without the need to place them in a pre-established hierarchy that only invites efforts to divest them of their privileged status, from whatever angle of skepticism or resentment.

Most of the efforts to "interrogate" the canon over the past two decades have not really questioned the need for hierarchy in organizing literary study. Indeed, the focus of much canon-busting has been on making room for other texts, sometimes on replacing existing canonical works with those deemed worthy for other than traditionally defined "literary" qualities. (In some cases, non-canonical works, such as *Their Eyes Were Watching God*, were shown to have such qualities despite their previous neglect.) The canon was altered or reconceived, not abandoned.

Canonization, it would seem, continues to be "socially useful," as Jenkyns explicitly puts it, while the idea of literature as something that mostly provides "shared references and resonances"--or at least should be made to do so--is further reinforced.

If all "great books" can do is allow us to resonate with one another, then I don't think finally abandoning the canon altogether would do much harm. It might do literature a great deal of good, if we can then more profitably think of reading it as a particular kind of experience the ultimate reward of which lies in the experience itself and can't be reduced to its political utility or its role in the academic curriculum. Jenkyns himself, in discussing the popularity of Jane Austen, convincingly maintains that literary works survive through a kind of bottom-up process whereby authors and books appeal over time through their "actual merits." This kind of informal canonization should be enough to keep the greatest books in circulation, while whatever "shared references" they also encourage are references that persist because they're really worth sharing.

Apparently Steve Wasserman believes that "The best reading experience is to occupy your time with the worthy dead rather than the ambitious living."

This remark (actually among the first words to come out of Wasserman's mouth during a July 14, 2005 *Open Source* radio interview) certainly tells us a great deal about why the *Los Angeles Times Book Review* never fulfilled its promise, or really even came close to being a reliable guide to contemporary letters.

The truth is pretty close to exactly the opposite of what Wasserman would have us believe. Not only is it the case that, as Ed Champion has put it at his weblog, *The Return of the Reluctant* (July 15, 2005), "the very form of the novel has evolved *precisely because* of efforts from the ambitious living" (one could say the same thing about other literary forms as well), but the "worthy dead" were probably the most intensely "ambitious" writers one could imagine--not necessarily ambitious for worldly success (although many would have no doubt gladly accepted it) but, because until the mid-nineteenth century (at the earliest) financial success as we would define it was more or less unthinkable (not enough readers), for "literary immortality." The great writers of the past literally wanted their work to survive through the ages, as testimony to their "success" as literary masters. (Remember the first stanza of *Paradise Lost?*: "Sing, Heav'nly Muse. . .I thence/Invoke thy aid to my advent'rous Song,/That with no middle flight intends to soar/Above th' Anonian Mount, while it pursues/Things unattempted yet in Prose or Rhyme." How audacious to think your poem could successfully "justify the ways of God to men"!)

Furthermore, one suspects that Wasserman finds reading the "worthy dead" the best way to occupy his time precisely because it doesn't have to be an overly strenuous "reading experience." After all, these writers have already been pronounced "worthy"; all one has to do is nod sagely while passively absorbing all the greatness previous generations of readers have been kind enough to pre-determine for you. What a nice way to pass a rainy day. Some people might even be impressed with your good taste and admirable discernment.

In fact, the best (defined as "challenging") reading experience is precisely to read the "ambitious living." Judgments have yet to be reached about these folks; their work has to be explored and assessed. Some of it even strikes out in directions with which one is unfamiliar, and requires more than ordinary concentration. This sort of writing has yet to be certified as Literature, and while reading it might not provide the same sense of security that one's experience will be "worthy," it does test one's ability to comprehend what makes literature literary in the first place.

Ultimately, Wasserman's pronouncement is at least as condescending to the "worthy dead" as it is to the "ambitious living." It implies that their work is safely ensconced in the collective literary mausoleum, no longer embroiled in the petty concerns of the living. It expresses a view of Literature that only makes living readers less likely to be interested in the literature of the past, held out by the likes of Wasserman as something so much grander than what the puny present could produce.

Younger readers especially recoil (justifiably so) at such a display of supercilious superiority (itself so thoroughly unjustified). In my opinion, if the literary work of the "worthy dead" is perceived as detached from the affairs of the present, with nothing to say to those who must live in it--and in many cases this is simply not the case--it doesn't have much value to anyone. It's not what is passed on to us from the worthy dead. It's just dead.

In the March issue of *First Things*, R.V. Young, an English professor at North Carolina State University, seeks to praise Shakespeare, and not to bury him. Here is the first paragraph of his essay:

> More than any other writer, Shakespeare embodies the distinctive principles of Western Civilization. Men and women of the West are drawn to Shakespeare because his plays and poems continue to express their aspirations, to articulate their concerns, and to confront the tensions and contradictions in the Western vision itself. He is admired not as an uncritical encomiast of his own culture and society, but rather as an exemplum of the spirit—both critical and conservative—that is among the West's most enduring legacies to the world. It is, therefore, no surprise that academic literary critics, who owe their very existence to Shakespeare and other great

writers, have cast doubt upon Shakespeare's exalted position at exactly the moment in history when the societies of the West have become most anxious about their own integrity and probity.

Now, I think Shakespeare is indeed the greatest writer in the English language (and I have read all of the plays). I also think the passage just quoted is garbage.

When I come upon essays like this one, ostensibly defending Shakespeare from all of his many supposed detractors, I also come as close as I ever do to feeling sympathy for the academic critics who have rejected "bardolatry" and used Shakespeare as one more opportunity to deprecate the "merely literary" and politicize literary study to advance their own agendas. These critics assume (wrongly, in lots of cases), that this sort of Western-Civ rah-rah was really the goal of academic literary study all along and have understandably enough recoiled from it.

But of course to uniformly boo and hiss at "the West" is no better than to always celebrate its wonders, and my sympathy is short-lived.

What I really seem to hear when reading passages like the one above is the sound of Shakespeare himself frantic to free himself from the grave if only to seek out the likes of Professor Young and throttle him. Shakespeare of course had no interest in the "distinctive principles of Western Civilization" (wouldn't have known what they were), did not in the least express something called the "Western vision," was certainly no "encomiast of his culture and society" (far from it), and sought to exemplify nothing but the possibilities of the forms in which he wrote and whatever personal "vision" of human existence he had managed to acquire. (And fortunately he did possess a vision that has seemed to express the aspirations and concerns of many of the rest of us--the one point on which I agree with Professor Young.)

But in Professor Young's "vision," Shakespeare's plays and poems disappear in favor of an "encomium" on behalf of Western Civilization. Shakespeare becomes a Great Figure to admire and exalt (but not to read), an opportunity for the Professor himself to posture and declaim. And Shakespeare is not the only writer to fall victim to this sort of reactionary praise ("reactionary" in the literal sense of the term, as it is a reaction to the perceived loss of prestige among the "great" Western writers). Sadly, writers from Milton and Swift to Emerson and Twain are accorded this dubious defense, their obvious enough human limitations in terms of racial attitudes or class solidarity not simply acknowledged or explained but erased. Young, for example, struggles mightily in his essay to demonstrate there's really nothing at all wrong with Shakespeare's depictions of Shylock and Othello, that in fact he really portrays Jews and "Moors" as stand-up guys. I would agree that there's great ambivalence in the portrayal of these characters, and that the plays in which they appear ought not to be merely dismissed, but there's no point in denying that some of the ambivalence is unattractive, to say the least.

Sometimes people come to have questions about even great writers not because they despise Western Civilization but because every new generation of readers has to be convinced anew that the work of these writers actually stands up to present scrutiny. (The sort of indoctrination Professor Young seems implicitly to favor never works.) "Criticism" of the kind this *First Things* essay represents doesn't help to resolve such questions because it ultimately discourages serious reading in the first place. An acquiescent and unequivocal esteem will do.

Nature writer David Gessner astutely observes:

As the 150th anniversary of "Walden" approaches on August 9, it may pay to remember that Thoreau's great book also has its share of fart jokes, including references to Pythagrians and their love of beans. Bad puns, too, but you get the feeling that that isn't what the anniversary party is going to focus on. Instead the same, tired old cut-out of Thoreau as nature saint will be dragged out, St. Francis of Concord, our sexless-- and increasingly lifeless --hero. It makes you wonder if anyone's actually taken the time to read his strange and wild book lately. If they did they would find sentences that fulfill Emerson's epigram:

"My moods hate each other." Sentences that are, in turn, defensive and direct, arch and simple, upright and sensual, over-literary (even for the times) and raw. Of course I'm not claiming that Thoreau's book is free of nature reverence, just that the pious tone is often contradicted--delightfully, thornily--by moments like his confession that, for all his reasoned vegetarianism, "I could sometimes eat a fried rat with good relish, if it were necessary." (*Boston Globe*, August 1, 2004)

In fact, I wouldn't be at all surprised to find that not many people, including most nature writers, have "taken the time to read [Thoreau's] strange and wild book lately." Indeed it wouldn't surprise me to learn that few people have really read *Walden* at all, at least as it really is and not through the prism of a romanticized revisionism that sees the book as the kind of prissified environmental tome most people take it to be. There's plenty in it that's cranky, imperious, inflexible, and manifestly not politically correct. Most of all there's Thoreau's sometimes dense and allusive style, which hardly seeks to describe nature in translucent language and dulcet tones, to elevate the "scenery" above the writer's own subjective perceptions. In effect, an image of Thoreau as a certain sort of nature-worshipper has replaced Thoreau the writer his texts actually present him to be.

One might say that this kind of inattention to what objectively characterizes the work of writers from the past, a failure to actually read it, is almost inevitable when these writers become known to us only--or at least mostly--through their inclusion in curricula of academic study--through being listed on course syllabi of various kinds. Familiarity with their books or plays or poems comes entirely in the "textbook" variety, although we don't necessarily read them only in literal textbooks. We read them in snippets, abridgements, condensed versions. It becomes very easy in this context for Thoreau to become the solemn nature-writer or Dickens to become the creator of Tiny Tim and other sentimental characters, or Hawthorne to become the grim chronicler of Puritanism, tags that efficiently describe them--or a version of them--and make it unnecessary to read them further.

Since the dominant attitude toward canonical literature among those who would otherwise be entrusted with educating readers or playgoers in the appropriate strategies for appreciating literature--that is, in the academy--has actually become a skeptical if not belligerent one, this situation will only get worse. The culture mavens will continue to insist on the spiritually pharmaceutical properties of Literature, and the professors will continue to use the snippets and abridgements to advance whatever preconceived agendas they have in mind.

Yet at some point it does become necessary to acknowledge that perhaps some writers, perhaps some great writers, just no longer engage present-day readers as effectively as they seem to have done in the past. Perhaps people no longer read *Walden* because its voice seems too alien, too prickly, for current sensibilities. Perhaps even the time will come when overcoming all the obstacles to understanding Shakespeare in his own language and according to the appropriate literary conventions will become too difficult, at least for all but the few. Neither insisting on the greatness of these writers nonetheless, nor attempting to reinterpret or literally retranslate them into contemporary idioms and assumptions will forestall this for long. It is true that we live in a time when any kind of difficult or unorthodox writing is often decried as an offense to the "common reader," and it is possible that at some time in the not so distant future such writing will again be welcomed. At that time the difficulties involved in reading works of literature from the past might again be seen as worth the effort as well. But there is effort involved, and it remains an open question whether "literary reading" will ever really be an interest shared by more than a small, if ardent, minority. And, if not, whether this would be such a bad thing.

PART NINE

Critics

II Morris Dickstein and Historical Criticism

Readers of Morris Dickstein's newest book, *Dancing in the Dark: A Cultural History of the Great Depression*, should find it an agreeable survey of the cultural expressions of the 1930s that reveals how the Depression years were portrayed and understood by those living through them. Readers of Dickstein's previous books will recognize its method, a fastidious interrogation of novels, films, and other works of art for their historical resonances and mutual assumptions, their ability to show how an entire culture at a particular time is "thinking." Readers less interested in Dickstein's signature critical approach or in the context his earlier books provide nevertheless could easily enough from *Dancing in the Dark* be made aware of "Depression culture" in a coherent and often insightful way. Dickstein's painstaking scrutiny of texts for their clues to cultural developments can occasionally get bogged down in some turgid writing, but that he can be an acute analyst of these texts within the framework of a consistently applied historical criticism is undeniable.

While I don't find this sort of historical criticism invalid-- there is ultimately nothing wrong with situating a work of art or literature in its period and cultural mileu, as long as the limits of this strategy as a way to "understand" the work are acknowledged--I do find Dickstein's relentless pursuit of the strategy frequently tedious and finally not much service to literature, although Dickstein often assures us it is. Since a great deal of his criticism has been focused on post-World War II American fiction, I think that Dickstein has especially done some misservice to contemporary fiction, my own critical bailiwick, distorting its achievement and finally reducing it to a function as barometer of the cultural and political changes that have taken place in the United States between 1945 and the present.

I make this criticism regretfully, as Dickstein's 1979 book, *Gates of Eden*, was probably more responsible for setting me on a path of study of contemporary fiction than any other critical book I read or any course I took. It introduced me to the work of experimental writers such as John Barth and Donald Barthelme, of whom I don't think I'd ever heard at the time, and although I could sense even when reading the book as a undiscriminating undergraduate that Dickstein didn't entirely approve of their fiction, especially the Barthleme of the late '60s and after, just the suggestion that Barthleme was "radical" (Dickstein meant to associate him with the decadent, Weatherman phase of 60s radicalism) was enough to make me want to read his books posthaste.

Actually, much of Dickstein's analysis of the fiction of the 1960s still holds up, as I discovered when I recently re-read the book, even if the tacit impatience with postmodernism seems more apparent to me now. (The term "postmodernism" is never used, however; Dickstein in 1979 preferred to identify writers like Barth and Barthelme as modernists, emphasizing the continuity between the formal experimentation of modernism and that which came to be called postmodernism. Dickstein thinks that late modernism radicalized itself beyond redemption in the work of writers such as Rudolph Wurlitzer, but while I can't agree that the experimental impulse inevitably leads to an aesthetic impasse, his implicit suggestion that the adventurous writing of the 1960s and 1970s was really a second flowering of modernism usefully emphasizes that "postmodernism" was first of all a phenomenon of literary history, not a reorientation of history itself.) Above all, his recognition that the fiction of the 1960s represents a significant achievement still seems audacious:

> In a topsy-turvy age that often turned trash into art and art into trash, that gaily pursued topical fascination and ephemeral performances and showed a real genius for self-consuming artifacts--an age that sometimes valued art too little because it loved raw life too much--novels were written that are among the handful of art-works, few enough in any age, that are likely to endure. It's a bizarre

prospect, but the sixties are as likely to be remembered through novels as through anything else they left behind.

Dickstein finds much that is praiseworthy in the fiction of Thomas Pynchon, Joseph Heller, Kurt Vonnegut, and even Barth and Barthleme, despite his judgment that they ultimately take things too far. However ambivalent his reaction to the most adventurous of adventurous fiction, and however much attention he gives to writers whose work will not, in my opinion, "endure," such as Bellow and Mailer, Dickstein's consideration of the experimental fiction of the sixties inspired me at least to take this fiction seriously and to discover for myself whether it produced work "likely to endure."

Unfortunately, the very passage I have quoted, I now see, also signals the real limitations of Dickstein's approach, of the assumptions about fiction's utility as a clue to culture. The last sentence arguably implies that the novels of the era will endure because they are the best way to "remember" the sixties. For those who lived through the era, they will continue to evoke it; for those future readers who did not, they will still enable a cultural "remembering" that will likely allow us to get a glimpse of the kind of "topical" and "ephemeral" attractions Dickstein describes in the rest of the passage. These novels will be "left behind" for scholars and others interested in that "topsy-turvy age" to recreate it, either critically or imaginatively. Fiction is ultimately of value, especially fiction particularly attuned to the social wavelength of its period, as a window onto history. It perhaps enlivens history in a way that straight historical narrative or cultural criticism, cannot, but otherwise it remains an adjunct to the study of culture in its historical manifestations.

My own initial response to *Gates of Eden* demonstrates that it is possible to read the book as an illuminating appraisal of American fiction of the 1950s and 1960s, but turning to Dickstein's other writing on postwar fiction only confirms that ultimately his purpose seems to be to pin postwar writers down as specimens of their time and place, at best figures in a procession of "tendencies." In the essays "The Face in the Mirror: The Eclipse of Distance in Contemporary Fiction" and "Ordinary People: Carver, Ford and Blue-Collar Realism" (both reprinted in *A Mirror in the Roadway*, Dickstein's explicit defense of realism), he extends his survey of postwar fiction into the 1970s and 1980s. In the first, he notes a shift in the 1970s toward novels "built around characters who are the very self and voice of the author," exemplified by Philip Roth, William Styron, and John Irving. In the second he discusses the rise of minimalism in the work of Raymond Carver, as well as the subsequent move away from minimalism to "a more expansive, more full-bodied fiction" in the work of Richard Ford and Russell Banks. In the latter he predicts a further shift to "some transformed and heightened version of the social novel." Clearly Dickstein is most interested in contemporary fiction as an opportunity to chart developments in fiction's way of registering social realities. Chronicling the rise and fall of trends in fiction is not necessarily a trivial activity, but in Dickstein's case the single-minded manner in which he pursues the task does threaten to make criticism an intellectual version of fashion journalism.

Leopards in the Temple (2002) is probably Dickstein's summary statement of the historical progression of postwar American fiction. Subtitled "The Transformation of American Fiction 1945-1970," it again focuses on the 1950s and 1960s, this time treating only fiction but otherwise covering much of the same ground scrutinized in *Gates of Eden*. The biggest change in approach to the fiction of this period is a considerable narrowing of the terrain on which Dickstein is willing to cast his critical eye, leaving experimental or postmodern fiction out of view almost completely. He instead devotes most of the book to discussions of well-publicized mainstream writers such as Gore Vidal, Truman Capote, Mailer, James Jones, Jack Kerouac, James Baldwin, John Updike, Bellow, and Roth, although there are a few welcome considerations of Paul Bowles, Nabokov, Heller, and Vonnegut. Dickstein's implicit dismissal of experimental fiction is perhaps best exemplified in his discussion of John Barth's *End of the Road*, which Dickstein calls "Barth's best novel" and is included in *Leopards in the Temple* in the first place mainly because it illustrates the "road" theme Dickstein traces from Kerouac to other writers of the '50s and early '60s. His attitude toward Barth's later metafiction, truly his most important achievement, well beyond *End of the Road*, is surely encapsulated in his observation that "In *Lost in the Funhouse* and *Chimera* Barth's genial narrators soon grow as heartily sick of [their] self-consciousness as we do."

One can legitimately find the work of John Barth and other metafictionists not to one's liking without distorting the fact of its prominence during the period Dickstein is examining. It is hardly credible to suggest that the 1960s are most appropriately represented by Bellow, Malamud, and James Baldwin, which Dickstein does in his final chapter by highlighting their work rather than the postmodern writers, whose work rebelled against the quiescent realism preferred by the gatekeepers of literary culture, much as others rebelled against the constraints of conformity and established practice in other arts and in politics during this time. A survey of the "transformation" of American fiction after World War II that willfully excludes this work is finally hard to take seriously.

Leopards in the Temple posits a postwar literary history that begins with war novelists, proceeds through the early fiction of certain writers who first came to public attention immediately after the war, such as Vidal and Capote, further through sensation-causing writers such as Kerouac and J.D Salinger, and, with some pauses along the way to acknowledge a few other noteworthy authors, winds up affirming the centrality of culturally sanctioned novelists such as Bellow, Baldwin, and Mailer. Another history of postwar fiction is possible, however, one that begins with, say, John Hawkes, emphasizes Nabokov's work beyond *Lolita*, carefully considers William Gaddis, includes James Purdy and Thomas Berger along with Joseph Heller, and takes as the apogee of the period the work of Pynchon, Barth, Robert Coover, and Donald Barthelme. Dickstein's history is a history of American culture as reflected in his chosen authors and books; the alternative history is more properly a <u>literary</u> history of the years 1945-60, one that focuses on the response of writers to the legacy and the challenges of modernism by extending that legacy through fiction that continued to challenge readers' expectations and that, in my opinion, more accurately encompasses the writers whose work will still likely be read once this period more firmly recedes into literal history.

What now alienates me the most from Dickstein's critical method, however, are the grand generalizations he makes about the practice of fiction, generalizations that interpose great distance between the critic and the texts he/she ostensibly tries to illuminate. He writes, for example, that novelists of the 1940s and 1950s

. . .were obsessed more with Oedipal struggle than with class struggle, concerned about the limits of civilization rather than the conflicts within civilization. Their premises were more Freudian than Marxist. . .Auschwitz and Hiroshima had set them thinking about the nature and destiny of man, and relative affluence gave them the leisure to focus on spiritual confusions in their own lives.

How does Dickstein know what "they" were thinking? How can "they," as opposed to individual writers, be thinking anything except insofar as the critic has self-selected a few of "them," invested them with "premises" and speculated about "their" social standing ("relative affluence") and the state of their souls ("spiritual confusions")? Occasionally Dickstein does offer an interesting critical reading of a particular text, as when he observes of *Catcher in the Rye* that "Holden's adventures in New York are really a series of Jewish jokes, at once sad, funny, and self-accusing," but the overwhelmingly dominant impression left by *Leopards in the Temple*, and by Morris Dickstein's books as a whole, is that fiction is most worthwhile as a leading indicator not just of just of writers', but an entire culture's temporal obsessions. If I thought this was the foremost reason to read novels, I'd probably never read another one.

II James Wood

It would seem that a significant number of people whose opinions I otherwise respect, including not a few literary webloggers, have great admiration for the British literary critic James Wood. (Or at least they profess to admire him--one could wonder whether some of those who have extolled his critical virtues aren't trying to stave off some of the critical barbs he might at some point hurl in their direction.) I would like to say I share the high opinion of Wood so many others have expressed, since in some ways he does continue a tradition of informed, wide-ranging literary criticism not tied to the careerist norms of the academy that desperately needs to be revived. But I just can't. Ultimately his reviews and essay-reviews are detrimental not just to the cause of literary criticism but to the continued appreciation of the possibilities of literature itself.

In a review of Wood's novel *The Book Against God* (*Harpers*, July 2003), Wyatt Mason made some telling points against Wood as a critic, some of them similar to those I will make here, and I would recommend reading Mason's essay for further discussion of the topic. However, I will use Wood's review of John Le Carre's *Absolute Friends* in *The New Republic* (April 05, 2004) to illustrate my particular problems with Wood's criticism. I should say that I am neither a fan nor a detractor of Le Carre. I have read a few of his books and found them entertaining enough. I would not be among those Wood takes after for elevating Le Carre above his merits to the status of "literary" writer. Perhaps thus I am even better able to see the limitations of Wood's approach to both criticism and literature than if he were attacking a writer I greatly esteem.

I will also say that I do not question Wood's intelligence, his preparation to be a critic, or his motives. I think he believes his approach to literature is the correct approach. (And unlike Dale Peck, Wood's harsh judgments are usually backed up with reasons, even reasons that have something to do with the book at hand.) I simply think that this approach exemplifies what's finally wrong with the kind of literary criticism he attempts to perpetuate.

It would indeed be easy to maintain that Wood sees literature as a kind of religion-substitute, a charge Wood has himself acknowledged and to an extent accepted. But it's not so much questions of religious belief or "philosophy" more generally that Wood wants to find addressed in works of "serious" fiction. It's that he wants to take literature seriously in the same way the devoted take their religion. Just as they often believe their religious tradition gets things right in a particular way, Wood wants to believe there's one true path to writing a serious novel, one which makes all other paths not just more full of obstacles but actual roads to perdition. Wood's attacks on writers like Don DeLillo or Thomas Pynchon can be seen as motivated by this larger belief.

In the case of Le Carre, his first sin is to have written genre fiction. Although Wood tries not to condemn the whole enterprise outright in this review, it's clear enough he has no use for it. We can't even say that in reading Le Carre we learn anything about spying because, Wood declares, "much of Le Carre's detail was entirely invented, including the terminology, and there were old intelligence hands who complained that his picture of the service, while intended as an anti-James Bond demystification, was itself a species of romance." Not only is Le Carre a genre writer, then, but he writes. . .fiction.

Next Wood goes after LeCarre's reputed "political complexity" (which of course Wood thinks is anything but):

> . . .In fact, instead of analyzing the political complexities of the Cold War, Le Carre's books narrate the functional complexities of the political complexities; that is, they show us, mainly, that the two espionage systems often worked in matching ways. This insight then locks the mazy plots in place, essentially closing the door on further analysis: the two-sided mirror dazzles further curiosity. And so the form of the books tends toward a self-cancelling amnesty, each side a little shabbier at the end of the story than it was at the start.

I sure hope I am not alone in finding this passage mostly gibberish. To be fair, it has probably come out this way because Wood is trying to hide, as he does through most of the review, what he really finds objectionable about Le Carre: he doesn't like the man's politics, especially the "anti-American" turn his politics has seemed to take of late.

We are told that Le Carre "can write very well," even in this latest book, which Wood clearly despises. However, after quoting a passage of ostensibly good writing, and even explaining why some might find it good, Wood eventually concludes that Le Carre's "prose announces, in effect: 'here is what the world looks like according to the conventions of realism.' It is a civilized style, but nonetheless a slickness unto death." Apparently even what Le Carre actually does well he doesn't do well at all. (Or, he writes well very badly.)

Which brings us to the real nub of the issue, the failing of Le Carre's that is most debilitating, the overriding purpose novels must embody that Le Carre doesn't understand. In his essay, Wyatt Mason observes that ""How somebody felt about something' is precisely what Wood wants from a novel; reaching into character is what he expects. Consciousness is the ultimate freedom, and its honest representation in fiction is what draws us into sympathy with the created, not with its creator. This is the hallmark of the work of those authors. . .for whom Wood has the greatest regard." Of Le Carre Wood says: [His] character portraits are not themselves complex, merely complex relative to the rolled thinness of most characters in contemporary thrillers." Le Carre's characters, like those of Hemingway and Graham Greene, "are, paradoxically, alert but always blocking the ratiocinative consequences of their alertness. Such characters are not minds but just voyeurs of their own obscurities."

Frankly this is just a very pompous way of saying that Le Carre--and by extension almost all of the writers who come up short in Wood's estimation--does not employ the technique of "psychological realism," the revelation of consciousness that seems to be for Wood the most important legacy of the modernist fiction writers. To this extent Wood is stuck in the early 20th century, taking what was indeed at the time an innovation in the presentation of character and a step beyond the realism of earlier writers as the final word about what novels ought properly to do. Clearly it fulfills his own needs as a reader of fiction, filling in whatever void was left when he abandoned religion, but to write this out as a prescription for what novels must be like for everyone else seems hardly tenable, just as other, differing prescriptions (for "plot," for "clarity," even for "originality") shrinkwrap fiction into easily storable commodities but don't allow for the flexibility of the form.

Wood is sometimes compared to the academic critic F.R. Leavis, and indeed Wood's prose does have some of the smug lecture hall certainty and harsh evaluative tone of Leavis at his worst. But Wood does not often convey the impression that he actually enjoys literature (sometimes a failure of Leavis's as well), even the work of those literary artists he appears to admire. Furthermore, Wood's own criticism is very seldom enjoyable--it creates the tense atmosphere suitable to a hanging judge.

Wood also shares something with the "moral critics" such as the poet-critic Yvor Winters or Lionel Trilling (or even Irving Howe.) With all of them, literature is a rather sour and sober affair, the critic its grave taskmaster. I will take Wood's word for it that *Absolute Friends* is spoiled by the inserted political rhetoric he describes, as fiction usually is by such propagandizing. But one can't help but feel that by the end of the review Wood has converted what should be an aesthetic flaw into a flaw of the author's own character ("this humanly implausible and ideologically enraged novel"--enraged at George W. Bush). If Le Carre is not exactly judged to be a bad man, he is judged to be a "bad writer" solely because he has ideas different than James Wood's, ideas about the world and about fiction. To this extent, Wood shows himself to be a remarkably intolerant critic, just as "ideological" in his way as Le Carre is accused of being.

It is a very peculiar definition of "comedy" in literature that values such comedy for the way in which it manages to restrain itself from actually producing laughter, and that identifies as among the greatest comic writers in modern fiction the likes of J.F. Powers, Henry Green, and V.S. Pritchett. But this is indeed the view of comedy that emerges from James Wood's *The Irresponsible Self: On Laughter and the Novel.*

I have nothing against the work of Powers, Green, and Pritchett (or, for that matter, many of the other writers Wood discusses in his book), but they are not the writers anyone surveying the landscape of 20th century Western fiction with any real concern for historical development or descriptive accuracy could plausibly select as exemplars of "comic fiction" as it has been practiced over the course of that century. They are instead exemplars only of Wood's particular, and particularly parched and narrow, preference for a kind of fiction "in which a mild tragicomedy arises naturally out of context and situation, novels which are softly witty. . . ." (Note the words "mild" and "softly"; they are the kinds of words Wood resorts to repeatedly--along with "gentle," which must be used a dozen times or more--in his descriptions of the "comic fiction" he most admires.)

Again, Wood has every right to prefer this sort of fiction, indeed, to write essays extolling the virtues of those writers who provide it and belittling those who don't, but to elevate this preference to a critical principle of universal salience is something else. Although, one has to simply accept that Wood's critical principle is both incontestable and universally applicable, since Wood doesn't really carry through his notion of "the irresponsible self" and the gentle comedy accompanying it in any kind of sustained argument. Once he has set out his case for what he calls the "comedy of forgiveness" in the Introduction, in many of the ensuing essays he at best merely assumes the reader will remember the previous discussion and apply it for him/herself to the subject at hand. Certainly Wood does not engage in much of the kind of close analysis an argument as sweeping as that which he wants to make about both comedy and modern fiction would require. Frequently there is no further discussion of comedy of any kind in the essays collected in this book, and there are some essays included on writers--Dostoevsky, Tolstoy, Joseph Roth--whose work hardly has any relation to comedy--certainly not as "humor"--at all. One essay is not about fiction at all, but is merely a review of V.S. Naipaul's *Letters Between a Father and a Son*.

Of course, it might be objected that these essays were written for publication separately, in various magazines and book reviews, and expecting them to cohere more systematically when collected in a book would be unfair. But what justification is there for them to be reprinted as a book if no real effort is made to make them readable as a book?

Although Wood ostensibly disparages the category of "religious comedy" (which he associates with satire), his own explanation of the secular "comedy of forgiveness" seems to me essentially religious in its expectations of fiction:

> The comedy of what I want to call "irresponsibility" or unreliability is a kind of subset of the comedy of forgiveness; and although it has its roots in Shakespearean comedy (especially soliloquy), it seems to me the wonderful creation of the late nineteenth- and early twentieth-century novel. This comedy, or tragicomedy, of the modern novel replaces the knowable with the unknowable, transparency with unreliability, and this is surely in direct proportion to the growth of characters' fictive inner lives. The novelistic idea that we have bottomless interiors which may only be partially disclosed to us *must* create a new form of comedy, based on the management of our incomprehension rather than on the victory of our complete knowledge. . . .

This is a notion of "comedy" that ignores what is comedic in comedy in favor of the revelations of character, a spiritual communion with "fictive inner lives." Wood further muddies, rather than clarifies, the conceptual waters by opposing this comedy of forgiveness against the "comedy of correction"-- satire--as if all other manifestations of the comic in literature were perforce satirical, only versions of what is to be found in Moliere or Swift. Such a reduction of the possibilities of comedy is not just an oversimplification; it completely ignores a vast body of comic fiction that is neither primarily satirical nor "tragicomic" in the "mild" and "gentle" mode Wood celebrates.

Mikhail Bakhtin described this kind of comedy as embodying an attitude of "radical skepticism" that excludes as just another form of "seriousness" both conventional satire, which does indeed, as Wood maintains, seek to eradicate vices and flaws, and the "comedy of forgiveness," which is a thin veneer indeed on a form of fiction that otherwise could not be more "straightforwardly serious" in its intent. (Sentimentally serious might be a better way to describe it.) It is the kind of comedy to be found in Joyce rather than Henry Green, Beckett rather than V.S. Pritchett, Nathanael West rather than J.F. Powers. It is the comedy of *Catch-22*, of *Gravity's Rainbow*, of *Mulligan Stew*, and of the fiction of Donald Barthelme, Robert Coover, and Stanley Elkin. If a book were to be written that was truly about "laughter and the novel"--not about "mild tragicomedy"--these would be the books and the writers that would have to be examined.

The closest Wood comes to assessing this brand of fiction is his back-of-the-hand dismissal of what he calls "hysterical realism." Wood identifies Don DeLillo, Salman Rushdie, and

Thomas Pynchon as the chief hysterics in question, but one suspects he would accuse many of these other writers I have mentioned of being unduly hysterical as well. He never really defines "hysterical realism" at any great length or with any great analytical precision, but the following passage comes pretty close to capturing the essence of the idea: ". . .there are also 'comic novels,' novels which correspond to the man who comes up to you and says, 'Have you heard the one about. . .?' novels obviously very busy at the business of being comic. *Tristram Shandy*, for instance, is in multifarious ways a marvelous book, but it is written in a tone of such constant high-pitched zaniness, of such deliberate 'liveliness,' that one finds oneself screaming at it to calm down a bit."

There are indeed comic novels that embody the sort of laughter associated with jokes and comic routines. (*Catch-22* is one of these, as is *Portnoy's Complaint* and most of Elkin's novels), and many more that are broadly funny in a fashion James Wood no doubt finds excessively "lively." Frankly, I am surprised to find that Wood admires Cervantes, since *Don Quixote* is quite a "zany" book (or so it seems to me), as are most of the many novels influenced by *Don Quixote* throughout the 18th and 19th centuries. Furthermore, few of these kinds of comic novels could convincingly be labeled "hysterical realism" because almost none of them are realistic in any credible sense of the term. In fact, comedy is almost by definition <u>not</u> realistic, depending as it does on a deliberate distortion of reality, even to the point of completely reversing its normal assumptions. To the extent works of fiction seek first of all to be "realistic," whatever comedy they might also contain is almost certainly going to be incidental, the sort of "mild" and "gentle" amusement Wood clearly enough enjoys.

(The one writer Wood discusses to whose work the term "hysterical realism" seems appropriate is Tom Wolfe, whose novels Wood accurately judges to be shallow and really not very funny. It is one of the few essays in *The Irresponsible Self* with which I unreservedly agree--one of the others is the essay entitled "Shakespeare and the Pathos of Rambling.")

Finally, both "hysterical realism" and the book's occasional analyses of comedy more generally seem really to be devices Wood has adopted in his essays to make a more compelling case for the kind of fiction he manifestly most esteems: loosely, the sort of late 19th/early 20th century fiction that added to the realism that had come to be valued by writers like Flaubert and Tolstoy and George Eliot a further "psychological realism" that located the real truth about human reality in the disclosures of consciousness. Much of this fiction remains vital and important, and many of the strategies developed by writers like James and Woolf and Henry Green continued to be adapted by later writers in different and interesting ways. But the pure form of psychological realism Wood continually returns to--"a state in which the reader may or may not know why a character does something, or may not know how to read a passage, and feels that in order to find these things out he must try to merge with characters in their uncertainty"--is not a method that most subsequent 20th century writers continued to practice as if it had been determined to be the "correct" way to write novels and stories. (Neither it nor "mild tragicomedy" have been greatly favored in, especially, American fiction, which by and large Wood doesn't emphasize much at all in *The Irresponsible Self*; in most of his critical writing Wood appears to be particularly dismissive of post-60s American fiction, which has most consistently sought alternatives to the approach Wood seeks to privilege.)

It doesn't bother me in the least that James Wood approves of psychological realism and the creation of the "irresponsible self" more than any other technique a writer of fiction might choose to employ. To each his own where taste in fiction is concerned. However, Wood's overriding critical precept, that things were done much better back when, that the way things were done then is the only right way, performs no useful service to either contemporary writers or their readers.

William Deresiewicz's review of James Wood's *How Fiction Works* (*The Nation*, December 8, 2008) provokes me to come to Wood's defense. Although Deresiewicz correctly points out the narrowness of Wood's conception of realism, ultimately he is less concerned with Wood's near-dogmatism on this subject than with what he considers the narrowness of Wood's approach to criticism. According to Deresiewicz, a great critic should exhibit "not great learning, or great thinking, or great expressive ability, or great sensitivity to literary feeling and literary form. . .but a passionate involvement with what lies beyond the literary and creates its context." In other words, literary criticism should not concentrate too strenuously on the "merely literary."

James Wood's greatest strength as a critic is that he does not spend much time and space on "what lies beyond the literary." He certainly could not be accused of lacking "a passionate involvement" with literary texts--even if he can be charged with restricting his involvement too exclusively to a certain kind of text--but to his credit he devotes most of his attention to a close reading of the fiction he considers and leaves what's "beyond" to those less interested in literature than he is.

According to Deresiewicz, the exemplars of modern criticism are the so-called New York critics, specifically Edmund Wilson, Lionel Trilling, Alfred Kazin, and Irving Howe:

Wilson, who wrote about everything during his teeming career, from politics to popular culture, socialist factions to Native American tribes, warned about "the cost of detaching books from all the other affairs of human life." Trilling's whole method as a critic was to set the object of his consideration within the history of what he called "the moral imagination." Kazin, whose criticism, like [Elizabeth] Hardwick's, focused on the literature of this country in particular, sought to illuminate nothing less than "the nature of our American experiences." The goal of Howe's criticism, he said, was "the recreation of a vital democratic radicalism in America." The New York critics were interested in literature because they were interested in politics, culture, the moral life and the life of society, and all as they bore on one another. They placed literature at the center of their inquiry because they recognized its ability not only to represent life but, as Matthew Arnold said, to criticize it--to ask questions about where we are and how where we are stands in relation to where we should be. They were not aesthetes; they were, in the broadest sense, intellectuals.

With the possible exception of Wilson (who did indeed write about many subjects but whose essays on literary works were attentive to form and style and did mark him as, in part, an "aesthete"), Wood is a much better critic than any of these writers. Trilling is one of the most overrated critics of the 20th century, unwilling as he was to consider works of literature as anything other than what even his acolyte Leon Wieseltier describes protectively as "records of concepts and sentiments and values," apparently unable to describe "the moral imagination" except in platitudes. Kazin is simply hopeless, a truly awful critic whose essays and books on literary topics are simply useless to anyone interested in criticism that might enhance the reading experience. *On Native Grounds* is a bloated assemblage of historical generalizations mostly about writers, not writing. It's full of "remarks" about literature but no actual criticism. Like Trilling, Kazin bypasses the literary in order to arrive at banalities about "the nature of our American experiences." Howe is somewhat better--he does often enough really examine the texts on which he is pronouncing--but why would anyone want to rely for insight into literary texts on a critic who confesses he is most interested in "the recreation of a vital democratic radicalism in America"?

It's really rather amazing that Deresiewicz seems to believe that the approach to criticism represented by the New York critics has somehow been lost. In reality, criticism that obsesses about "politics, culture, the moral life and the life of society" is the dominant mode of criticism today, especially in academe and even more especially among so-called "intellectuals." These critics condescend to put "literature at the center of their inquiry because they recognize its ability not only to represent life but. . . to ask questions about where we are and how where we are stands in relation to where we should be," blah, blah, blah. James Wood stands out as a critic willing to challenge this tedious preoccupation with "context" and to make an "inquiry" into the literary nature of literature his "center" rather than the intellectual pomposity of "questions about where we are," questions that for Deresiewicz's preferred kind of critic take precedence over all that "aesthetic" fluff, finally over literature itself. In my opinion, it is all in Wood's favor that "what has happened in England since the end of World War II--anything that has happened in England since the war, politically, socially or culturally--simply doesn't enter into his thinking," and a testament to the force of his style, sensibility, and, yes, learning that he has managed to become widely known as a critic through publication in magazines that otherwise insist on relevance to politics and "the life of society."

Some of the responsibility for casting Wood in this particular sort of negative light undoubtedly lies with the magazine publishing Deresiewicz's article, *The Nation*. Left-wing editors, journalists, and "intellectuals" have always been particularly suspicious of "aesthetes," of writers and artists who emphasize the formal elements of their work and are too far "removed from commerce with the dirty, human world." Indeed, one hardly ever finds in *The Nation* reviews of fiction or poetry that isn't either obviously politically intentioned or can't be made to seem so. (Mostly, it has increasingly seemed to me, the magazine just doesn't review fiction or poetry much at all.) Attacking James Wood as a pointy-headed aesthete is a convenient way for the magazine to restate the long-standing "progressive" disdain for art in any of its non-partisan manifestations. I don't question that Deresiewicz believes all the things he says about Wood's failure to engage with the world "beyond the literary," but his conception of the role of both literature and criticism is clearly enough consistent with the Left's utilitarian attitude toward both.

Deresiewicz observes that Wood "ignores the meanings that novelists use [their] methods to propose. . . Wood can tell us about Flaubert's narrator or Bellow's style, but he's not very curious about what those writers have to say about the world." This actually makes me feel reassured about James Wood's prominence in current literary criticism. At least there is one critic with access to high-profile print publications who knows it isn't the novelist's job to "propose" anything and focuses his attention on writers' art rather than on what they allegedly "have to say."

III Harold Bloom

Since the publication of *The Western Canon*, Harold Bloom has become something of a caricature, derided on the one hand for the vehemence of his displeasure with the direction literary study has taken over the past quarter century, his opposition to the politicized, anti-aesthetic criticism he identifies collectively as the "school of resentment," while on the other he is frequently invoked as a kind of cultural mandarin dismissive of the pleasures ordinary people take in the products of popular culture and contemptuous of all books that can't be assigned to the canon of high literature. (Although James Wood accuses him of abandoning the role of critic for that of "populist appreciator," his populism surely extends no farther than to those who might conceivably be convinced of the greatness of what Bloom calls "strong poets," whose work certainly cannot be dumbed down in order to reach the masses.)

This image of Bloom as traditionalist curmudgeon is considerably at odds with the impression one might have gotten from his critical writings of the 1970s and 1980s, in which Bloom advances his own intricate (if ultimately rather private, even hermetic) theory of literary production and reception that does indeed focus on poetic greatness but hardly defends tradition for tradition's sake. Bloom makes elevated claims for the value of poetry, but these are not claims for the utility of poetry in the service of "culture" as moral critics would define it nor an Arnoldian attempt to construct a version of literary history that isolates works of literature as "the best" of their kind. Bloom's theory of literary influence certainly does assume a continuity of vision over the course of this history (although it also frequently alludes to writers and writing not necessarily considered to be "literary" per se), but the core principle of his theory--that great poetry is always a "misreading," sometimes radically so, of "precursor poets"--in essence holds that literary history is actually in a perpetual state of disruption and revision.

In my opinion, Bloom's 1982 book *Agon: Towards a Theory of Revisionism* provides the most complete and coherent account of his ideas about both literary history and the role of the literary critic, and thus will probably be the book of his that survives into the next generation of literary study (although Bloom's approach is idiosyncratic enough--deliberately so-- that a future cadre of neo-Bloomians is certainly an implausible notion). Indeed, this passage from the book's essay on John Ashbery is as succinct a statement of Bloom's prevailing assumptions as readers of his work are likely to find:

> A strong poem, which alone can become canonical for more than a single generation, can be defined as a text that must engender strong misreadings, both as other poems and as literary criticism. Texts that have single, reductive, simplistic meanings are themselves already necessarily weak misreadings of anterior texts. When a

strong misreading has demonstrated its fecundity by producing other strong misreadings across several generations, we can and must accept its canonical status.

Yet by "strong misreading" I mean "strong troping," and the strength of trope can be recognized by skilled readers in a way that anticipates the temporal progression of generations. A strong trope renders all merely trivial readings of it irrelevant. ..

There is a true law of canonization, and it works contrary to Gresham's law of currency. We may phrase it: in a strong reader's struggle to master a poet's trope, strong poetry will impose itself, because that imposition, that usurpation of mental space, is the proof of trope, the testing of power by power. . . .

"Misreading" (or "misprision," as Bloom would have it) is the motivating force, the ultimate inspiration, behind all poetry (which, in Bloom's critical universe, is synonymous with "literature" and is not to be attributed solely to self-identified poets). In the effort to emulate and finally surpass "anterior" texts, poems that fire the poet's passion for poetry in the first place, strong poets "misread" these texts in a psychoanalytically defensive gesture that allows the "something new" of literary creation to occur. Milton misreads Shakespeare, Blake misreads Milton, etc. Weak poets merely imitate their predecessors, fail to engage with the deeper and more unwieldy impulses that ultimately account for great poetry.

And it is these impulses that are ultimately responsible for all strong poetry. As Bloom writes elsewhere in *Agon*: "No one 'fathers' or 'mothers' his or her own poems, because poems are not 'created,' but are interpreted into existence, and by necessity they are interpreted from other poems. Whenever I suggest that there is a defensive element in all interpretation, as in all troping, the suggestions encounter a considerable quantity of very suggestive resistance. All that I would grant to this resistance is its indubitable idealism, its moving *need* of the mythology of the creative imagination, and of the related sub-mythology of an 'objective' scholarly criticism." Again the perception of Bloom as hidebound conservative does not fit well with assumptions like these. How far are they from the notion that there is "nothing outside the text," that language authors poems, not writers? (Although Bloom rejects this latter idea; to him this formulation reduces "language" to "the very odd trope of a demiurgical entity. . .acting like a Univac, and endlessly doing our writing for us.") "Creative imagination" and "objective scholarly criticism" are equally feeble concepts for describing what is really going on in the production and reception of poetry as Bloom understands it.

A "strong trope" is a use of language (whether in individual lines or phrases or the poem as a whole) so powerful in its implications that, as he puts it in another book, it creates meaning that "could not exist without" it and produces an "excess or overflow" that "brings about a condition of newness." Indeed, its force is so irresistible that it "will impose itself," although such a struggle with the text is carried out only by the "strong reader" who seeks to come to terms with it through an act of troping of his/her own. When he complains about the "school of resentment" or about the politicization of literary criticism more broadly, he is reacting against the establishment of a mode of academic criticism that validates weak reading, that diminishes the power of literature and the passion of reading. He is not lamenting the loss of "sweetness and light" as a goal of literary study, nor the rejection of New Critical formalism, which he considers a form of rhetorical criticism that equally fails to accentuate what is truly at stake in the "troping" of both poetry and criticism.

In what he apparently takes to be a telling criticism of Bloom's practice as a critic, Benjamin Balint remarks that "We might say that Harold Bloom is the Rashi of misreadings, a kind of contemporary sage who, due perhaps to the excesses of reading itself, himself misreads—sometimes forcefully, sometimes weakly" (*Claremont Review of Books*, Spring 2006). But of course Bloom already admits this, dismissing the notion that criticism involves something like accuracy of interpretation:

To read actively is to make a fiction as well as to receive one, and the kind of active reading we call "criticism" or the attempt to decide meaning, or perhaps to see whether meaning *can* be decided, always has a very large fictive meaning in it. I continue to be surprised that so many literary scholars refuse to see that every stance in regard to texts, however professedly humble or literal or prosaic or 'scientific' or 'historical" or "linguistic" is always a poetic stance, always part of the rhetoric of rhetoric. . . .

Balint further proposes that Bloom "turns out to be a reader par excellence, but also perhaps merely a reader," suggesting that he is finally unable to distinguish between his beloved texts and non-literary spiritual or religious "encounters." This surely fails to recognize that for Bloom "reading" is more than an "encounter" with words (although it begins there), just as " poetry" is more than a composition in verse. I would not go so far as to say that for Bloom reading <u>is</u> religion, but one might conclude from most of his books that the kind of experience to which reading works of literature gives access is for him about as close to what could be called a religious experience as is possible in a universe in which God probably does not exist.

This is perhaps where most readers depart company with Bloom, concluding that his kind of reading is finally an idiosyncratic and insular one, Bloom himself seated aloft in his own peculiar aesthetic empyrean. This is a mistaken impression, not least because it takes Bloom's very real passion for literature as a preoccupation with the aesthetic such as ordinary "rhetorical criticism" would describe it. James Wood asserts that whenever Bloom's commentary verges on becoming "openly evaluative, it becomes Freudian and biographical" and that "if he were just choosing one poet over another for purely aesthetic reasons, then he would have no need of his Freudian system of anxiety and repression." This assessment has validity, and aptly sums up the major weakness in Bloom's critical system. One reads Bloom for inspiration, for further amplification of the way in which his account of literary influence applies to specific writers or texts, for the occasional insight that reinforces the general claim of Freud's work on literary criticism, but not for sustained and careful explication of individual texts. That Bloom initially developed his theory of poetic influence to directly contest the New Critics' dismissal of subject-centered criticism and of Romanticism in general of course explains this absence, but I often wonder whether in his dismay at the direction literary study has taken he doesn't sometimes think he might have done more justice to New Criticism and its insistence that the aesthetic attributes of literature ought to be the proper focus of criticism.

Perhaps the most intriguing feature (to me) of *Agon* is Bloom's attempt to align his own approach to criticism with that of American pragmatism. Partly this is due to his admiration of Emerson as an American "seer," a fellow strong misreader whose habits of thought provided the true source of pragmatism. But pragmatic thinking also offers Bloom a touchstone that further vindicates his own self-reliant mode of reading:

> . . .American pragmatism, as [Richard] Rorty advises, always asks of text: what is it good for, what can I do with it, what can it do for me, what can I make it mean? I confess that I like these questions, and they are what I think strong reading is all about, because strong what it does to the poem is right, because it knows what Emerson, its American inventor, taught it, which is that the true ship is the shipbuilder. If you don't believe in your reading, then don't bother anyone else with it, but if you do, then don't care also whether anyone else agrees with it or not. . . .

I must say this seems a fairly ordinary reading of Emerson (who surely does ask of poetry, "what can it do for me?") and a weak misreading of Rorty (as well as Dewey and James before him). Putting aside the fact that both Rorty and Dewey believe literature does serve some generalizable good (for Rorty, helping us to become "less cruel," for Dewey, clarifying the nature of experience), it is very convenient for Bloom to exploit this overly literal interpretation of pragmatism's goal-oriented analysis so that it winds up justifying critical eccentricity for its own sake. For me, a thoroughgoingly pragmatic literary criticism might indeed put aside the question "Am I getting this poem right?" but would still find the question "Am I getting literature right?" an appropriate one to ask. Does "literature" as a category exist primarily to allow Harold Bloom or other like-minded critics to misread, strongly or otherwise, in any way they want, or does it also carry out a useful purpose by identifying a kind of text upon which some agreed-upon constraints do apply? Couldn't we say that both writing and reading works of literature pragmatically involves observing these constraints so that the activities themselves might be sustained?

I always find reading Harold Bloom's books a bracing experience, but I don't think I'm prepared to regard them as contributions to the elucidation of pragmatism.

Tom Lutz, on the other hand, wants to associate Bloom with the New Critics. In an essay in *Slate* (March 8, 2007), Lutz contends that Bloom believes the current generation of politicized literary scholars (what Bloom terms the "school of resentment") "are all looking at something besides the text itself, by which they mean a book that is read without theory, without reference to other values, and without mediation of any kind."

Lutz identifies this view with New Criticism, but nowhere in his essay does he reveal (if he knows) that Bloom was actually hostile to New Criticism. He considered its approach so limiting and so dismissive (in the practice of most of the New Critics, at least) of the Romantic poets, whose work Bloom so loves, that he deliberately designed his own theory of poetic influence as a corrective, if not an outright rejection, of New Critical biases. Lutz goes on to associate both Bloom and New Criticism with such disparate figures as Mortimer Adler, E.D. Hirsch, and John Sutherland, simply because they appear to endorse the idea that learning to appreciate the "text itself" is an important part of literary education.

In a move apparently intended to show that Bloom doesn't practice what he preaches (or doesn't understand the foundation of his own practice), Lutz cites H. L. Mencken's attacks on "The New Criticism" (as delineated by J. E. Springarn in 1911), which putatively show that academic criticism is inherently theoretical, "criticism of criticism of criticism." But again, since Bloom is/was not a New Critic, it's hard to see how this undermines Bloom's own approach to the "text itself." The New Critics did indeed have a "theory" of the literary text as something dynamic and inherently dramatic (and reading as the experience of the text's dynamism), but it is not Bloom's, however much he might accept the underlying emphasis on the integrity of the literary text, free of the demands made on it by those with their own personal and political investments.

But of course Bloom does have a theory. No one who remembers the scholarly debates of the 1970s and 1980s could think otherwise, as Bloom played a major role in these debates precisely as a theorist of literature, a proponent of the Freudian notion of the "anxiety of influence." Far from being considered a conventional formalist, someone who believed a text should be read "without mediation of any kind," Bloom was taken as a radical, even a postmodernist, a critic who was taking literary study away from its proper focus on the "text itself" into very a-textual speculations about the role of poetic influence and its rather violent Freudian implications. Anyone who's read and taken seriously books such as *The Anxiety of Influence*, *A Map of Misreading*, *Kabbalah and Criticism*, and *Agon* would know that the accusation Bloom is some kind of retrograde enemy of "theory" is ridiculous on its face.

Thus, at least as far as Bloom is concerned, Lutz's invocation of his name as one of those who demands a book be read "without theory, without reference to other values, and without mediation of any kind" is simply incorrect. This is not a matter of interpretation. Some investigation of Bloom's work, even of secondary explications of that work (a simple Google search, perhaps) would immediately reveal that Lutz's account is a caricature of the role Bloom has come to play in current literary discourse (the aging curmudgeon) but has nothing to do with what he's actually written. Even a book such as *How to Read and*

Why, a deliberate simplification of Bloom's ideas about the value of literature, reveals that he does not hold the naive view of reading Lutz attributes to him.

Unfortunately, the caricature of Bloom is widely accepted. Sandra at *Bookworld* (otherwise a nice, thoughtful litblog) has opined that she had contracted "Bloom Syndrome," a "condition in which the sufferer is unable to read any work of literature unless it is deemed Significant by Harold Bloom and which often results in the reader losing the will to live/read, crushed under the weight of canonical imperatives" May 7, 2007). To the sin of thinking that the "text itself" is what literature is all about (and in Bloom's case looking to account for the text by emphasizing the writer's confrontation with his predecessors, an emphasis that highlights the continuity-through-conflict of literature) is added the annoying belief that the literary tradition is meaningful and worthwhile, that "some books are better than others." It's telling that in our culture someone who becomes associated with beliefs such as these is lampooned as a pathetic fogey who apparently thinks those old books are important or something.

IV Susan Sontag

I do not at all understand what David Rieff thought could be the justification for his book, *Swimming in a Sea of Death*, about the death of his mother, Susan Sontag. It contributes nothing to our understanding of Sontag's work as critic or novelist, and even as a chronicle of Sontag's harrowing death it seldom seems more than tacky and sensational. Sontag herself isn't even given much of a role to play beyond that of victim and object of Rieff's endless rationalizations about his own behavior during Sontag's struggle with the blood cancer that finally killed her. Besides leaving us with an unpleasant depiction of Sontag in her last months, the book is difficult to admire simply for its repetitious, turgid prose, which constantly circles around Sontag's illness, always seeking to extenuate Rieff's response to it.

The portrait of Susan Sontag that does emerge is of a woman utterly unhinged by the prospect of her own death. She is unable to summon any degree of composure or self-possession, and is unwilling, at least in Rieff's account, to acknowledge the reality of her situation. She comes off as cowering, irrational, selfish. Perhaps this is an accurate portrayal of Susan Sontag in her confrontation with death, but I am reluctant to accept it as such, since so much of *Swimming in a Sea of Death* keeps returning to the effects of this confrontation on David Rieff, on his own struggle with how to mitigate his mother's inappropriate responses. This narrated struggle seems to me both narcissistic and futile, since ultimately he doesn't really do much of anything, preferring to passively acquiesce to Sontag's illusions. If it was the case that Sontag was unable to face the truth about her condition, I am not going to take this book as evidence.

The implicit damage that *Swimming in a Sea of Death* does to Susan Sontag's legacy as writer and critic will be registered primarily by the degree to which its "revelations" about Sontag's difficult death will come to dominate future discussions of her work. These revelations will be trotted out again and again as some sort of clue to "vision," dominated by her fear of death and her own puzzling sense of immunity to it as that vision must surely have been. The image of Susan Sontag as, in Sven Birkerts's words, "an isolated, deluded figure, terrified of death and filled more with regret than any satisfaction at her achievements" (*Boston Globe*, (February 10, 2008) will linger. The biographical will triumph over the exegetic, as it always does in our gossip-obsessed excuse for a literary culture, and even though Sontag's work, especially the criticism, is focused on the sheer pleasure of life as represented by our encounter with art, the terror of mortality rendered in David Reiff's book will overshadow continuing encounters with Sontag's essays and books. How lamentable that this process will have been initiated by her own son.

The lure of the biographical can also be seen at work in Daniel Mendelsohn's review (*The New Republic*, April 10, 2009) of Sontag's journals. (Although the primary culprit in encouraging biographical readings is again Rieff, who made the decision to publish the journals in the first place.) Although I agree with much of Mendelsohn's commentary on Sontag's writing per se--that her criticism is much more important than her fiction, that her taste in fiction became much narrower and more conservative in her later years, in particular that she had a large and debilitating blind spot where American fiction was concerned--I cannot countenance the basic split in Sontag's sensibility that Mendelsohn finds by focusing on her personality, on her supposedly conflicted sexuality.

"Here again you feel the presence of an underlying conflict: Sontag the natural analyst against Sontag the struggling sensualist," Mendelsohn tells us. He would have us believe that her reticence to speak about her sexuality somehow indicates a "hidden emotional life," that she was essentially asexual. (I don't really know how otherwise to interpret his gloss on Sontag's sexual life: "So the sex is not that good. That leaves the ambition.") From the fact that Sontag apparently didn't use her journals as an opportunity to emote, Mendelsohn concludes that "the outsized cultural avidity, the literary ambition to which these pages bear witness, seems eventually to have occluded the more tender feelings." How does Mendelsohn really know the degree of Sontag's sexual desires or the extent of her "tender feelings"? Should we be making any judgments about Sontag's emotional life based on the selections from these journals? (If she preferred to use them as a way of recording "the cognitive and the analytical" in her experiences, does this make her emotionally enfeebled?) Above all: Should we be using stray comments in a writer's journal and speculations about her sexual nature as the basis of a theory about the disposition of the work?

Mendelson further contends that Sontag, in her practice at least, was not really "against interpretation" at all:

> The essays in *Against Interpretation* and in *Styles of Radical Will* may champion, famously, the need not for "a hermeneutics but an erotics of Art," but what is so striking is that there is not anything very erotic about these essays; they are, in fact, all hermeneutics. In the criticism, as in the journals, the eros is all from the neck up.

A little later he asserts that

> this astoundingly gifted interpreter, so naturally skilled at peeling away trivial-seeming exteriors to reveal deeper cultural meanings--or at teasing out the underlying significance of surface features to which you might not have given much attention ("people run beautifully in Godard movies")--fought mightily to affect an "aesthetic" disdain for content.

Mendelsohn is pretty clearly attempting to turn Sontag's own strengths as a critic--"peeling away" and "teasing out"--against her in order to question the critical agenda with which Sontag began her career as literary critic, and for which she is still most prominently known. To so baldly label her an "interpreter" is to dismiss her early efforts to rescue the aesthetic pleasures of art from the maw of interpretation and its attempts to "dig 'behind' the text, to find a sub-text which is the true one." She was an interpreter all along and thus the "disdain for content" she expressed could only be an affectation.

Furthermore, Mendelsohn finds that Sontag is untrue to her call for an "erotics of art" because her essays mostly fail to confine themselves to the "sensuous surface" such a call seems to emphasize. Partly this accusation is a necessary gesture in reinforcing Mendelsohn's biographical approach to Sontag's work, through which he maintains that her purported sexual inhibitions fundamentally determined the orientation of her critical responses. "I do not doubt that [Sontag] genuinely wished to experience works of art purely with the senses and the emotions," writes Mendelsohn, "but the author of these celebrated essays is quite plainly the grown-up version of the young girl who, at fifteen, declared her preference for 'virtuosity ... technique, organization. . . .'" If there is truth in Mendelsohn's remarks on this subject, however, I don't see why it's necessary to speculate about her sexual hang-ups in order to account for it. In some of her essays Sontag is more of a theoretician than a close reader, but this hardly disqualifies her from holding at the center of her theory about the appropriate response to art a view that such a response ought to be closer to "erotics" than to hermeneutics.

A criticism that lingers over the "sensuous surface" could indeed provide a valuable service, especially if it's a "surface" that might be overlooked in the rush to uncover "content." But it hardly seems contradictory or inconsistent to go beyond the immediate surface to consider, say, the way various aspects of the surface work together, the way surface sometimes occludes other aesthetically relevant elements, such as the more subtle effects of point of view in fiction or of editing in film. Ultimately, to expect a critic, even one ostensibly dedicated to "sensuous surface," to confine herself to describing those surfaces is to ask her to self-proscribe other critically useful tactics that might be employed. Moreover, it is possible to approach a work of art in a move that might be called "interpretation" but that does not amount to interrogating the work for "content." The critic might go beyond obvious surface features to point out less discernible qualities that are relevant to an <u>aesthetic</u> appreciation and do not attempt "to translate the elements of the [work] into something else," as Sontag puts it in "Against Interpretation."

Mendelsohn is suggesting that to be consistent Sontag should have contented herself with the innocent pleasure to be found in the surface features of art, but as Sontag herself reminded us in "Against Interpretation," "None of us can ever retrieve that innocence before all theory when art knew no need to justify itself, when one did not ask of a work what it *said* because one knew (or thought one knew) what it *did*. From now to the end of consciousness, we are stuck with the task of defending art." Sontag wanted to defend art against those who would say that "sensuous surface" is merely a distraction, that the role of the critic is to assure the audience the work is "about" something. For the interpretive critic:

> interpretation amounts to the philistine refusal to leave the work of art alone. Real art has the capacity to make us nervous. By reducing the work of art to its content and then interpreting *that*, one tames the work of art. Interpretation makes art manageable, conformable.

To combat this anti-aesthetic emphasis on "content," Sontag naturally enough sought for a criticism, especially literary criticism, that "brings more attention to form in art":

> If excessive stress on content provokes the arrogance of interpretation, more extended and more thorough descriptions of *form* would silence. What is

needed is a vocabulary--a descriptive, rather than prescriptive, vocabulary--for forms.

This sort of focus on the manifestations of form, more than on the "sensuous" per se, is really what "Against Interpretation" wants to encourage. Sontag wants us to stop looking past the aesthetic thing-in-itself toward the "meaning" it supposedly conceals. This approach to criticism is just a way of making art "manageable," ultimately of making art itself essentially irrelevant. Why go to the trouble of fashioning a "sensuous surface" in the first place if all we're interested in is the latent "content"? Artists just get in the way of our making sense of things.

"Sense" understood as intellectual comprehension. Otherwise, of course, "sense" is precisely what Sontag herself wants to retrieve from the interpreters, although this includes the sensory as part of a unified experience:

> Interpretation takes the sensory experience of the work of art for granted, and proceeds from there. This cannot be taken for granted, now. Think of the sheer multiplication of works of art available to every one of us, superadded to the conflicting tastes and odors and sights of the urban environment that bombard our senses. Ours is a culture based on excess, on overproduction; the result is a steady loss of sharpness in our sensory experience.

All the conditions of modern life--its material plenitude, its sheer crowdedness--conjoin to dull our sensory faculties. And it is in the light of the condition of our senses, our capacities (rather than those of another age), that the task of the critic must be assessed.

If anything, the conditions making "sharpness in our sensory experience" difficult to attain have only become more pronounced since Sontag wrote this paragraph. Our sensory faculties are surely even duller than they were in the early 1960s, which in retrospect seems a golden age of quiet contemplation. Although I think more than just <u>sensory</u> experience is at stake in the effort to restrain interpretation ("experience" extends to a purely cognitive level as well), that the critic must not take "the sensory experience of the work of art for granted" still seems to me a first principle of criticism.

Sontag's essay "On Style" (*Against Interpretation*) contains many passages to warm an aging aesthete's heart. First, a selection:

Indeed, practically all metaphors for style amount to placing matter on the inside, style on the outside. It would be more to the point to reverse the metaphor. The matter, the subject, is on the outside; the style is on the inside. As Cocteau writes: "Decorative style has never existed. Style is the soul, and unfortunately with us the soul assumes the form of the body." Even if one were to define style as the manner of our appearing, this by no means necessarily entails an opposition between a style that one assumes and one's "true" being. In fact, such a disjunction is extremely rare. In almost every case, our manner of appearing *is* our manner of being. The mask is the face. . . .

Most critics would agree that a work of art does not "contain" a certain amount of content (or function--as in the case or architecture) embellished by "style." But few address themselves to the positive consequences of what they seem to have agreed to. What is "content"? Or, more precisely, what is left of the notion of content when we have transcended the antithesis of style (or form) and content? Part of the answer lies in the fact that for a work of art to have "content" is, in itself, a rather special stylistic convention. The great task which remains to critical theory is to examine in detail the *formal* function of subject-matter. . . .

To treat works of art [as statements] is not wholly irrelevant. But it is, obviously, putting art to use--for such purposes as inquiring into the history of ideas, diagnosing contemporary culture, or creating social solidarity. Such a treatment has little to do with what actually happens when a person possessing some training and aesthetic sensibility looks at a work of art appropriately. A work of art encountered as a work of art is an experience, not a statement or an answer to a question. Art is not only abot something; it is something. A work of art is a thing in the world, not just a text or commentary on the world. . . .

Inevitably, critics who regard works of art as statements will be wary of "style," even as they pay lip service to "imagination." All that imagination really means for them, anyway, is the supersensitive rendering of "reality." It is this "reality" snared by the work of art that they continue to focus on, rather than on the extent to which a work of art engages the mind in certain transformations. . . .

In the end, however, attitudes toward style cannot be reformed merely by appealing to the "appropriate" (as opposed to utilitarian) way of looking at works of art. The ambivalence toward style is not rooted in simple error--it would then be quite easy to uproot--but in a passion, the passion of an entire culture. This passion is to protect and defend values traditionally conceived of as lying "outside" art, namely truth and morality. but which remain in perpetual danger of being compromised by art. Behind the ambivalence toward style is, ultimately, the historic Western confusion about the relation between art and morality, the aesthetic and the ethical.

For the problem of art versus morality is a pseudo problem. The distinction itself is a trap; its continued plausibility rests on not putting the ethical into question, but only the aesthetic. To argue on these grounds at all, seeking to defend the autonomy of art. . .is already to grant something that should not be granted--namely, that there exist two independent sorts of response, the aesthetic and the ethical, which vie for our loyalty when we experience a work of art. As if during the experience one really had to choose between responsible and humane conduct, on the one hand, and the pleasurable stimulation of consciousness, on the other!

Much of Sontag's essay is concerned to break down the opposition between "style" and "content," but unlike others who sometimes complain about the persistence of this opposition but do so mostly in order to banish "style" from critical discussion altogether--it's just the writer's way of communicating his/her content--Sontag maintains it is content that should recede, becoming simply the word for a "special stylistic convention." Style is the real substance of art, content its outer decoration, the enticement to the reader's attention that allows the "experience" of art that style enables.

Sontag was unfortunately denied her wish that critical theory might move "to examine in detail the *formal* function of subject-matter." Academic criticism has gone in precisely the opposite direction, dismissing form altogether in order to focus on the "subject-matter" that satisfies the critic's pre-established theoretical disposition, while there's very little "critical theory" at all in general-interest publications of the sort that once published writers like Susan Sontag. Essentially, the debate over the fraught relationship between "style" and "content" is about where Sontag left it.

Unfortunately, she left it presumably resolved to her own satisfaction, but not in a way that satisfies any current attempt to advance the argument that "style is on the inside." Since the notion that subject-matter is mostly a formal function seems if anything more outlandish even than it must have in 1965, a case needs to be made for it that extends beyond Sontag's somewhat idiosyncratic account and that avoids what I consider her more serious missteps.

The most serious problem with "On Style," in my opinion, is that Sontag can't finally unburden her argument of the criticisms of aestheticism made by the moralists she otherwise castigates. It seems to me her observation that it is quite easy to keep separate "responsible and humane conduct" from "the pleasurable stimulation of consciousness" without the latter contaminating the former would entirely suffice as a rebuttal of these criticisms, but she spends a great deal of her essay--the heart of it, really--defending the notion that art should not be judged by the standard of "humane conduct, " since art and the experience of art are phenomena of "consciousness," not actions requiring moral scrutiny. In fact, immediately after making the observation she begins to back off, assuring skeptics that "Of course, we never have a purely aesthetic response to works of art--neither to a play or a novel, with its depicting of human beings choosing and acting, nor, though it is less obvious, to a painting by Jackson Pollack or a Greek vase."

Since we never have a "pure" response to anything, I can't see that this proviso is necessary. If it isn't obvious to readers that a depiction of "human beings choosing and acting" is not the same thing as human beings choosing and acting and that it would be irrational "for us to make a moral response to something in a work of art in the same sense that we do to an act in real life," then any further attempt to heighten those readers' aesthetic awareness isn't going to accomplish much in the first place. Although Sontag argues that "we can, in good conscience cherish works of art which, considered in terms of 'content,' are morally objectionable" (her brief defense of Leni Riefenstahl's documentaries is the best-known illustration of this possibility), finally she can't let "morality" go as an issue relevant to the creation and experience of art. "Art is connected with morality," she asserts. "The moral pleasure in art, as well as the moral service that art performs, consists in the intelligent gratification of consciousness."

Much is elided in that formulation "intelligent gratification." Is "unintelligent" gratification immoral, or just lack of artistry? Is lack of artistry itself a moral issue, or simply a critical/evaluative judgment? Does only the greatest art perform the "moral service" Sontag associates with the "intelligent gratification of consciousness"? I don't object to the formulation itself--John Dewey would probably have found it usefully synonymous with his own notion of "art as experience"--but to insist that it must have a moral dimension seems to undo almost completely Sontag's case--which she admits she has made "uneasily"--for the autonomy of art:

> But if we understand morality in the singular, as a generic decision on the part of consciousness, then it appears that our response to art is "moral" insofar as it is, precisely, the enlivening of our sensibility and consciousness. For it is sensibility that nourishes our capacity for moral choice, and prompts our readiness to act, assuming that we do choose, which is a prerequisite for calling an act moral, and are not just blindly and

unreflectingly obeying. Art performs this "moral" task because the qualities which are intrinsic to the aesthetic experience (disinterestedness, contemplativeness, attentiveness, the awakening of the feelings) and to the aesthetic object (grace, intelligence, expressiveness, energy, sensuousness) are also fundamental constituents of a moral response to life.

Again, there isn't much here with which I would fundamentally disagree, but Sontag comes close to suggesting that art needs this moral justification, that "contemplativeness" and "attentiveness" are not in themselves sufficiently desirable qualities. They are "moral" insofar as they are good things to exercise, but I can't see that an explicit justification of them--and thus of aesthetic experience itself--on moral grounds is otherwise relevant. Either art needs no moral justification to strengthen its appeal or it is an impetus to moral action after all. Sontag wants to believe the first, but really seems to believe the second.

At the center of Sontag's discussion of style in "On Style" is her emphasis on the role of "will" in the creation and reception of art:

Perhaps the best way of clarifying the nature of our experience of works of art, and the relation between art and the rest of human feeling and doing, is to invoke the notion of will. It is a useful notion because will is not just a particular posture of consciousness, energized consciousness. It is also an attitude toward the world, of a subject toward the world.

The complex kind of willing that is embodied, and communicated, in a work of art both abolishes the world and encounters it in an extraordinarily intense and specialized way. This double aspect of the will in art is succinctly expressed by [Raymond] Bayer when he says: "Each work of art gives us the schematized and disengaged memory of a volition." Insofar as it schematized, disengaged, a memory, the willing involved in art sets itself at a distance from the world. . . .

`Art must distance itself from the world in order to become visible as art in the first place. It comes into being as a <u>version</u> of the world, as an aesthetic reproduction, and for this to be accomplished as thoroughly as is necessary, both for artist and audience, an act of "will" is required. And this act could be described as "dehumanized," since

in order to appear to us as art, the work must restrict sentimental intervention and emotional participation, which are functions of "closeness." It is the degree and manipulating of this distance, the conventions of distance, which constitute the style of the work.

Although I really don't understand how this effort of aesthetic willing could itself be identified as a work's "style" (more on this below), otherwise the concept of "will" as the imposition of a purely formal status on a text, image, or soundscape seems a cogent enough formulation. Most readers of novels, viewers of paintings or sculpture, and listeners to music want to disregard art's distancing effects and recover a notional "closeness" Sontag duly reminds us is antithetical to the very creation of art.

But again Sontag can't seem to accept the full implications of her position. She must add a codicil:

> A work of art *is* first of all an object, not an imitation; and it is true that all great art is founded on distance, on artificiality, on style, on what Ortega [y Gasset] calls dehumanization. But the notion of distance, (and of dehumanization, as well) is misleading, unless one adds that the movement is not just away from but toward the world. The overcoming or transcending of the world in art is also a way of encountering the world, and of training or educating the will to be in the world. . . .

This encountering of the world is what Sontag calls the "function" of art, which she thus substitutes for "content" in opposition to the art "object." She appears to believe that in so doing she is banishing "content" as a subject of critical discussion, but I can't really see how "function" operates as any less of an obstacle to the appreciation of style--which for Sontag remains the only "substance" of art--as the content it effectively displaces. If previously a work of art could be judged by the moral or social ramifications of its "content," what, under Sontag's formulation of "function," would prevent it from being judged by how acceptably it performs the task of "educating the will to be in the world"? Art would still be valued at least as much--probably, inevitably, more--for its utilitarian intervention in "the world" as it would as a self-sufficient creation, an act of aesthetic will.

The function of a work of art is to be itself. It doesn't engage in "training" for anything other than subsequent, perhaps more "educated" experiences of art. No doubt some people regard some works of art as having provided them the kind of enhanced re-engagement with the world of "real" experience that Sontag invokes--keeping in mind that works of art themselves belong to the world of experience--but to posit that art has a function that makes it useful to the world for reasons other than being available to experience, and this function applies at all times for all people, only gives away to the philistines what Sontag otherwise seems to want to preserve--the integrity of art.

Part of the reason for Sontag's readiness to trade "object" for "function" may lie in the ultimate imprecision of her notion of "style" in art, especially as style is embodied in works of literature: "Style is the principle of decision in a work of art, the signature of the artist's will." "If art is the supreme game which the will plays with itself, 'style' consists of the set of rules by which the game is played." "To the extent that a work seems right, just, unimaginable otherwise (without loss or damage), what we are responding to is a quality of its style." "An artist's style is, from a technical point of view, nothing other than the particular idiom in which he deploys the *forms* of his art." "[E]very style embodies an epistemological decision, an interpretation of how and what we see." Nowhere in "On Style" is there discussion of color or brushstroke, tone or harmonics, phrases, sentences, or paragraphs. "Particular idiom" in poetry or fiction is never associated with specific effects of language, with the use of words.

The closest Sontag comes to a real analysis of style is this brief discussion of Gertrude Stein:

> The circular repetitive style of Gertrude Stein's *Melanctha* expresses her interest in the dilution of immediate awareness by memory and anticipation, what she calls "association," which is obscured in language by the system of the tenses. Stein's insistence on the presentness of experience is identical with her decision to keep to the present tense, to choose commonplace short

words and repeat groups of them incessantly, to use an extremely loose syntax and abjure most punctuation. Every style is a means of insisting on something .

It would be hard not to notice Stein's "circular repetitive style"--her particular idiom of "commonplace short words" and "extremely loose syntax"--but this sort of focus on style as the deployment of language is relevant to all writers worth our notice, and otherwise "On Style" defines style much more abstractly as "principle of decision," "set of rules," and "epistemological decision." And even here Stein's prose style is summed up as an aspect of will, as the "means of insisting on something," rather than as the enlistment of words in an aesthetically compelling verbal composition. A writer's "style" can be examined for its successes and failures in meeting the latter goal; as an embodiment of "will" it remains, for me at least, rather too mistily metaphysical.

On the other hand, Sontag seems correct to me when she concludes the essay by reminding us that "In the strictest sense, all the contents of consciousness are ineffable," that "Every work of art, therefore, needs to be understood not only as something rendered, but also as a certain handling of the ineffable."

In the greatest art, one is always aware of things that cannot be said. . ., of the contradiction between expression and the presence of the inexpressible. Stylistic devices are also techniques of avoidance. The most potent elements in a work of art are, often, its silences.

I would only add that the "silences" cultivated by great art are "present" because the work makes room for them in a concrete way. They are incorporated into the work as "ineffable" but real. (The New Critics might have called this ineffable quality "ambiguity," something half-said but not fully said.) The specific way in which, through its style, the work of art invokes a fruitful silence is always still worth attention.

www.ingramcontent.com/pod-product-compliance
Lightning Source LLC
LaVergne TN
LVHW022258060326
832902LV00020B/3154